62.95/ 47.21

P9-AQT-770

TECHNICAL COLLEGE OF THE LOWCOUNTRY
LEARNING RESOURCES CENTER
POST OFFICE BOX 1288
BEAUFORT, SOUTH CAROLINA 29901-1288

Project Scheduling *and* Management *for* Construction

Updated Second Edition

Formerly
*Project Planning & Control
for Construction*

David R. Pierce, Jr.

RS**Means**
CMDGROUP

Project Scheduling *and* Management *for* Construction

Second Edition

David R. Pierce, Jr.

TECHNICAL COLLEGE OF THE LOWCOUNTRY
LEARNING RESOURCES CENTER
POST OFFICE BOX 1288
BEAUFORT, SOUTH CAROLINA 29901-1288

RSMeans
CMDGROUP

Copyright 1998

R.S. Means Company, Inc.

Construction Publishers & Consultants
Construction Plaza
63 Smiths Lane
Kingston, MA 02364-0800
(781) 585-7880

R.S. Means Company, Inc. ("R.S. Means"), its authors, editors and engineers, apply diligence and judgment in locating and using reliable sources for the information published. **However, R.S. Means makes no express or implied warranty or guarantee in connection with the content of the information contained herein, including the accuracy, correctness, value, sufficiency, or completeness of the data, methods and other information contained herein. R.S. Means makes no express or implied warranty of merchantability or fitness for a particular purpose.**
R.S. Means shall have no liability to any customer or third party for any loss, expense, or damage, including consequential, incidental, special or punitive damages, including lost profits or lost revenue, caused directly or indirectly by any error or omission, or arising out of, or in connection with, the information contained herein.

No part of this publication may be reproduced, stored in a retrieval system, or transmitted in any form or by any means without prior written permission of R.S. Means Company, Inc.

The editors for this book were Mary Greene, manager, Reference Books; Marla Marek, copy editor; and John H. Ferguson, PE, manager, Engineering Operations, R.S. Means Company, Inc. The production manager was Michael Kokernak; the production coordinator was Marion Schofield; Michele Able supervised electronic publishing; Composition was by Paul Hebert; the book and cover were designed by Norman R. Forgit.

Printed in the United States of America

10 9 8 7 6 5 4 3 2 1

Library of Congress Cataloging in Publication Data

ISBN 0-87629-533-2

47.2/

Dedication

This book is dedicated to Arlan and Deborah Toy, Alan Hall, Lorie Gold, Jodie Feldman, Doris Parker Roberts, Joanne Goldberg, and especially to Bob and Tillie Carter.

It is also dedicated to Loren, Erica, and Karen Mannard; and especially to Jennifer Harp, soccer player extraordinaire and all-around great stepdaughter.

Table of Contents

Foreword

Construction projects are becoming more and more complicated, and a Project Manager's work is becoming increasingly difficult as a result. Every tool a Project Manager can find to help manage the hectic process of building is one more asset that can help bring the project in on time. This book is intended to give the Project Manager one of those key tools—a technique that helps the project team to effectively plan the schedule and keep track of progress. If used as described, the techniques described here will give any Project Manager a significant head start.

The scheduling techniques covered are all based on the Critical Path method of scheduling, which has become the standard means of planning and keeping track of construction progress. Too many works on this subject simply show that CPM schedules are made up of activities, and that network calculations are done thus and so. This book is different in that it shows the Project Manager how to think through the details of a work sequence the way it is actually done by experienced construction personnel, and discusses the "nuts and bolts" of the process as "real world" people actually do it. In that sense, it is "short on theory and long on practice". Also, the techniques are demonstrated using a straightforward sample project that provides an excellent learning tool. In addition, sample computer output is provided, which is in keeping with modern practice. Up-to-date scheduling practices include the use of microcomputer-based software; this text includes samples from SureTrak®, which is among the latest and best software available.

The first two chapters outline the basic concepts of project scheduling and how these concepts are translated into a model that can be used to develop a schedule system and procedures for a construction project. A sample building project is introduced at the end of Chapter 2, and this project is used throughout the book to illustrate the principles of scheduling and the actual steps necessary to build a full project schedule and control its progress. Chapter 3 identifies key project team members and spells out the essential steps for getting a project schedule started out on the right foot.

A primary key to good scheduling and control is a thoroughly thought out initial plan. Chapter 4 introduces the primary tool for accomplishing this, i.e., the Critical Path Method. Chapter 5 covers specific, detailed tasks of planning the project—breaking the project down into its component elements and tasks, and deciding on a sequence of work. Chapter 6 follows up with how to schedule the tasks—determining how long each part should take and how to calculate the overall time for the project. Chapter 7 then covers how the Project Manager can best display and utilize the information found in the schedule. Since all projects encounter delays and difficulties, and a primary task of a Project Manager must be to identify these problems, Chapter 8 deals with how a project's progress can be monitored, and how action can be taken to bring the project back on track. In addition to time and schedule, Project Managers must also be concerned with how to manage the resources used for the project. Chapters 9 is therefore included to show the basics of how a Critical Path schedule can be used to plan and track resources, as well as how to use the schedule to adjust workload to use resources more efficiently. Finally, Chapter 10 covers how a schedule can be used to plan, track and control the procurement process and its inevitable paperwork. Several appendixes are included, among them a complete estimate and logic diagrams for the sample office building project, as well as some tips for developing logic diagrams.

Acknowledgments

The author would like to express grateful appreciation to all the individuals and companies who contributed to the preparation of this book by sharing their experience and knowledge over the course of the author's career in construction teaching and practice.

Particular appreciation is due to Dean Evans, Kevin Evans and Brent Bartenfeld of Evans Technologies, Incorporated, for their support in developing the software exhibits for the book, and to Joel Koppelman, President of Primavera Systems, Inc., who has been unstinting in his support of professors all over the country who have been charged with teaching construction scheduling.

Introduction

Scheduling and management of a construction project is a three-step process that requires the involvement of all the parties on a job site. It demands that the participants look ahead at the work to be done, plan strategies for getting it done, and then monitor the work to ensure completion according to plan. Each step requires the commitment and dedication of all project team members. All are essential to the successful outcome of a construction project, and to the long term success of a construction firm.

The first step is establishing a plan of action for carrying out the construction work. This involves breaking the job down into a series of manageable sub-parts, deciding on an order of placement, and determining the time and cost for each part and for the job as a whole. This early planning results in a "road map" to be followed by all persons and companies on the job—to finish the project on time and within budget. There is no one best plan for each project, just as there is no one correct estimated cost. There are only choices among possible plans. The task of the project manager is to make the right choices to ensure that a reasonable and effective plan is devised, one that reflects the intentions and desires of those who will be responsible for its accomplishment.

After the plan has been developed and accepted, it must be communicated effectively to all those on the job. The quality and plausibility of this plan and the degree to which management personnel are involved in its development set the tone for the work itself. Once the job is under way and the plan is being carried out, events inevitably occur that will force changes in the job. To cope effectively with these events, the project manager must ensure that the second management setup is carried out.

The second step in project scheduling and management is regular monitoring of the job. This includes comparing the progress of the work to the original plan to see which aspects of the job are going according to plan, and which are not. To check progress, individual parts of the job are tracked to determine if they are completed within the time limits of the schedule. With information gathered from this tracking and monitoring, the project manager must find out where the job is off track.

Finally, in the third step, the project manager must determine the causes of any delays that have occurred, and then follow through. This means working with the personnel responsible for the job's progress to ensure that corrective action is taken to bring the troubled parts of the job back into line. In order to do this, the project manager must involve all the working managers in the problem-solving process to determine causes and corrective actions. This process frequently involves re-planning and aggressive follow-up. These actions are essential, however, if the job is to be properly controlled and a late and unprofitable finish avoided.

Project scheduling and management is a difficult task, but one that must be performed well to realize both short- and long-term success in the construction business. The process requires taking a close look at field procedures and plans, and at the ways in which field managers and subcontractors are managed and scheduled. The rewards of effective project management are time saved and money earned. When vigorously pursued by the project manager, these methods help prevent the problems of late job completions and cost overruns. This book is intended to provide all project management professionals with effective skills and tools to carry out these planning, monitoring, and follow-up tasks, and to show how these tasks can be carried out with the least possible cost and effort to the individuals and their companies.

What Is
Project Management?

1

What Is Project Management?

The goal of this book is to help the reader become a more effective construction project manager, or to help a construction company carry out more effective project management and control. A major element in the process of project management is that of scheduling the work of the project, and then keeping the work on track and on time as the project unfolds. This book is devoted specifically to that part of the project management. However, if we are to schedule as effectively as possible, it is important for us to understand the underlying principles of management as they relate to project management generally and scheduling specifically. These general principles form the basis for specific tasks we must execute as we schedule and control a project. The following chapter is therefore aimed at helping the reader understand these principles as a starting point for subsequent chapters.

What Is Management?

- It is the planning, organizing, staffing, directing, and controlling of resources to achieve a company's goals.
- It is deciding, for both individuals and groups, the use of resources and implementing such decisions.
- It is controlling and directing human resources toward a goal.
- It is the rational, systematic process of decision making, to achieve specific goals.

These general definitions introduce some key elements:

Goals

Process

System

Decisions

Rational Process

Personnel

Resources

Planning

Control

At the very beginning, we recognize that **goals** are always involved. In a philosophical sense, without a set of goals, there is no point in even taking actions. In practical terms, a construction company or manager must have profit as an overall goal. Establishing smaller and more focused short-term goals is a very important part of the overall task of project management.

Process can be defined as a set of continuing actions over time. The management process must be carried on continually throughout the life of the job or company. Management must be done in a **systematic** way, which means an orderly, regular, and dependable way, using a set of established procedures or methods.

Management also means that **decisions** must be made in order to achieve the goals of the project or company. These decisions must be made **rationally**, that is, based on facts, not hunches or inaccurate information. One of the primary reasons for setting up a systematic, orderly method of management is to deliver accurate, timely information to the decision makers on the job.

Personnel are always a management consideration. On a job site, there are craftsmen, subcontractors, suppliers, designers, and owner's representatives, among many others who must work together in the process of getting a project built. The necessary personal and organizational interactions make the process complex and challenging. The decisions made by managers must take into account the requirements, opinions, and attitudes of all these concerned parties. A good project manager brings these parties together regularly, to encourage a shared effort toward achieving the project goals.

We must also be concerned with the expenditure of **resources** as the job progresses. Labor must be hired, and effectively and efficiently controlled; material bought at the right time and price; subcontractors employed and properly scheduled; and owner-furnished materials supplied and properly installed. Again, the system we establish must provide for the use of these resources in the best possible way toward achieving the project goals.

Once a sound project management system is in place, the project manager may use it to carry out the more specific functions of **planning** and **controlling**. *Planning* can be defined as scheduling the tasks that will accomplish the goals of the project. This means establishing realistic schedules and budgets, coordinating resources to get the work done, and most importantly, making sure everyone knows what the plan of action is.

Controlling is the final action in the management process. To achieve and maintain control, the project manager monitors the progress of the job. When short-term goals are not being met, the project manager must take action to get everything back on track.

What Is Project Management?

The previously listed concepts are the basis for effective construction project management. The tasks listed below grow out of these concepts and are the focus of this book.

1. Establish and focus on goals that will be general at first, then increasingly specific and job-oriented.
2. Establish an effective management process that will operate in a systematic manner.
3. Use this management process, or system, to make the best possible rational decisions for efficiently using resources, coordinating personnel on the job, and planning and controlling the work throughout the life of the job.

Having defined the three major project management tasks, we can begin to focus on the more specific jobs of the project manager.

1. Setting Goals

The first task of the construction project manager is establishing goals. Many goals have already been set by the project estimate and contract documents. A primary purpose of the estimate is to arrive at a cost for the project, while the contract establishes the time required for completion. Neither of these goals—cost or time—can be altered in any significant way by the project manager. However, the project manager can set intermediate goals for the construction process, goals that meet the ultimate requirements of cost and time.

2. Creating a Project Management System

After setting goals for the project, the next task of the project manager is to establish control through an effective management system. There are two approaches to project management. They are: 1) proactive—aggressive management ensuring that the job proceeds as planned by the manager; or 2) reactive —spending money and reacting as events occur, letting circumstances run the job. The latter, reactive scenario tends to occur if the manager fails to set up a properly organized, thorough, and methodical management system. This approach almost certainly guarantees that a job will overrun time and budget allowances, and generally cause much grief to all concerned.

The management system should be designed to address the following elements:

Time: A plan of action must be established to assure the work is done in the correct order or sequence and within the time allowed.

Cost: The work must be performed efficiently if the contractor's goals are to be met.

Resources: It must be determined in advance when and how much of each resource (such as particular categories of labor, equipment, or materials) is needed to do the work. One must then ensure that the resource is provided when and where needed. Resource management supports the effort to control time and cost. The information used by the project manager to perform this task is developed from the time and cost information data.

Finances: Ultimately, time and resources translate into dollars. Thus, the financial control function means accurately predicting the amount of cash needed to support all the work done on the job.

3. Managing the Project

The third task of the project manager is to manage the project as it proceeds, using the project control system to best advantage. In the simplest terms, is the project heading in the right direction to meet its goals? Project control is best illustrated as a *feedback loop*, shown in Figure 1.1.

Managing the project begins with the input of data on labor, materials, and equipment—the resources used to build the project. As the work is performed, the output, or productivity, is measured to see if it is meeting the goals set for the project. If it is not, corrective action must be taken.

Project control can be illustrated by comparing it to a feedback loop used in machine control. For example, a cruise control on a car measures the speed of the car, compares it to the preset speed, and if there is a variation, either adds or reduces throttle to return the speed of the car to the preset limit. If the cruise control fails to function properly, the car either takes a long time to reach its destination, or the driver gets a ticket. Using feedback to manage and control a construction project, however, requires a few more steps. The project manager must perform the following tasks.

Plan: Realistic, usable schedules and budgets must be established for all phases of the job. These guidelines will serve as a "blueprint" for building the job. The schedules and budgets should be based on the original estimate and contract requirements. They must reflect the commitment of the people who will have to carry them out.

Communicate: Once developed, the plans must be communicated clearly and effectively to the people who will be executing them. Emphasis must be placed on providing clear, usable visual displays, particularly for scheduling.

It is also wise to recognize that the professionalism shown by the project manager in planning and communicating on the job site has a very real effect on employee morale and effectiveness. A sloppy plan, poorly organized and executed, gives employees the impression that they work for a slipshod organization. Pride in their work will be affected accordingly.

Monitor and Control: After the plans have been developed and communicated, they must be carried out by project personnel. Realistically, some unexpected events could interfere with the original plan. If this occurs, the project manager must take steps to ensure that the project goals are met. This means taking action to bring the job back in line with the original plan, or revising the plan to fit the new situation.

If the project manager is to effectively deal with delays, the management system must provide him with the most current information. This monitoring function involves collecting data on time and cost, and comparing this information to original projections.

Once the project manager is aware of the current job status as compared to the original plan, actions can be taken to meet the original goals. These actions can range from adding more crews to speed up sheetrock installation, to completely changing the installation sequence of complex formwork.

Two other points should be made about the feedback loop. First, construction job sites can be very busy places, with many activities going on at one time. Therefore, it is important that the management system be *exception-oriented*. That is to say, the system should be designed to specifically point out those items that are at variance with the plan, and to essentially ignore those that are proceeding on schedule. Without an *exception-oriented system*, the project manager is in danger of being overwhelmed with detail, while key areas may be overlooked.

Second, the information provided must be timely, so that problems are caught and recognized early in the game. Problems on a job tend to worsen at an accelerating rate. It is important to catch them before they have a chance to become major disasters.

The key to monitoring and control by project management is making frequent checks of job status and, if necessary, taking action to ensure that the project's goals are met. Failing in either checking or acting will result in a failure to meet the project goals.

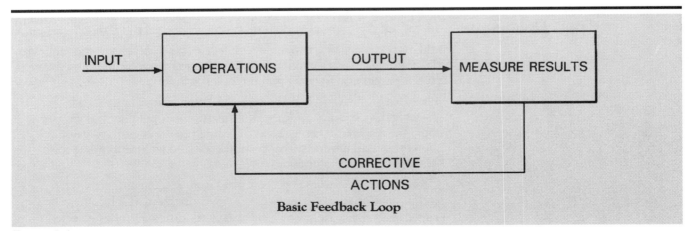

Basic Feedback Loop

Figure 1.1

Why Use Project Management?

In the previous sections, we have recommended an overall strategy for project management and control. There is still, however, some feeling in the construction industry that all this management and paperwork is not really necessary—that one can monitor the job effectively enough by walking around the site to ensure on-time completion and a profit. In reality, the current state of the construction industry is such that more effective techniques for control and management on the job are essential.

The recent history of some construction projects is sadly one of the reasons why old methods of project control are no longer effective. Today's construction projects are complex and very different than in the past. For example, building environmental control systems have replaced simple heating systems. Structures may now consist of high-, early-strength, post-tensioned concrete floor systems with shear walls, where we once had simple flat slabs and columns. Windows have become complete "exterior enclosure systems." This means a greater variety of jobs to be done, and a greater percentage of subcontractors. Architects and owners have a much wider range of materials and systems to choose from; thus, very few projects are the same.

The increased variety of construction materials and methods has generated more detail than can be managed effectively by one person. In the past, one individual could carry out most of the management tasks since only the basic trades were involved, there was an architect and an owner, and the contract was straightforward. Today's project manager must coordinate specialized subcontractors and work with design specialists who are, in effect, subcontractors of the architect. Many regulatory agencies have also entered the picture. The total management work load has increased to the point that a team with a comprehensive, well-designed system of control is essential. Contractors who attempt to deal with this new situation in the same old ways have encountered enormous problems.

At the same time, a kind of revolt has been taking place on the part of owners, who are themselves faced with some difficult circumstances. The highly volatile marketplace of recent years, which has been aggravated by periods of high inflation and high interest rates, has put extreme pressure on owners for on-time and within budget project completion. As a result, owners tend to increase pressure on contractors for better and quicker performance. A contractor not using up-to-date methods is at a serious competitive disadvantage. In some cases, owners have even dictated changes in operating methods to contractors. The demands of clients provide yet one more argument for good project controls.

Good project controls can help keep us out of the legal arena—first by making it more likely that we will perform better, thus reducing the reason for legal action—and second, by providing us with a better set of documents with which disputes may be more easily resolved.

The Benefits

Having reviewed today's situation and having seen the need for an improvement in management, the question arises—why use scheduling? Above all, it should be used because it has proven effective on construction jobs. In particular, the use of Critical Path Method (CPM) scheduling (and the implementation of this method using computers) is clearly both workable and cost-effective.

While a computer and good control systems are not a panacea and will not do the manager's job, they are very helpful in providing a way to set up target plans, track events on the site, and examine alternate ways to correct the schedule of work in the event of deviation from the original plan. A good control system is especially helpful to the manager in pinpointing the problem areas, and therefore helps to manage and reduce the information overload. While such an approach may not guarantee success in terms of cost and time, the intelligent use of control systems definitely increases the odds that success will follow the project manager's efforts.

Better Organization

One of the benefits of using good management systems is that they encourage, or even force, better organization and planning. This is a vital influence since one of the biggest failures of managers in industry is a lack of planning. Effective monitoring and control must start with a workable plan. It has even been said that 75% of the value of creating a CPM schedule is the initial planning that must accompany the process. This statement may be an exaggeration and probably reflects the fact that people in the field sometimes tend to be less rigorous about updating and monitoring a schedule as the project progresses. Nonetheless, a well organized initial plan starts the job off right.

Using control systems also forces the manager to look at how all of the available resources will be assembled and used. It encourages better purchasing and timing, and reduces wasted motion.

A Good Basis for Coordination

A major problem for many contractors is subcontractor scheduling. A big part of the solution is communication. If the project manager and superintendent maintain an up-to-date schedule and require the subs to attend regular job schedule meetings, all the parties on the job will be operating from a base of common agreement. Also, the regularly scheduled meetings encourage subcontractor participation in the scheduling process. This participation promotes a sense of commitment to the project.

In general, better coordination benefits all of the parties to a project—the owner, contractor, designer, and subcontractor. Delays are prevented rather than reacted to, costs are contained early, claims prevented or resolved earlier and more amicably. The result is a better profit for all.

Management by Exception

As noted, a major challenge for today's project manager is tracking vast amounts of detail. Computers provide an advantage as they are very good clerical and record keeping devices. Most of the computer-based management systems used today take advantage of this capability, and promote the exception-based management approach. The systems can be set up to track all work, but report only those elements of job progress that deviate significantly from the original plan. This leaves the project manager free to devote his or her construction knowledge and skill to the problem areas, leaving the on-schedule areas to proceed to completion.

Another key point in a computer-based management system is providing early detection of problem areas, thus helping to prevent unpleasant surprises. This early detection is critical to correction, since as we all know problems on construction sites never get better without attention; they only get worse.

Better Decision-Making

A good, up-to-date management system and the associated techniques will in all cases provide the basis for better decisions on the job. Accurate information is an absolute necessity for sound decisions. Such a system should be designed to display the essential data, and to weigh the effects of alternate plans of action. Many experts suggest that a better term for *project control systems* is *management information systems*. Regardless of the name applied, a good system properly used will result in better decisions, and thus, better results.

Variables That Affect the Project

While the benefits of project management are clear, it must be noted that a good project management system—whether manual or computerized—cannot be implemented without an investment of money and time on the part of corporate management. It is, however, an investment that brings a definite and positive return. It is certainly worthwhile to review some of the common problems associated with developing better project management. Forewarned, one can at least minimize these problems. Later chapters of this book will cover the procedures and possible pitfalls in more detail.

Personnel

In any change, people must be the first consideration. First, the installation or development of new project management techniques must directly involve the people who will be responsible for the results. Probably the worst possible approach is to simply choose a technique or system, and mandate, "you *will* use this system." The people involved should be recognized as knowledgeable, competent, and concerned about their job performance. Their professionalism will also be helpful in choosing and operating any new and better procedure. They must be brought into the decision-making and changeover process.

Job-site personnel may be somewhat intimidated by new methods. For example, a superintendent may fear that a new scheduling or cost system will have the home office looking over his shoulder. Or a project engineer may feel uncomfortable with a new, unfamiliar system, fearing failure due to lack of knowledge. The solution to these kinds of problems lies in: 1) honest dealings with the persons involved, with an emphasis on team improvement and the removal of threatening elements, and 2) training, which will clearly demonstrate the company's commitment to improvement and willingness to continue investing in its employees.

Cost and Organizational Concerns

The project manager must recognize that implementation of better management techniques will cost real dollars and will require some organizational changes and adjustment. As previously noted, the benefits justify the investment of time and money.

Organizational changes clearly involve people. To begin with, any improvement in the system must start with the wholehearted commitment and backing of the company's management. Without it, it is difficult for a single project manager to undertake significant improvement in techniques.

It is also important that company management approach the problem professionally. If, for example, the company president's attitude toward installing and developing a new project control system seems sloppy and half-hearted, company personnel will perceive that the president does not really care about good project control. The development of a better project control system is probably doomed from the start in this circumstance, since the people who have to carry it out will not devote anything like their best effort to a project that they feel the president will not reward.

Another organizational concern is inflexibility, or rather the fear of it, among construction people. The personalities who do well in the construction field are traditionally self reliant and individually competent. They prefer to work with little supervision and to be judged on results, not methods. Also, most field supervisors have more than a few good ideas themselves, which they are willing to share with upper management. A new technique or method should therefore be flexible enough to allow for this kind of individual approach in the field. The emphasis should be on making the burden as light as possible for the field, with the information as accessible and usable as possible.

One final note concerns the importance of communications. When new procedures are being discussed and changes are in the wind, rumors are inevitable and may hurt morale and cripple the effort to change for the better. Such rumors are best countered by full and open disclosure to project personnel whose lives and professions are directly affected.

Use of Computers in the Construction Industry

It is a fact of life in the construction industry that computers are here to stay. Many contractors have successfully adopted computers for appropriate uses in their organizations and have become more competitive as a result. As is always the case with new management procedures, the implementation and use of computers necessarily involves an investment of both money and managerial time.

The actual investment takes several forms. At the very beginning, management time must be devoted to deciding what kind of hardware and software to purchase and implement. Once these decisions are made, machines and software must be purchased and personnel trained. The training period is apt to be a time of relative inefficiency, since old methods and systems will probably have to be maintained at the same time that the new one is being brought on line. Further, the people being trained in these new methods will be less efficient due to their individual learning curves. After the new procedure is in use, there are ongoing operating expenses.

There is no doubt that computers and software, properly used, are helpful and productive management tools. The challenge is learning how to implement them to greatest advantage. More than anything else, persuading employees to accept computers and software as useful tools is a matter of helping them use the tools easily and effectively. This means that the company must invest in adequate training for all users. Modern software systems have advanced enormously from those available at the beginning of the micro-computer era, but they still are not such that an untrained user can simply turn on the machine, click a few times, and turn out useful information. At the very least, a construction company should make sure that all field personnel who are involved in scheduling have enough training to understand the basic concepts of critical path methods. Also, those persons who will be actually operating the software should receive specific course work in whatever package the company uses. Finally, construction managers should promote and encourage the use of critical path methods and software. One highly effective method is to insist on receiving regular reports developed using computer technology. Not only does this give a manager a better picture of job progress, it also forces the field managers to examine their own performance.

Summary

In this first chapter, we discussed the ideas behind the specific program management tools and techniques we will develop later in this book. These ideas have been well-known for many years, in construction and in other industries as well. Also, since there still tends to be some resistance to using modern scheduling techniques in construction, we discussed some of the benefits that can result from adopting these techniques. In the next chapter, we will discuss the extension of the basic management ideas, and in particular, we will expand the concept of the feedback and control cycle into what is known as the Project Control Cycle. This Cycle is a more detailed version of the concept, adapted especially for construction, which a Project Manager can use as a model for setting up his or her own techniques and procedures.

2

The Project
Control Cycle

2

The Project Control Cycle

We have discussed monitoring and controlling, functions that are at the heart of the project manager's job. The goals of monitoring and controlling can also be used as a model for setting up the operations of our project management system. The simple feedback loop (see Figure 1.1) does not, however, cover all of the details that must be dealt with on an actual project. The *Project Control Cycle*, shown in Figure 2.1, illustrates the practical workings of project management.

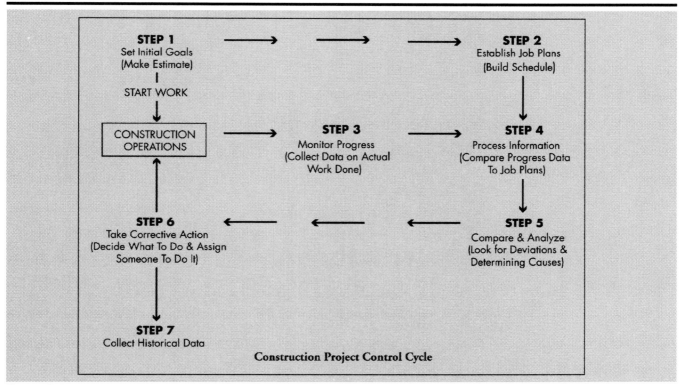

Figure 2.1

Basic Management Functions

Step 1: Set Initial Goals

The first step in the project control cycle is setting initial goals. This step typically occurs before the job is even awarded to the contractor. The initial goal is generally no more than a profit goal for the project, in the form of an estimate. Regardless of whether that estimate is conceptual or fixed, or something in between, it serves as a limiting factor, along with the time allowed in the contract documents. Simply put, no future budget for construction should exceed the costs anticipated in the estimate, nor can the time planned in a schedule exceed the number of days permitted under the terms of a contract. The detailed development of estimates is not within the scope of this book. However, using the estimate and contract documents to develop the intermediate goals and job plans is covered in detail.

Step 2: Establish Job Plans

This second step, establishing job plans, typically occurs after the job has gotten underway, and crews and equipment have moved onto the site. It may not seem advisable to start without a control mechanism completely in place. However, initial conferences will typically have been held during the period right after contract award. Information gleaned during this time may provide a good basis for initial decisions. Such decisions are later developed into detailed job plans.

Establishing job plans for scheduling is done in a three-step process. First, the overall job is broken down into workable parts or *activities*. These activities can be analyzed and planned independently for maximum efficiency. Second, the activities are strung together in a realistic order of work, which is then converted into a logic diagram, or network. The third and final step involves network calculations to determine at what time and on what dates each activity should occur. The final result is a comprehensive plan which serves the following two functions: it is a guide to action by all those involved with building the job, and it can later be used to effectively cope with the inevitable changes that will occur.

Step 3: Monitor Progress

After the job is underway and detailed plans have been drawn up in the form of a budget and schedule, the job monitoring system must be established and used by the project managers. The first part of this process is carried out on the construction site at regular intervals, and involves monitoring the actual events which occur on the project, to be compared with the schedule later in the cycle.

Schedule monitoring is done on an activity-by-activity basis, again reflecting the very important concept of dealing with workable-sized units of the job at all stages. Typically, each activity is labeled with the following information: start time, duration of work, and anticipated final completion.

Step 4: Process Information

This activity occurs throughout the monitoring and control process. A computer or manual procedure is used to manipulate the data collected during the monitoring phase. The data is set up so that it can be compared with the plans developed earlier. This processed information enables the project manager to determine whether or not the project is deviating from the planned order or rate of progress, and if that deviation is significant enough to warrant action.

The key element in this information processing phase is the management of the project control *system*, as distinct from managing the project. The processing and use of the plans and monitoring of data depends in large part on having logical and workable coding systems. Also needed is a regular, efficient, and workable procedure for quickly and accurately developing comparison reports for management.

As projects grow larger, managing the project control system becomes more and more a full time job for a specialist. However, this does not mean that a project management system cannot be operated without specialized job site personnel. The key is having a system that is appropriate for the job at hand.

Step 5: Compare and Analyze

In Step 5, the project managers review the information developed by the system in the last stage in order to determine the actual state of the project. Report formats must be selected for typical job decisions, and other methods established for efficient exception reporting. The greater the efficiency, the more the project manager's efforts can be directed to those areas of the project which are most in need of management attention.

Step 6: Take Corrective Action

Taking corrective action represents the final step—acting to rectify an aspect of the job which is not going according to plan. A complete evaluation of Step 6 would include a wide range of topics, since the project manager must deal with technical questions relative to the actual delay or cost overrun.

It is fairly common in construction for deviations from plan to be noted, but not followed up by project personnel. This is equivalent to not monitoring the job at all, and means that not only is the effort spent in developing a project management system wasted, but the job is also likely to end up behind schedule and over cost. The project management feedback cycle must have all its parts working in order for the job to be properly run.

Step 7: Collect Historical Data

Step 7 occurs on the expanded project control cycle, but does not occur on the general feedback cycle. It involves collecting data on what has happened on the job. Ideally, the results of the job are recorded for two purposes: first, to serve as a basis for planning future jobs; and second, to serve as a thorough record of actual events in case claims arise.

Introduction to the Sample Building Project

Now that we have discussed—in general terms—the main steps that are performed in the scheduling and controlling process, we can begin to look at them in detail and explore techniques for actually running a project. Subsequent chapters develop these ideas and tools step by step, using a sample office building project, which is included in this chapter. The goal is to provide the reader with a demonstration of what real scheduling would be like. The reader is therefore invited to become familiar with the sample project, just as he or she would on a real project, and then follow the process through as the chapters unfold. Ideally, at the end of the book, the reader will then have some real skills in scheduling and a sense of how the process proceeds. The sample project itself is a multi-story office building with a basement parking garage. The structure is built on a typical suburban site with the usual parking lots. The structure for the parking garage and main floor is concrete waffle slab, and for the upper stories, structural steel with steel decking and concrete topping. There is also a penthouse structure of concrete masonry units with steel joist roof which contains mechanical equipment. The main tower enclosure system is aluminum curtain wall. The interiors of all three office floors are minimally finished, as would be the case if the space had not been leased yet. The ceilings are, however, fully finished, as are the floors. The plans for the building are shown in Figures 2.2 through 2.19 and a complete estimate can be found in Appendix A.

In reality, such a building would require many more sheets of plans, though construction schedules are often developed from schematic or design development drawings of a similar level of detail as these sample drawings. A set of specifications would also be included with an actual set of plans. However, for purposes of illustrating scheduling principles, these drawings provide sufficient information. Assumptions have been made for items not shown in the sample drawings that would normally be included in the plans and specifications for a building of this type.

TECHNICAL COLLEGE OF THE LOWCOUNTRY
LEARNING RESOURCES CENTER
POST OFFICE BOX 1288
BEAUFORT, SOUTH CAROLINA 29901-1288

Summary

In this second chapter, we outlined in detail the specific steps of the Project Control Cycle, which is the underlying concept behind all the actions and steps a Project Manager must perform to properly control the schedule of a construction project. If, as the reader continues through the book, learning the actual tools and concepts of scheduling, he or she refers back to the appropriate step in the Cycle, the logic behind the tool or action will be clearer, and the reader can understand the total process, rather than simply learning to apply a series of steps in isolation. Also, we introduced the sample project, which serves as an illustrative device for teaching the specific tools. If the reader can become thoroughly familiar with this hypothetical building, he or she will more easily understand each step, and can more easily translate the ideas to his/her own projects. In the next chapter, we will start describing the actual process of scheduling, beginning with the preliminary information gathering which should precede any actual work planning.

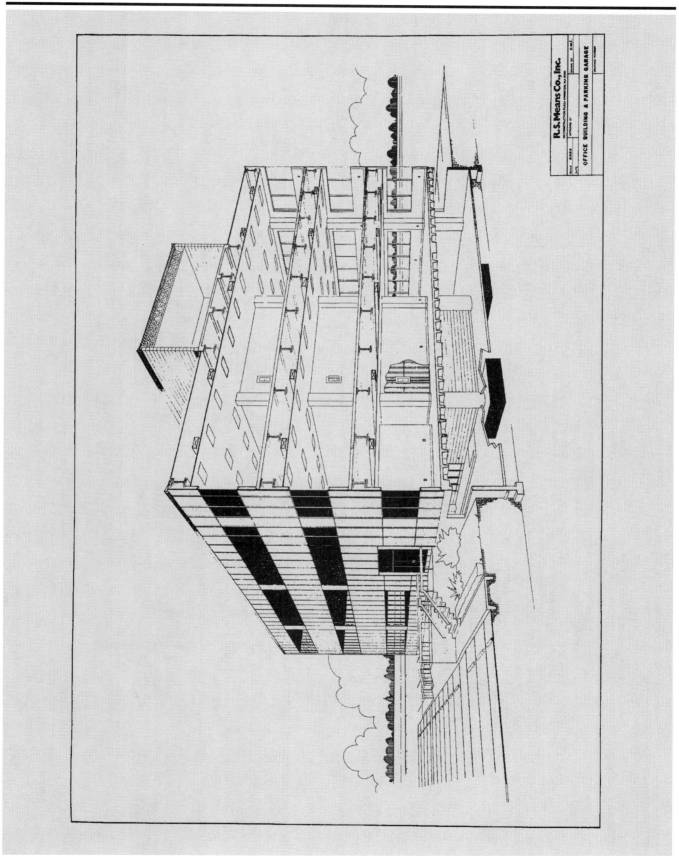

Figure 2.2

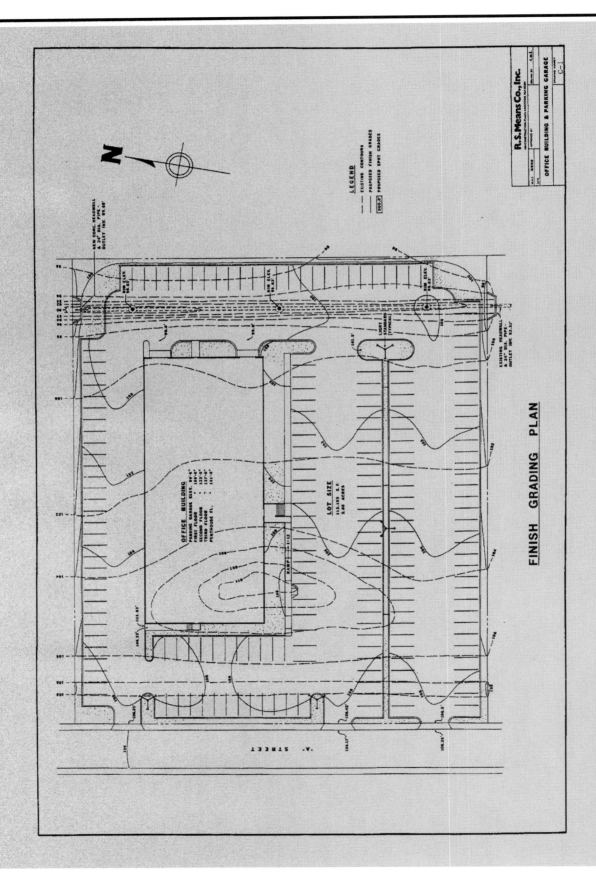

Figure 2.3

18

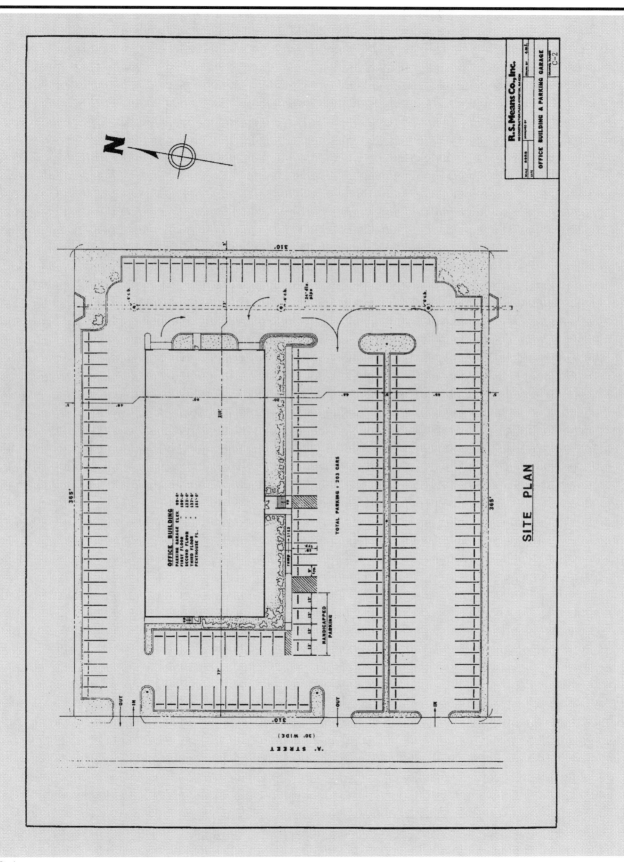

Figure 2.4

19

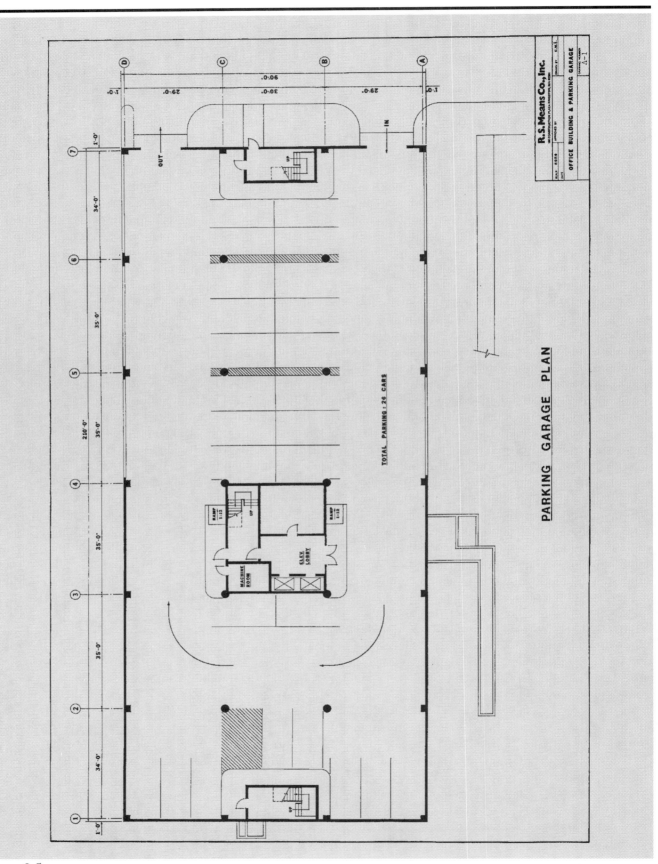

PARKING GARAGE PLAN

TOTAL PARKING : 26 CARS

Figure 2.5

20

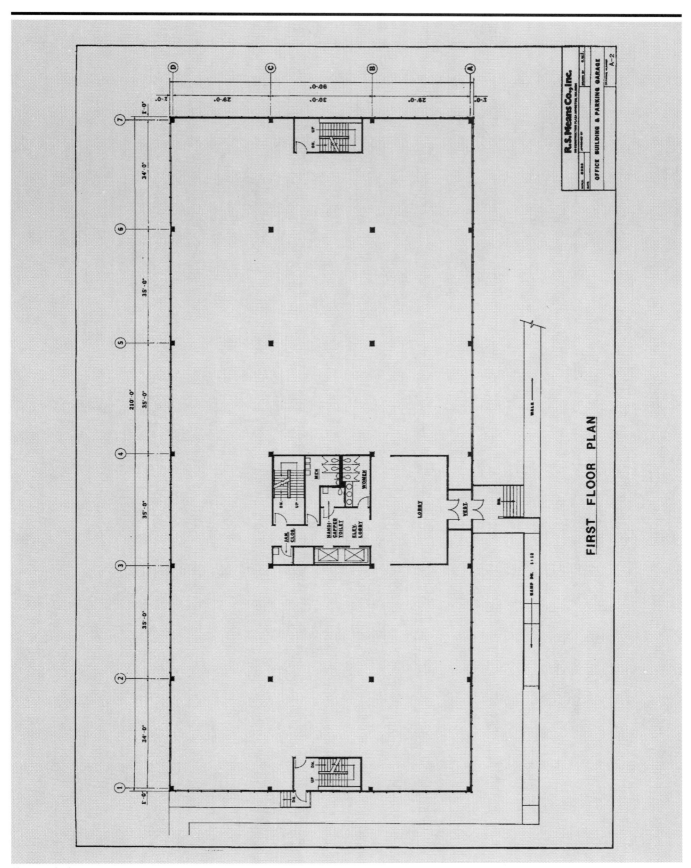

Figure 2.6

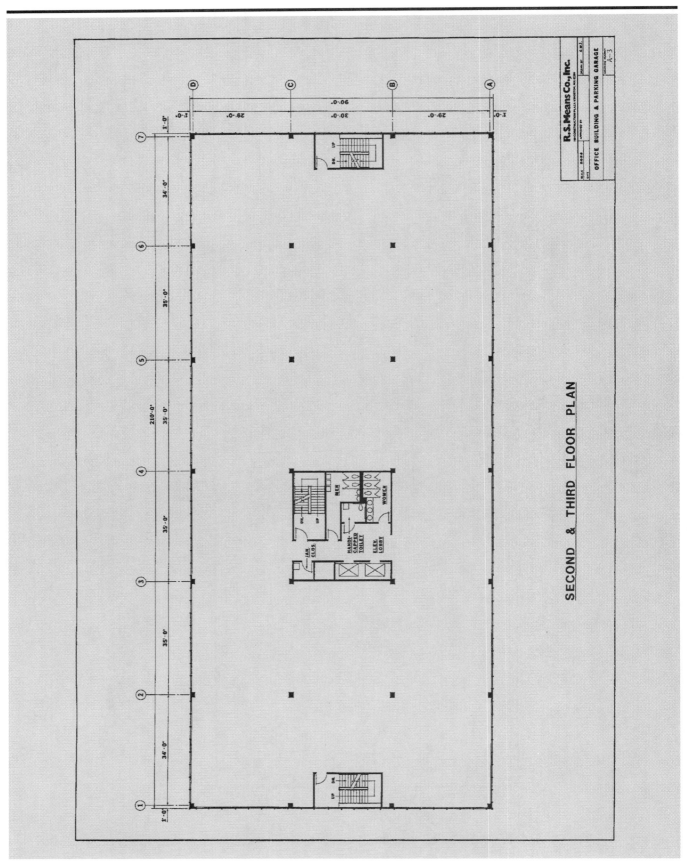

SECOND & THIRD FLOOR PLAN

Figure 2.7

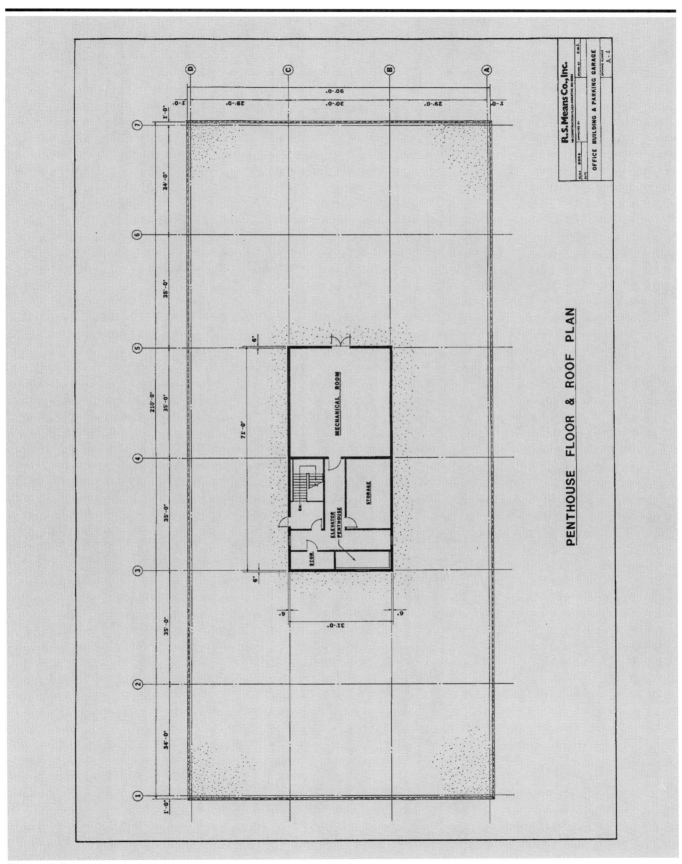

PENTHOUSE FLOOR & ROOF PLAN

Figure 2.8

23

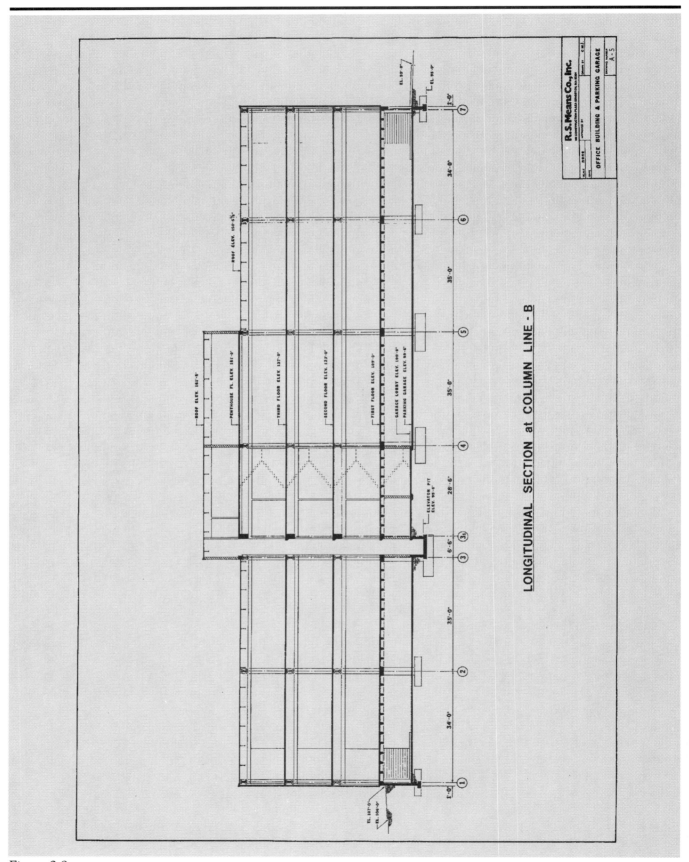

Figure 2.9

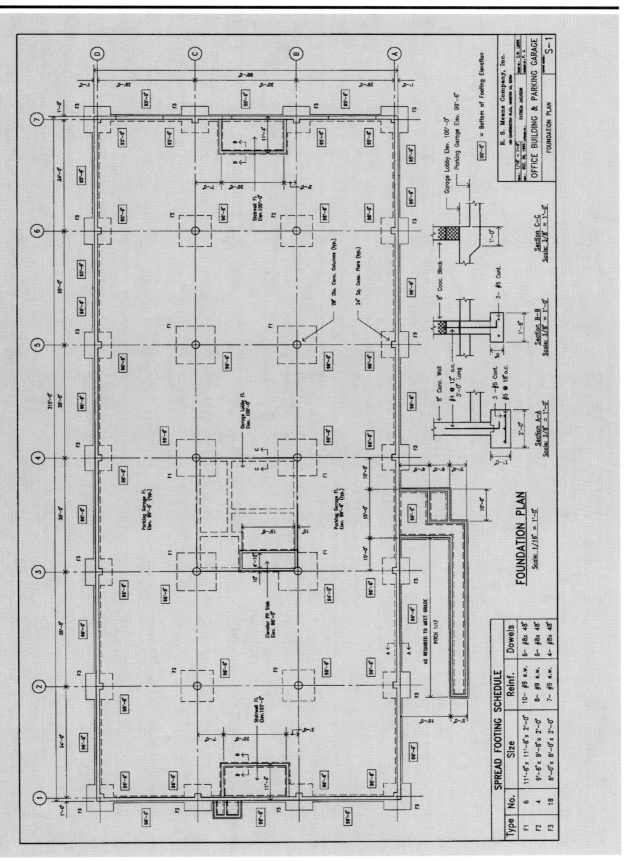

Figure 2.10

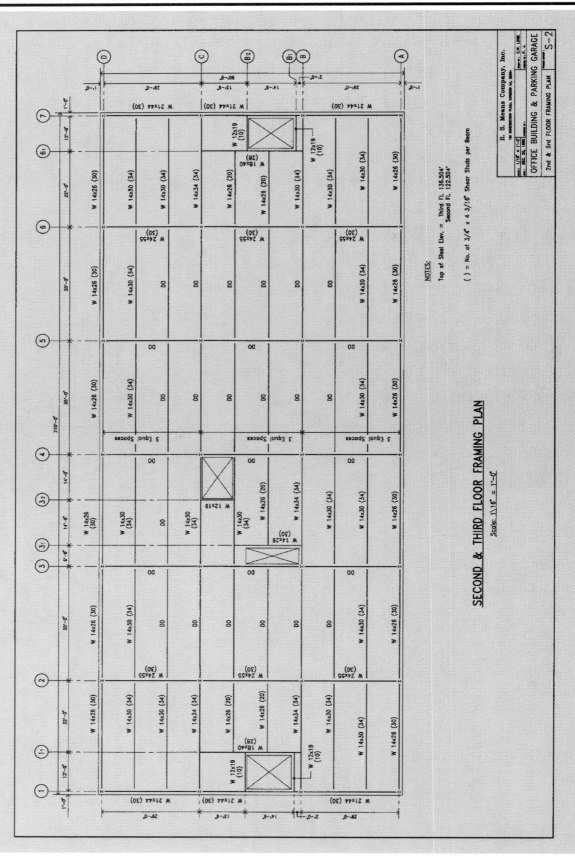

SECOND & THIRD FLOOR FRAMING PLAN

Scale: 1\16" = 1'-0"

NOTES:

Top of Steel Elev. = Third Fl. 135.50±'
                     Second Fl. 122.50±'

( ) = No. of 3/4" x 4 3/16" Shear Studs per Beam

Figure 2.11

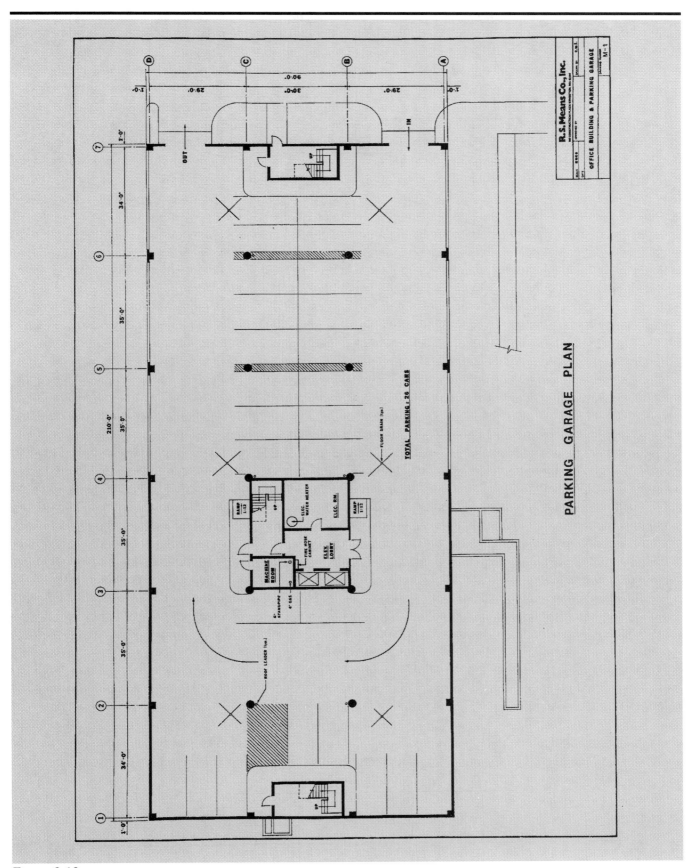

PARKING GARAGE PLAN

Figure 2.12

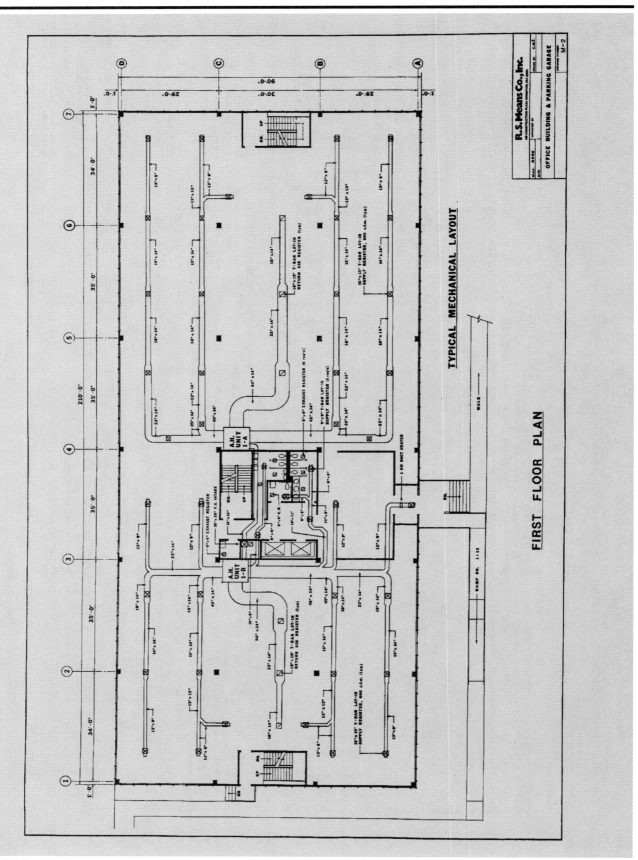

Figure 2.13

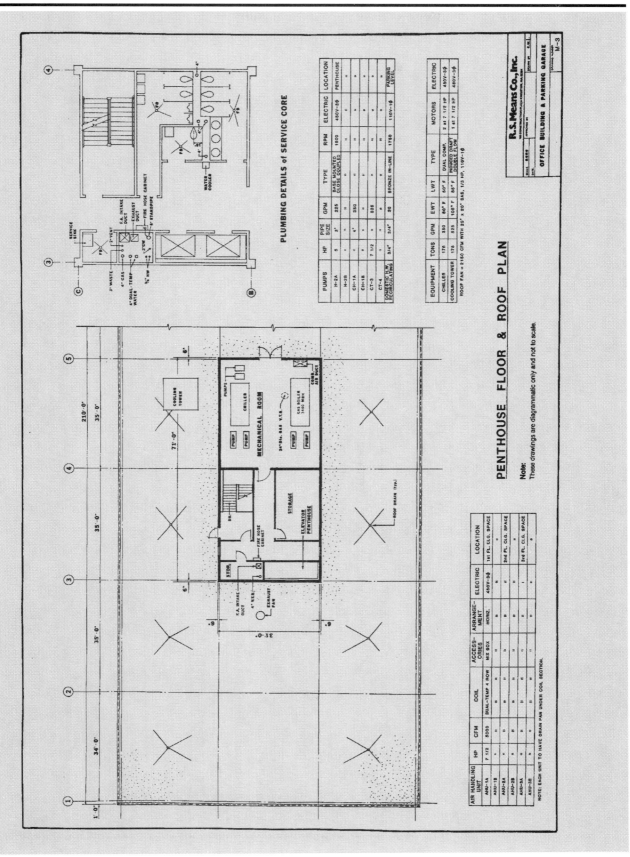

Figure 2.14

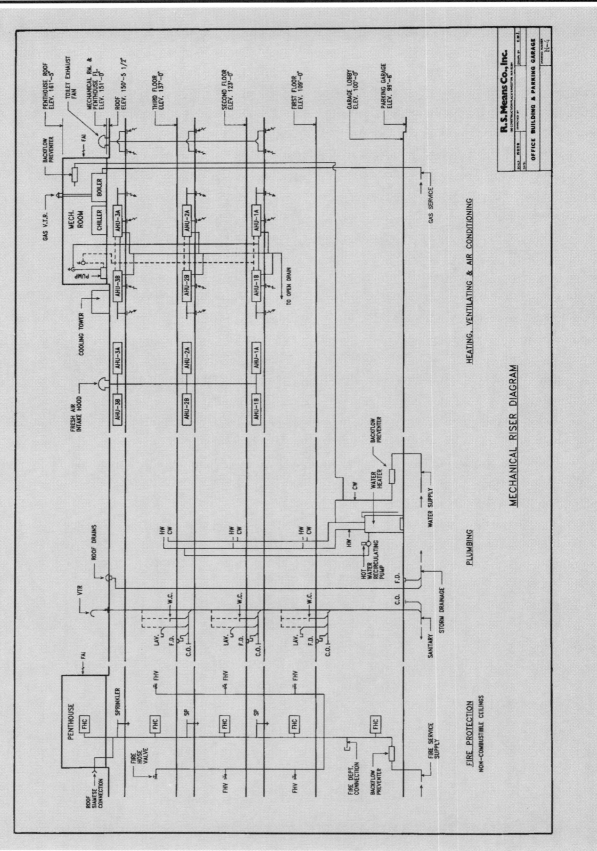

Figure 2.15

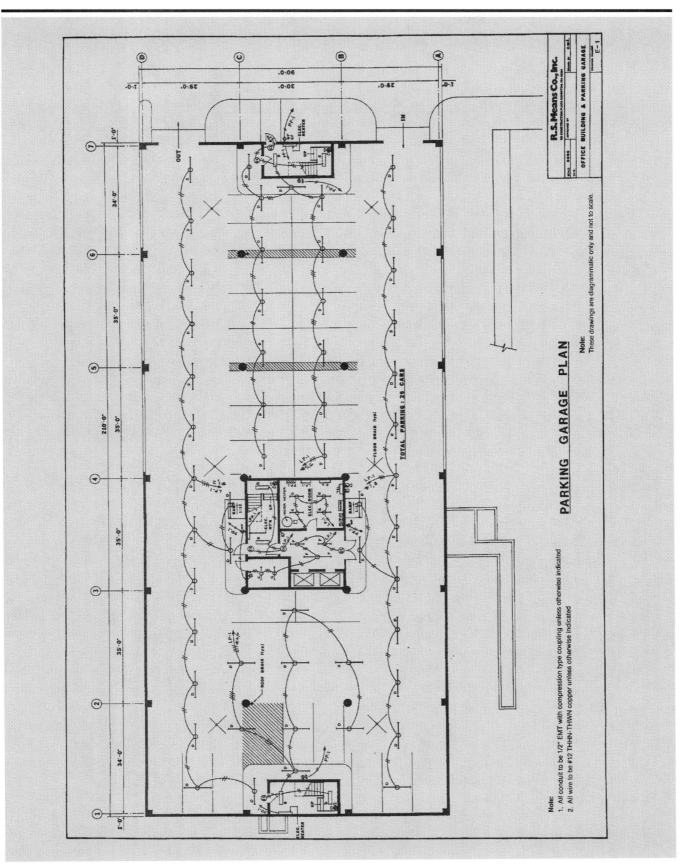

Figure 2.16

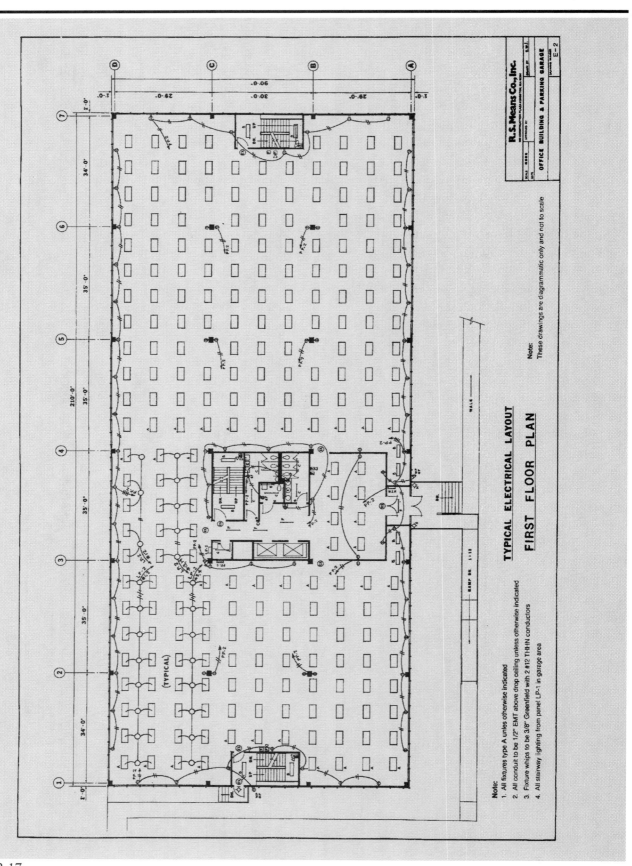

Figure 2.17

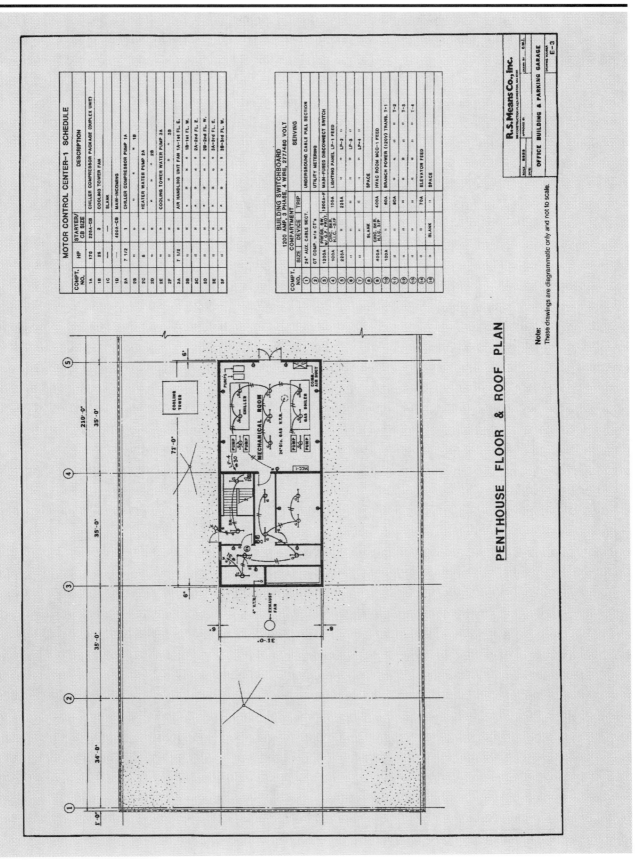

Figure 2.18

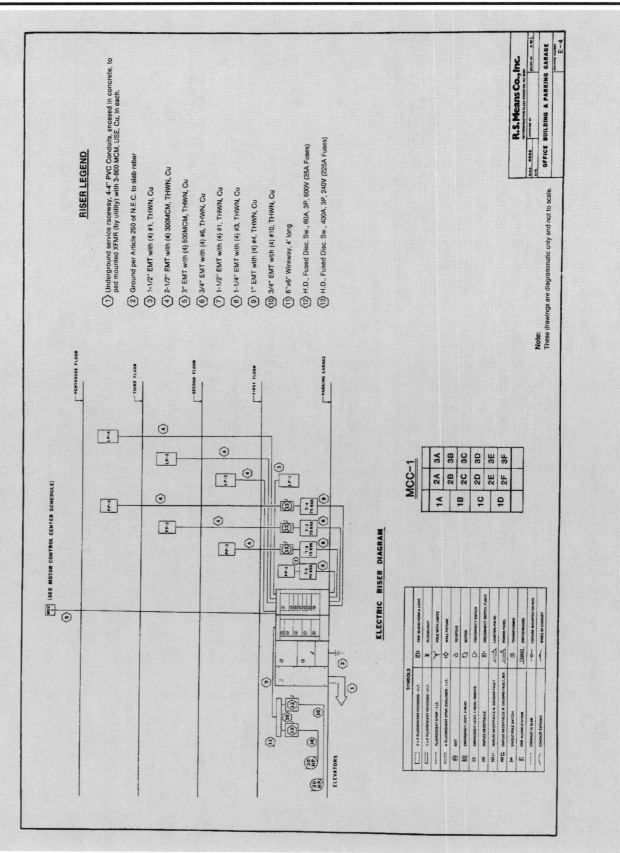

RISER LEGEND

1. Underground service raceway, 4-4" PVC Conduits, encased in concrete, to pad mounted XFMR (by utility) with 3-800 MCM, USE, Cu, in each.
2. Ground per Article 250 of N.E.C. to slab rebar
3. 1-1/2" EMT with (4) #1, THWN, Cu
4. 2-1/2" EMT with (4) 300MCM, THWN, Cu
5. 3" EMT with (4) 500MCM, THWN, Cu
6. 3/4" EMT with (4) #6, THWN, Cu
7. 1-1/2" EMT with (4) #1, THWN, Cu
8. 1-1/4" EMT with (4) #3, THWN, Cu
9. 1" EMT with (4) #4, THWN, Cu
10. 3/4" EMT with (4) #10, THWN, Cu
11. 6"x6" Wireway, 4' long
12. H.D. Fused Disc. Sw., 60A, 3P, 600V (35A Fuses)
13. H.D. Fused Disc. Sw., 400A, 3P, 240V (225A Fuses)

Note:
These drawings are diagrammatic only and not to scale.

R.S.Means Co.,Inc.

OFFICE BUILDING & PARKING GARAGE

E-4

ELECTRIC RISER DIAGRAM

MCC-1

1A	2A	3A
	2B	3B
1B	2C	3C
	2D	3D
1C	2E	3E
1D	2F	3F

Figure 2.19

Pre-Construction
Planning

3

Pre-Construction Planning

After the contract has been awarded and the notice to proceed has been issued, the project manager must develop a project management plan. The best place to start this process is with a phase most accurately described as *pre-construction planning*, or *setting up for project control*. During this phase, the project manager establishes the basis for good job planning, and for efficient and effective monitoring as the job proceeds. Effective project control is an orderly process, which depends on accurate, reliable information distributed to project personnel. Setting the system up properly ensures effective performance from the beginning.

The project manager sets the tone for the job during this pre-planning phase. The quality of the initial set-up of a construction job has a profound effect on the entire project. If project personnel perceive a professional, well-thought-out approach, the job is more likely to proceed in the same manner. It is the project manager who is responsible for the job as a whole, and the entire project team looks to him for direction.

One of the major tasks of the project manager is coordinating all of the parties in the management process, and this, too, begins in the early planning stage. All should be encouraged to participate and share information about the project and its processes. Participants should also be made aware of their responsibilities—both during the set-up part of the process, and for regular procedures once the job is underway. Communications with project personnel involve more than simply recording in a manual the various requirements. It must be an active process in which the responsibility is assigned and acknowledged, and the tasks monitored to see that they are accomplished. There is no room for assumptions.

The project manager takes on the leadership role at this early stage, and maintains it throughout the job. He must communicate the requirements, and once the work is underway, perform follow-up procedures to ensure completion.

These early activities can be viewed as a twofold process, and will be treated as such in this chapter. First is the task of information gathering. We will cover possible and desirable sources of data, how the information may be best obtained, and who should undertake this task. The second part of the process is management—including establishing procedures. We will focus primarily on the ongoing decision-making, and on the record-keeping needed to support project control. While other aspects of construction management, such as safety and personnel administration, are also very important, the emphasis of the discussion in this chapter is in keeping with the scope of this book, i. e., schedule control.

The recommended procedures and checklist included here are not comprehensive, as it is not possible to cover every construction situation in one book. It is recommended that the individual project manager use these guidelines as a starting point, then expand and modify these procedures based on experience and the direction of his/her career. For example, the recommended file classifications could be used on a first job. During the course of the job, these categories might be expanded and culled appropriately, and the revised version used as the basis for starting the next, and presumably larger, job. Within a few years, a comprehensive file list will likely have been developed. The general guidelines presented here cover most project management situations.

Identifying Key Personnel

The first task that the project manager must undertake is to mobilize the company's resources. Part of this task is identifying key personnel. Depending on the size of the job, these individuals could range from a superintendent to a staff consisting of project manager, office engineer, scheduler, cost engineer, and secretary. Home office personnel who will not be assigned permanently to the job, but who will be responsible for specific tasks at particular stages of the project, may also be part of the project team.

Providing Data to the Project Team

The next step is to note all sources of information for use by the project team. In these early stages, there are few sources of information that are available to everyone. Typically, all of the data is derived from the contract documents and estimate, plus the knowledge accumulated by the estimators during the bidding or procurement process. An excellent starting point is making sure that project personnel have access to the estimate data and contract documents. Ideally, copies of both would be issued to key team members. If this is too costly, copies of the documents should be provided in an easily accessible location and team members should be assigned the responsibility of familiarizing themselves with the contents of these documents.

Contract Document Review

A review of the contract documents should provide each project team member with an overall understanding of the job. The project team has a further opportunity to question any unclear aspects during a later meeting with the estimators. It is essential that the members of the project team have a clear understanding of the project. This is accomplished by simply spending as much time as necessary reviewing the plans, specifications, and estimate. During this document review, project team members should be looking for the following:

- **The size and scope of the project, including physical features of the structure.** The point here is that no one would start building from a set of foundation plans without knowing what was to be erected above the foundation.
- **Required construction procedures.** Contract documents do not typically describe specific construction procedures; each team member should visualize the process and then agree on the actual plan in the team meeting.
- **Special conditions and features.** This element should also be considered by individual team members and agreed upon at the project team meeting.
- **Physical limits of the site.** This category includes special construction problems that might be caused by the character of the site, by virtue of remoteness or surrounding structures.
- **Unusual situations.** The reviewer should look over the contract documents, taking note of those items which may cause unusual problems.

In addition to reviewing the plans and specifications, the team members should also review the general and special conditions. Information in this section should include:

- **Contract time allowed.** This figure sets a limit on the duration of the initial schedule. Any intermediate milestone dates that must be met, or portions of the project that must be delivered to the owner prior to the project's completion should be noted, as they clearly affect the project plan.

- **Owner's schedule, payments, and other administrative requirements.** Some owners, particularly public owners such as the U. S. Army Corps of Engineers, have specific requirements that must be met during the building process. These stipulations may have little to do with the actual construction. For example, pay invoices may have to be based on a critical path schedule rather than a traditional schedule of values. If there are specific requirements for the submission of schedules, it may be that only certain software packages will provide this capability. If the company does not already own a suitable system, it might first have to be procured. Setting up a new system creates purchasing and training requirements which must be considered.

- **Inspection and notification requirements.** Some contracts require a minimum notice for all inspections. Failing to take note of this requirement can result in otherwise avoidable delays during which work stands idle while waiting for the inspector to appear.

- **General administrative requirements.** Many owners require contractors to attend to administrative matters relating to public laws, financial institutions, etc. The contractor must set appropriate procedures for those needs on the job site.

- **Claims requirements.** In today's legal climate, many owners are establishing time limits for submitting claims for extra compensation. The team should pay particular attention to the notice requirements. Certainly no contractor wants to be in the position of losing an otherwise valid claim because of having failed to meet these requirements.

Estimate Review/ Estimator Meeting

After reviewing the contract documents, the team members should review the estimate thoroughly. The project manager should then schedule and conduct a meeting with the estimators, allowing the team an opportunity to ask questions. This meeting should be one of the earliest, and certainly before any meetings with "outsiders," such as subcontractors or owners.

In the early stages of a project, the estimators and their documents are probably the best and most complete source of information in the company about a given project. It is not enough, however, to simply read the estimate and look at the numbers. The information in an estimate is not arranged to help the actual management of a project. It is arranged to help make the bid process accurate and efficient.

As such, it may need some interpretation by the originating estimators to make it useful to project management. A meeting between the estimators and the project team ensures that the assumptions built into the estimate are reflected in the project plans.

In reviewing the estimate and questioning the estimators, the project team should look for the following.

Special Conditions and Features
In addition to the special conditions and features picked up by the project management personnel, the estimators may be aware of other situations which are not readily apparent in the estimate documentation. It should be the estimator's responsibility to pass this information on to the field personnel, but it cannot be assumed that this will be the case. The estimator may well be deeply involved in preparing another bid, so members of the field team must ask specific questions.

Assumptions and Limitations
Even in straightforward projects without special features, the estimator will have made assumptions about how the project is to be built. Typically, these assumptions are made in the interest of getting the bid put together on time. While such assumptions

are usually valid, it should be noted that the project team is not obliged to assume that they are completely infallible. In fact, the management team should be encouraged to find a better solution to problems of production. Any improvement, after the bid is won, results in pure profit, not money left on the table. At a very minimum, questions should be asked about the following areas:

- **Weather.** Weather can be thought of in terms of two different factors: location and time of year. Location is clearly not alterable, but the time of year may be flexible. For example, while the use of overtime is usually not a good idea, there may be cases where the shrewd application of overtime to structural work in good weather may permit indoor work to take place in winter weather in an enclosed building. A "normal" schedule, on the other hand, would simply mean waiting for the spring before resuming structural work.

- **Crew composition.** The management team clearly needs to know what crew make-ups were assumed in planning both the unit costs and the scheduled time in the estimate. Initial crew assumptions serve as a starting point in the scheduling process, but should not be taken as absolutely reliable without checking. It is possible that the estimator has allowed too few crews, or crews which are too small.

- **Equipment.** It is also necessary to determine what equipment has been assumed, particularly since equipment has such an impact on other parts of the job. Estimates often contain equipment assumptions based on a particular piece of gear being on the job for a period of time, rather than tying the equipment to the cost of specific tasks. This approach is especially common with large pieces of equipment such as tower cranes. Problems can arise if the equipment is either too small to handle all that is expected of it, or if the time allowed on the site is not adequate to do all the jobs for which it is intended. Equipment choices also have an impact on crew assumptions in that the time allowed for a piece of equipment on site may be predicated on a crew moving at a given rate; if the crew is too small to move at that rate, then clearly, the size of the crew or the time frame for the equipment must be altered. The estimator may also have made certain assumptions about renting, leasing, or buying. Such decisions may be governed by company policy (i.e., if the company owns it, we use it). Again, the project manager may not be obliged to use the estimator's plan, but it does serve as a starting point for the actual decisions as to equipment use.

Note: The project manager should be aware of any deals made by the estimator with the subcontractor regarding the use of general contractor-owned equipment. This issue can be very complex, particularly on high-rise jobs where only a limited amount of equipment can fit onto the site at any one time.

- **Location.** As previously mentioned, the location of a site can have a great influence on construction cost and schedule. The two types of sites that tend to cause the greatest problems are those that are either isolated or tightly restricted. Both tend to increase production costs and schedule time, by virtue of the difficulty and expense associated with getting material and/or labor to the site.

- **Logistics and procurement.** While site location is an important factor in logistics, it is not the only one. In general, any situation that requires materials or equipment that are subject to manufacturing and delivery problems requires special attention. The estimator should be questioned on this point since, hopefully during the process of compiling the bids, he will have identified the items to be installed which will take longer than normal to be delivered. Once these items have been identified by the project team, they can be properly factored into the schedule. Tracking these items during the job is also extremely important. Promised delivery dates are seldom moved up; they are much more likely to be put off, and during construction adjustments will have to be made.

- **Subcontractors.** Of all the items that must be discussed with the estimator, subcontract arrangements are among the most important. The scope of work of each subcontractor is never clear immediately after a bid opening. The time pressures of bid day are simply too great to permit precise definition of scope at that time. Also, the documentation of the subcontractor bidding, including all the call-ins, bid alterations, and price cuts, are invariably confusing and require explanation by the estimator. In particular, the project manager will be responsible for executing the buy-out with the subcontractors as the job proceeds. He or she must know the conditions under which bids were tendered by the subs. The project manager must also know the identity of each subcontractor, the scope of work for which the subcontractor bid, and the price quoted. The project manager should also be made aware of any special contractual exclusions made by the subcontractors, and any long-lead-time items within the subcontractor's scope of work.

- **Quantity Takeoffs.** Finally, the project team should inquire as to the nature of the material takeoffs done by the estimators, and should understand the format thoroughly. This part of the estimate serves as a handy source of information for the field production planning and scheduling which will occur as the job progresses. These original quantity surveys will probably have to be reworked in part, but they provide a good starting point.

Initial Project Team Meeting

After reviewing the contract documents and the estimate, and after meeting with the estimators, the project manager should meet with the project team. The purpose of this meeting is to set goals for accomplishing the remainder of the pre-job planning tasks, and to assign responsibility for getting those tasks done. Such a meeting also provides an opportunity to solicit ideas and comments from the project team members, both for building the job and for starting the ongoing project control procedures. Ideally, there should be a corporate operations manual in existence to guide new personnel. If there is no manual, one should be created and should include the above-mentioned planning procedures.

During the initial meeting, the team should consider the following:

- **Overall job approach.** It is very rare that a company gets a job of a type that no one in the company has seen before. In fact, it makes sense to assign most of the personnel to a job on the basis of their having done that kind of work before. The team should therefore be able to decide fairly quickly on the primary methods of construction. In the event several possibilities exist, an appropriately knowledgeable team member should be assigned the task of investigating alternatives and reporting the results to the project manager.

- **Most critical parts of the job.** In most types of construction, the most difficult or likely trouble areas can be identified by the team members based on past experience. All members of the team should be made aware of these areas. By getting this information out onto the table, decisions can be made as to the best course of action, which will result in the most effective construction sequence.

- **Project control needs.** Since the intent of the meetings is to set up the most effective project management process possible, the team will also be considering the control system to be implemented. While many of the systems, such as cost, may be dictated by company-wide requirements, some, such as scheduling, are up to the team. The size and character of scheduling systems to fit specific jobs are discussed later in this book, but it is worth noting here that during these initial meetings, the team and the project manager must start to consider how scheduling is to be implemented. Scheduling choices are based, primarily, on the degree of detail desired, the way in which the information is to be displayed, and how often that information is needed. Also, the responsibility must be assigned for maintaining the scheduling system.

- **Project administration.** Complete coverage of this subject is beyond the scope of this book. However, project administration is an important topic that should be discussed in these early meetings when the project team sets up procedures. These procedures will be determined by such diverse needs as corporate policy, the owner's requirements, and local ordinances.

  It is important at this point to assign the responsibility for creating rough drafts of major subcontracts. This is done in anticipation of the buy-out meeting which will fix the scope of work and the price, drafting the major material purchase orders for mailing to suppliers, and last but not least, identification of submittal data requirements by job items.

- **Remaining pre-job planning.** Finally, the team should plan the actions and assign the responsibilities for dealing with the pre-job planning which must occur with agencies and parties outside the company. These parties and items will be discussed in the next section.

Pre-Planning with Other Parties

As is the case with employees, subcontractors and other "outsiders" respond well to professional management and respond poorly to sloppy procedures. The project team should use the same professional approach in dealing with these other parties to the contract. While there are many similarities, each outside party has its own peculiar set of requirements for the most effective construction process.

Subcontractors

According to some experts, the most challenging aspect of construction today is the effort to achieve effective, on-time use of subcontractors on job sites. While the subcontracting process does relieve the general or prime contractor of much of the risk stemming from labor cost overruns, the problems associated with scheduling and actually getting the work accomplished are, in some ways, worse. The reasons for this situation are many. One problem is that each subcontractor is a separate corporate entity with obligations beyond the job site; few are on the job site full-time. Early, effective pre-planning can do much to prevent the problems associated with extensive subcontracting.

The general process for dealing with subcontractors can be described in the following three steps:

1. Setting up the contract, in a process which is known as "buy-out."
2. Involving the subcontractor extensively in the initial planning and scheduling process.
3. Involving the subcontractor in the monitoring and any subsequent re-planning processes that may occur.

The first of these phases is discussed in the following paragraphs; the last two are covered in detail in subsequent chapters.

The buy-out is the process in which the general contractor makes the final subcontractor selections, negotiates scope of work and price, settles contractual terms, and signs the subcontract. Also considered at this time are initial scheduling concerns, meeting and notice requirements, subcontractor representation in dealings with the owner, and the submittal data and equipment delivery issues associated with the subcontractor's work.

The first of these concerns is the definition of scope of work and price. As previously noted, the bidding process leaves no time for adequate definition of scope of work. This task is best accomplished later in meetings between general and subcontractor, at which all of the items of work are very carefully defined. Defining scope of work and price is a task involving great amounts of detail; it is a job that is best done one piece at a time. A set of drawings and specifications is used, on which each item of work for which the subcontractor is responsible is marked in color. From the drawings and specifications, a list is developed which both parties can keep as a part of the contract. This list should cover both included and excluded items, and should be as specific as possible. While this method of marking up drawings and specifications is not the only way to conduct a buy-out meeting, the purpose of the process is to remove all possible ambiguity from the subcontract. One of the benefits of creating a well-defined set of contractual obligations for the subcontractor (which will in itself prevent future claims), is the fact that it is probably not possible to talk about *what* will be done without talking about *how* it will be done.

At this time, the project manager and subcontractor should also address scheduling issues. As the activities are defined, a commitment must be obtained from each sub regarding the duration of each activity. The submittal data is required before an activity can begin, and it must be known what material must be ordered and delivered prior to the start. These items should be included in the list of contractual obligations for the subcontractor. The information will be used in the development of the critical path scheduling sequence and times.

The subcontractor must also be made aware of the ongoing scheduling requirements for all parties on the job. The basic idea is that the project manager must conduct regularly scheduled meetings during the course of the work; attendance and participation will be required of all parties. Despite the fact that many contractors and subcontractors consider meetings a waste of time, experience in the industry has shown that well-conducted, regularly scheduled meetings, in which subcontractor ideas are encouraged and used, and subcontractor commitment is required, are the most effective means of achieving the real coordination which is so vital to successful job progress.

Suppliers

In addition to the subcontractors, the major material suppliers must also be contacted and the information they contribute worked into the planning process. During the bidding, suppliers, like subcontractors, are working under the pressures of time, and while their quotes typically contain terms and dates of delivery, it is always best to confirm that data. The project manager cannot assume that the estimate contains information on all items that have the potential to delay the schedule. For example, because of time pressures, the estimator may commonly use average, current prices for a bid submission, rather than specific quotes. There will also be no information gathered about delivery times at this stage.

The specifications and plans must be thoroughly reviewed for the following purposes: to identify all articles of material which must be ordered and delivered, to identify and contact suppliers, to confirm prices, and to obtain delivery commitments. This information must then be incorporated into the budget and schedule.

Even materials that are not difficult to obtain must be reviewed in terms of their effect on the scheduling process. Many owners, especially public agencies, require submittal data on even the most common of materials, such as lumber and concrete. These submittal data requirements can affect the project schedule if the submissions and subsequent approvals are not carried out on time.

The purpose of the pre-planning process is to identify and assign responsibility for the activities of the job. Effective pre-planning prevents the problems associated with making purchases just as installation is due to begin. The administrative task of setting up logs and continually tracking the status of these items must also begin at this point.

Owners and Their Representatives

One of the universal characteristics of construction owners is their desire to monitor how their project is being built and how their money is being spent. Most of the owner's attention is, understandably, directed toward ensuring good quality in the finished product. Owner involvement frequently creates administrative work for the contractor in the form of progress reports and additional record keeping requirements at the site, such as insurance confirmations and lien releases. The vast majority of these requirements are clearly designed to protect the owner's interests.

Many owner requirements are covered in the contract documents and will therefore have been discovered during the document review. However, a pre-job meeting between owner and contractor will almost always be required. It is at this meeting that the contractor can discover the "unwritten rules" and clarify issues which may not be totally clear in the contract documents. This meeting will also be the start of personal working relationships between the owner's and contractor's representatives. These contacts can sometimes degenerate in an atmosphere of acrimony and distrust. It is therefore important to begin and remain on as positive and professional a footing as possible. A contractor must recognize the fact that the owner's concerns and fears are legitimate, since a large amount of money is typically at stake. The contractor should be properly organized for the initial meeting with the project team, and display a cooperative attitude toward the information needs of the owner's representatives.

During the initial meeting, the following topics are of primary concern to the project manager. First, make sure that any items not clearly expressed in the contract documents now become known and understood. Very often a few words in a contract document will not even begin to describe a potentially complex situation. For example, it is common for a contractor to perform work while an owner continues to operate a business in the same structure. Under these circumstances, the contractor must know how to avoid damage to existing equipment and work, and the procedure for coordinating the various activities of construction with the closing or opening of various parts of the building. There may even be other contractors who have been hired by the owner and who are working at the facility at the same time. This situation usually requires frequent and effective communication among all concerned parties for the life of the project. First meetings with the owner set the tone for this aspect of the project as well.

There are many other issues that must be coordinated with the owner in the initial stages. For example, most construction projects require temporary utilities. These are often coordinated with the utility companies through the owner. Frequently, there is also the matter of owner-furnished materials or equipment which must be identified, delivery dates verified, and installation details confirmed. It should also be noted that the contractor must inform the owner of the specific, potential impacts on the schedule if delivery of owner-furnished materials or equipment are not made on time.

Public and Government Agencies

Almost all construction projects must meet the requirements of a regulatory government body. It has traditionally been the contractor's responsibility to acquire permits for the construction process, but that requirement has become much more complex in recent years. For example, many permits, such as environmental approvals, must be obtained by the owner prior to the start of design, with an additional permit for actual construction obtained by the contractor at the start of work. Some permits are predicated on the issuance of other permits; this whole issue has the potential to become a complex and difficult business.

There are several actions that the project manager can take in order to cope effectively with permits. First, a comprehensive list of required permits and the parties involved should be made. This list must include: all the parties involved with individual permits, identification of those responsible for obtaining and paying for the permit, and the requirements for obtaining the permit. This list should be carefully cross-checked and coordinated with the owner and subcontractors.

Most construction contracts assign the contractor the responsibility of complying with local laws without saying what those laws are. The project team must therefore do some careful research in order to determine exactly which local laws and ordinances require the contractor's compliance. The project team can get this information by going to the local building department and environmental agencies and obtaining literature on the local requirements. It may be helpful to establish personal contact with the officials involved after reading the department's literature.

Unions and Labor Suppliers

Finally, the contractor and project manager must be aware of the procedures, problems, and pitfalls of obtaining labor in the location of the job. Basic information about labor availability and rates should have been known at the time of the bid. The project manager will, however, have to follow up in order to find out what the actual procedures are for hiring in a designated area. Aside from the more obvious source— local business agents and other union officials—it is a good idea to contact local contractor associations and government employment development agencies.

Setting Up Management Procedures

Concurrent with the information gathering process, the project manager must also begin setting up management procedures for the project. Clearly, some of these procedures will be influenced by the specific requirements of a particular project. Most, however, will be similar in nature from project to project, especially for a series of projects performed for the same owner, or in the same local area. Some basic guidelines for these procedures follow.

Assigning Responsibility

The assignment of responsibility is a task that continues throughout the project. It is, however, often neglected in the early stages. As a result, many important tasks do not start off as regular, monitored events, and are consequently discovered not done at a critical time.

The basic concerns in assigning responsibility are as follows: First, make sure that every ongoing task is identified—especially those related to cost and schedule. Second, a competent individual must be assigned to monitor each task on a regular basis. For example, in scheduling, who is to track the progress of each activity on a periodic basis, and how often is the tracking to be done? Or, in the case of daily labor time cards used to record the expenditure of labor-hours, who is to fill the card out? Who checks it, and who transmits it to the home office for processing? The project manager must follow up to see that the responsibility assigned is in fact assumed by the assigned individual.

Coordination on the Job Site

Construction projects are complex endeavors, and procedures must be established to ensure effective communication among all parties involved in the project. Communication requires both informing and listening to all participants. For example, schedule obligations should be clearly explained to subcontractors. In fairness and in the interest of maintaining productive harmony on the job, the subcontractors' concerns must also be heard prior to decisions being made about their assignments. The means of communication can take many forms, but consist primarily of: 1) regular meetings of the concerned participants, and 2) recording and distributing the results of the meetings in written form.

The first element, regular meetings, must be made productive by the project manager. Otherwise, the other parties will simply come to regard the meetings as a farce, with no attention being paid to the results. To use scheduling as an example, a regular meeting should be held every week. In this meeting, the schedule for the previous week and upcoming two weeks would be discussed. The project manager must ensure that an up-to-date schedule and agenda are provided to all parties required to attend, and that the discussion is productive and to the point.

Following the discussion, the project manager should announce his decisions, basing the schedule he proposes on the commitments given publicly by each subcontractor. The new schedule should then be distributed in written form within one day.

In holding schedule meetings on this basis, the project manager invites participation by the subs, which helps to establish an overall team commitment. He also obtains "public" commitment from the subs, which is more likely to be met than a privately made promise. By distributing the results promptly, the project manager provides written documentation for the job, and re-confirms in everyone's mind the decisions made. Effective use of the project meeting is one of the project manager's most powerful tools.

Coordination with Other Parts of the Company

In addition to coordination of the subs and other on-site parties, most jobs also require some degree of coordination with the home office. These procedures are typically less demanding than those directly related to the construction work, but are no less important. For example, all companies have a set of procedures for accounting and payroll. These procedures are company-wide and must be dealt with at each job site. Ideally, they are defined in a company operations manual or guide, and need not be re-invented for each new project. If such a manual does not exist, then company efficiency would be well served by creating one.

Setting Up a Good Record Keeping System

Finally, in order to control the many documents generated by a typical job, the project manager must see to it that a consistent and workable record-keeping system is established and maintained on the job site. A job site filing system must be created, and responsibility must be assigned for keeping each file. The job secretary may not be the most logical person to keep all of the files. For instance, working files, such as those for scheduling, might more logically be the responsibility of the scheduler or other individual who is responsible for maintaining the schedule. Again, record-keeping should be consistent throughout the company, but in the event it is not, the following filing breakdown may be used as a starting point.

A. Correspondence

One file for incoming, one for outgoing, arranged chronologically.

1. Owner/Client
2. Architects/Engineers
3. Subcontractors (by specification division)
4. Regulatory & Inspection Agencies
5. Suppliers (by specification division)
6. Miscellaneous

B. Transmittal Letters

One file for incoming, one for outgoing, arranged chronologically.

1. Owner/Client
2. Architects/Engineers
3. Subcontractors (by specification division)
4. Government & Inspection Agencies
5. Suppliers (by specification division)
6. Miscellaneous

C. Meeting Notes and Minutes

Arranged chronologically.

1. Regularly Scheduled:
   a. Weekly Job Conference
   b. Weekly Subcontractor Scheduling Meeting
   c. Other

2. Non-Regularly Scheduled:
   a. Owner/Client
   b. Designers

D. Contracts

1. Owner/Prime
   a. Main Contract
   b. Addenda (by number)

2. Prime/Subcontractors
   (by specification subdivision)

3. Outside Consultants
   a. Surveyor
   b. Form Design Consultant
   c. Other

E. Changes and Scope of Work

1. Specifications

2. Requests for Information
   (consecutively number all R.F.I.'s)

3. Responses to R.F.I.'s (by number)

4. Bulletins/Design Changes

5. No Cost Change Orders/Field Directives

6. Change Orders Pending

7. Approved Changes

8. Unapproved Changes

9. Claims in Process

10. Delays/Time Extensions

F. Project Control

1. Cost/Budget
   a. Original Estimate
   b. Bid Analysis
   c. Budget
   d. Weekly Labor Cost Summaries
   e. Weekly Equipment Cost Summaries
   f. Monthly Material Cost Summaries
   g. Monthly Job Cost Summaries
   h. Other Regular Cost Reports

2. Schedule
   a. Activity Work Sheets
   b. Networks
   c. Periodic Schedule Reports & Runs
      (arranged chronologically)

      1) Planning Schedules

      2) Bar Charts

3) Other Runs

G. Invoices and Payments

   1. Schedule of Values

   2. Invoices to Owner

   3. Payments Received

   4. Invoices from Subs (by specification section)

   5. Payments Made to Subs (by specification section)

   6. Invoices from Suppliers (by vendor)

   7. Payments Made to Suppliers (by vendor)

H. Reports

Arrange chronologically.

   1. Daily Job Logs
      a. Project Manager
      b. Superintendent
      c. Project Engineer
      d. Other

   2. Telephone Logs

   3. Progress Photos

   4. Weekly/Monthly Job Progress Reports

   5. Change Order Status Reports (by change order number)

   6. Submittal Data Status Reports
      (by specification section and by subcontractor and supplier)

   7. Material Delivery Status Reports
      (by specification section)

I. Tests & Inspections Reports

   1. Inspection Logs
      (by specification section)

   2. Inspection Reports
      (by inspecting agencies and companies and by specification section)

   3. Test Reports
      (by inspecting agencies or company and by specification section)

J. Material Procurement and Deliveries

   1. Master Material Order List
      (by specification section)

   2. Material Order Status List
      (by specification section)

   3. Purchase Orders
      (by specification section)

K. Submittal Shop Drawing Logs
      (by specification section and by subcontractors and suppliers)

Summary   As we have noted in this chapter on Pre-construction Planning, early information gathering and preparation are key to building a complete and comprehensive schedule that covers all aspects and parts of a project. The reader will have no doubt noted that these preparations are what good Project Managers usually do anyway. This chapter simply put those preparations in the context of scheduling, plus provided some tools to help a Project Manager make the process even more effective. Once this preparation has been done, a Project Manager must get into the "nuts and bolts" of scheduling, which may be new ground for some readers. The next chapter therefore provides an introduction to the specific steps for scheduling and provides the reader with some background which will help him or her understand the detail.

4

Introduction to Scheduling

Introduction to Scheduling

As noted in Chapter 1, it is essential that construction companies maintain and use good scheduling systems so that projects can be kept on track and can be completed on time. The next several chapters of this text specifically address the subject of time control, including the step-by-step process of setting up scheduling procedures. Before proceeding with the specifics, however, it is useful to look at some basic facts and ideas about the process of scheduling and how it works.

The Critical Path Method

The emphasis of this book is on the use of critical path method (CPM) techniques of construction scheduling. Of all the techniques available to a project manager, CPM has proven to be the most useful and effective means of developing and displaying the information needed to control the time variables on today's job sites. The basic CPM technique was developed in the late 1950s, primarily for the purpose of controlling large manufacturing and construction projects. It has been further developed and refined since, and has evolved into a tool that is well suited to the construction process.

Most people familiar with the construction process recognize the fact that a project is composed of tasks which are separate, yet interdependent. For example, in building a house, both foundation and stud wall are essential elements. The crew that forms and places the foundation is very different from the one that erects the stud walls. Nevertheless, these tasks are interdependent in that the walls cannot begin until the foundation is complete. The most difficult task in construction is keeping track, and deciding the correct order and timing, of a large number of these individual, yet interrelated tasks; the critical path method of scheduling addresses this issue.

The CPM technique is simpler and more flexible than it might first appear. It takes the building process one step at a time and separates the project into workable sub-parts or activities. A plan is made for each activity to be performed in the correct sequence. The task of scheduling becomes a systematic, one-piece-at-a-time endeavor.

The basic steps, or phases, of scheduling are as follows.

A. Planning
B. Scheduling
C. Monitoring and Controlling

Each of these phases has sub-steps. The first phase, *planning*, involves:

1. Breaking the project down into workable sub-tasks, commonly called *activities*.
2. Deciding the order in which these activities are to be performed.

The result of the planning phase is a *logic diagram*, or *network*, which is an initial graphic representation of a plan of what to do and the order in which to do it. This phase of the process is illustrated in Chapter 5.

The second phase, *scheduling*, adds a time element to the planning phase; the sub-steps for this phase are:

1. Determining a reasonable duration for each individual activity.
2. Calculating the duration of the project as a whole.

The product of this second phase is a series of time plans, typically presented as *planning schedules*, or *bar charts*. This type of display is shown in Chapter 6 and in Appendix A.

The last phase, *monitoring* and *controlling*, consists of:

1. Measuring the progress of the project.
2. Comparing the actual progress against the schedule developed during the scheduling phase.
3. Taking corrective action if the actual progress deviates significantly from the schedule.

The monitoring and controlling phase is covered in detail in Chapter 8.

Learning CPM Techniques

Many people who have tried to implement the critical path method have found it a difficult task. Most of this difficulty stems from not recognizing the basic simplicity of the process, and from being overwhelmed by the "gurus" of scheduling who have made the process seem far more complex than it really is. Much of this book is devoted to straightforward, workable techniques for CPM scheduling. As these techniques are presented, it is helpful to keep in mind the following general guidelines.

First, take the process one step at a time. The chapters of this book are presented in the same, step-by-step manner, outlining each of the major tasks that must be performed in order to achieve effective construction project management. These tasks and methods are discussed in the actual order in which they would occur on a project.

Second, recognize that the CPM technique is a way of representing what a manager intends to do; it does not require that the manager build in an unfamiliar way. Modern CPM techniques and software systems have more than enough flexibility to represent virtually any possible plan of action desired, so there is no reason to have the "tail wag the dog."

Third, the project manager and other project personnel should recognize that using CPM effectively will require an investment of time and energy on their part. Using CPM requires skill, and no skill can be developed without some effort in learning it. To use an analogy, no one in construction would expect to use a new laser surveying system without some training and practice. CPM is like the new laser surveying system in that it is a better productivity tool, but requires an initial investment of time as well as money. CPM is also like the new surveying system in that no contractor is likely to continue with an old tool when his competitors are using a new and more productive one.

Fourth, developing schedules is a creative process. It is analogous to an architect developing a set of plans for a building. No one ever created a set of working drawings without first going through a lot of sketches on tracing paper, then schematic and design development drawings, and finally, working drawings. Those developing a CPM schedule should be prepared to do a lot of erasing and rewriting as decisions are made and altered, and the plan of action develops.

Potential Pitfalls of Using CPM

First and foremost among CPM's potential pitfalls are those related to the human element. It is very common, for example, for a contractor to require the use of CPM for scheduling projects, and to use schedules that are developed and presented by professional schedulers. These professional schedulers have no stake in the outcome of the project, and may fail to consult the project manager and other project personnel. The result is a schedule which frequently does not reflect reality, and certainly not the project manager's reality. In this situation, those who are responsible for the performance of the project are, in effect, being told how to run the job, and may, quite understandably, be resentful. As a result, the schedule may be largely ignored by field personnel and become useless as a monitoring tool. In this case, the job as a whole suffers and the management of the company is unable to monitor progress until it is too late to correct the overruns.

The best way to avoid an unrealistic schedule is to provide project management with the tools and training to develop and use CPM effectively, and for top management to require its use in tracking and reporting progress. This is the ideal, in which every field manager regards good scheduling as an essential part of his or her job, and has the skills to use it properly. In the real world, the company's management must be sure that any schedules developed by others reflect the thinking of the field personnel, and that field personnel see the schedulers and the schedule as serving them and not as an imposed duty. If the schedule does not reflect the thinking of the people who have to live with it, it will not have their commitment, and cannot be effective.

Second among potential pitfalls is over-complexity. This problem can usually be identified when the schedule reports tend to gather dust rather than fingerprints. The schedule may be particularly susceptible to this problem when a "sophisticated" computer system is used. The problem brought on by complexity is that the schedule does not serve the project managers, but rather becomes an end in itself, and is ultimately ignored. The computer's capacity for generating large amounts of paper seems to be very difficult to resist and quite often one or more of the following occurs.

- Huge volumes of reports are generated which are so complex and bulky that it is difficult to read them all, much less pick out the important ones;
- The reports are confusing or are in an inappropriate format, and do not concentrate on the problems at hand, i. e., they do not promote management by exception;
- The project manager is flooded with detailed reports when, in fact, summary reports are needed; or vice versa;
- There is a severe lack of flexibility in the reports or in the schedule itself.

Summary

As we noted earlier, the point of this short summary was to give the reader an overview of the more detailed parts of the scheduling process. If during the process, the reader has trouble figuring out where a given step fits into the overall process, he or she can refer back to this chapter for a refresher on the overall picture.

5

Planning the Project

5

Planning the Project

As noted in Chapter 4, the first major step in the scheduling process is planning, which consists of:

1. breaking the job down into "sub-tasks," and
2. establishing the sequence of work.

This chapter describes each of these parts of the process in detail, and shows how the two are linked.

Breaking the Job Down into Activities

The first part of the scheduling process, breaking the job down into sub-parts, is probably the easiest. In fact, anyone who has worked in construction is probably aware that a foreman, superintendent, or project manager performs this task, either intuitively or deliberately, as a normal part of managing. Construction managers typically think of a job as a series of distinct steps, separate from one another. This separation process begins in the estimating stage, and continues through the hiring and scheduling of subcontractors, and in the setting up and directing of construction crews.

In using CPM techniques, the separation of sub-parts is more formal and more complete. There is no absolute way to go about this subdividing process, but the following guidelines can help to ensure that activities are not overlooked or ignored.

Activity Types
Listing the parts of the job can begin very early in the life of a project. For example, during the reviews of plans and specifications, a construction manager will probably already be thinking of the different tasks that have to be performed. The subdivision process is best begun using the basic construction documents, the plans and specifications, and then expanded based on additional information from other sources.

General Activity Types
The easiest and most general way to view the task breakdown is by recognizing all activities as falling into one or more of the following categories.

1. **Production Activities:** directly related to construction, involving crews, materials, and installing elements of the building. Examples are "erect steel studs," or "place foundation concrete."
2. **Procurement Activities:** required to order, purchase, and ensure delivery of the materials and equipment that are to be used in erecting the project. Examples are "order condenser units," "fabricate storefront frames and glass," or "deliver hollow metal door frames."

3. **Administrative and Support Activities:** "secondary" to the construction process, but vitally important in the complex and litigious environment that exists today. Examples are "submit water fountain shop drawings," or "approve steel shop drawings."

For every element installed in a project, there is an administrative process that must take place before actual construction can begin. To illustrate this idea, visualize the steps that must be performed in order to get structural steel for the sample office building project in place. These steps might include:

- Prepare structural steel shop drawings
- Review structural steel shop drawings
- Order structural steel
- Fabricate structural steel
- Deliver structural steel
- Erect structural steel

The first two steps are administrative in nature, the next three involve procurement, and the last is the actual construction. The reader will note that of these six steps, only one actually involves crews and construction on the job site. Nevertheless, all are necessary for the installation of structural steel.

Specific Activity Types

After breaking the job down into general activities, a manager or scheduler developing a construction schedule further divides these categories into more specific items. This classification process might be based on the following features:

Physical Elements of the Project: This is the most basic of the groupings and the one that comes to mind most readily. In fact, anyone who works in construction tends naturally to view a project in these terms. In looking at the sample office project, it would be logical to think in terms of "foundations," or "columns," or "waffle slab." Clearly, each of these three parts of the building must be scheduled with different formwork, and in all likelihood, different crews will perform the work. Also, it is clear that the columns rest on the foundation and must therefore be installed after the foundations are complete. All of these factors make it necessary to separate the activities.

Trade, Skill, or Crew Involved: The various trades used to erect the parts of the building must be directed by different foremen, and must therefore be kept separate in any schedule. Again, looking at the office project, typical activities might be, "form concrete retaining walls," "erect masonry walls," "erect structural steel," and "erect metal stud walls." Each of these activities involves a different trade or skill: carpenters, masons, and ironworkers, respectively. Each activity is managed and directed separately, and should therefore be kept separate in the schedule.

Contractual Divisions: In today's construction projects, increasing amounts of the total work are subcontracted. Each subcontractor is a separate corporate entity, with its own set of contractual obligations to the general contractor. There are several reasons why each subcontractor should be kept separate on the schedule, if possible. First, each subcontractor is managed and scheduled for work individually. The electrical subcontractor will probably be scheduled to perform the rough-in after the heating, ventilating, and air-conditioning subcontractor. Examples of this type of subdivision on the sample office building might be:

Rough-in electrical—main floor

Rough-in ductwork—main floor

Install storefront—front entrance

The second reason for keeping the subcontractors separate is that payment to each depends on progress. It is generally regarded as good practice to clearly separate one subcontractor's documented progress from that of another. In this way, disputes over the responsibility for lack of progress are prevented. In the event a dispute does occur, separation of the subcontractors helps the general contractor accurately assess who is at fault. The process of claims resolution is also greatly simplified if the schedule keeps all contractors separate—an important consideration.

Organizational Responsibility

This idea of subdividing also applies to the organizational subdivisions set up by the general contractor. For example, if a project is large enough to require two field superintendents, the activities for which each is responsible should be separately listed. Or, if a different part of the company is involved (such as a separate formwork design department which was part of the home office), then the task of "design formwork- waffle slabs" should be kept and tracked separately from the field work.

Physical or Geographic Area: Often, if a job is large enough, it might be organized along what could be called geographic lines. This practice is very common in such projects as petroleum process plants, which are spread out horizontally over large tracts of land. In these cases, it is important to be able to track progress across the site. The principle can be applied to a project as small as the sample office building. For instance, the two roof areas might well be installed at separate times, leading to two separate activities, such as:

Install roofing–penthouse
Install roofing–main roof

In the case of vertically-oriented buildings, it is important to be able to track progress up the building by area. A manager needs to see activities organized in this way, since it is very likely that similar crews could end up working at several levels at the same time, for example:

Install metal studs–main floor
Install metal studs–2nd floor, tower
Install metal studs–3rd floor, tower, etc.

System for Description

In developing a list of activities, it is recommended that a consistent system be used to describe them. A system that works well in practice describes each activity in terms of:

1. An action being taken
2. The building element involved in this action
3. A location identifier for the element

Such a system results in the following kinds of activity descriptions:

Place concrete–garage footings
Erect masonry wall–north side
Install tubs–3rd floor

The following examples show the kind of flexibility a classification system may offer.

Separating Actions

Form foundations–garage area
Place foundations–garage area

In this case, the types of work are kept separate, even though the element being worked on and the area are both the same.

Separating the Work Items

Form foundations–garage area
Form columns–garage area

In this case, foundations are kept separate from columns, even though both are in the same physical area.

Separating Areas

> Form foundations—garage area
> Form foundations—dining and kitchen area

In this case, the garage area work is clearly kept separate from the dining/kitchen area, even though both are foundation work.

While this system may seem somewhat rigid, it points up some important distinctions in the activity lists. These issues are often ignored, only to find out later (after several hundred activities have been listed) that the listing, "concrete," has left the user of the schedule with no idea where the concrete is or what phase of the concrete work is being done.

The Concept of Level of Detail

So far, we have discussed how to divide work into activities and how to describe them in such a way as to prevent confusion later in the scheduling process. It is relatively easy to describe individual activities. After all, a footing or a wall is a simple element of the building, and anyone experienced in construction can probably visualize the work necessary to build one of these elements. However, when we are faced with the job of developing an entire list of activities for a large project, the task is somewhat more complicated by the fact that we rapidly find our lists becoming so large as to be unmanageable. If this occurs, it becomes difficult to use a schedule effectively, and in a worst case scenario, we may lose control of the schedule altogether because our information is not organized enough to be of any use.

The Level of Detail concept is one of the tools available that helps avoid this problem. In basic terms, it works as follows. All projects can be visualized in terms of a series of general phases that usually occur on projects of a like type. Within each of these phases, there is usually a similar set of physical elements or parts of the job, and for each element, there is a similar set of tasks that must be performed in order for that part to be built successfully. In a nutshell, we break the project down into its component parts by going from the general to the specific to the detailed.

The General Phase List

Using the office building project as an example, we can illustrate how the Level of Detail concept is applied. First, any commercial office building can be divided into several major phases, listed below.

- Site Preparation
- Foundations
- Structure
- Envelope
- Rough-ins
- Finishes
- Final Site Work

This is, of course, not the only set of phases that could be used for an office building. Also, if we are working with a different type of project, the phases would be different. For instance, industrial projects are often broken down along the lines of engineering disciplines; and civil projects might be broken down along the lines of major structural features. Any scheme is acceptable as long as it is appropriate to the type of work, and can be understood by the scheduler and by project personnel.

The Specific Physical Element List

As we continue to break down the project into phases, we can use the Foundation phase as an example of the process. Looking at the project estimate and plans, we can see that the foundation consists of the following physical elements:

Building Excavation

Footings

Elevator Pit Slab

Foundation Walls

Foundation Columns

Slab on Grade

Foundation Waterproofing System

This further development gives us a list of every piece of the phase that must be installed.

The Detailed Task List

Again, continuing with the process, we can develop a task list for construction of the footings, which is as follows:

- Excavate for Footings
- Form Footings
- Reinforce Footings
- Place Footings
- Strip Footings

The overall concept is illustrated in Figure 5.1, where each phase is shown to be the "sum" of its elements, and each element is the "sum" of its tasks.

This "downward" detail technique allows us to do a number of things which make our schedule better and more effective. First, it helps us ensure that nothing is left out. Second, it keeps our data organized, and prevents us from being overloaded with pieces of paper listing unknown and untraceable activities. Third, it allows us to proceed in a methodical and orderly manner and will probably speed up our work in the long run.

We should note, however, that it is not necessary to develop every schedule to its maximum possible level of detail, down to individual tasks. Many schedules need be developed only to the level of physical elements, for example, and some may only need the major phases outlined. Each project and project manager has different requirements, but the basic idea of going from the general to the specific should be retained.

Figures 5.2 and 5.3 show sample activity lists of the sample office building projects. These lists contain both high and low levels of detail as illustrative examples.

Tips on Activity List Development

The following guidelines may be helpful in quickly putting together a good activity list.

- "Brainstorming" can sometimes help. A group of project personnel may meet and, together, record the list on a chalkboard.
- It is generally better to come up with a large list, and then cull, rather than the other way around.
- One of the best ways to get a sense of required building activities is to look at the wall sections and read upwards.
- Procurement and administrative activity lists can often be gleaned from a careful reading of the specifications, taking note of submittal data requirements.
- The estimate is typically a good source of information about subcontractor work activities, and identifies the responsibilities of each.
- One should be prepared to go through a series of lists. The first one never has everything right.

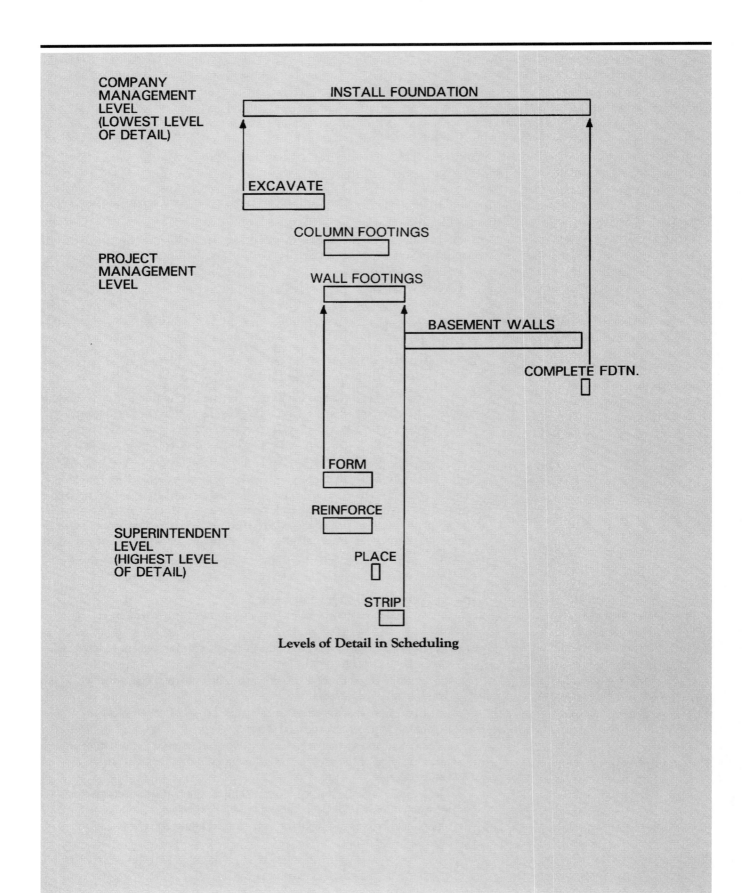

Levels of Detail in Scheduling

Figure 5.1

Activity List - Means Office Building (Low Detail)

Site Work
- Clear Site
- Grade Site
- Install U/G Utilities
- Parking Lot
- Landscaping

Foundation
- Foundations
- Elevator Pit
- Foundation Columns
- Foundation Walls
- Foundation Drain
- Slab on Grade

Structure
- Masonry
- Waffle Slab
- Structural Steel
- Elevated Slabs

Rough-ins
- Rough Ductwork
- Studs and Framing
- Sprinkler Piping
- Rough Plumbing
- Rough Electrical
- Insulation
- Rough Paint

Finishes
- Ceiling Grid
- Light Fixtures
- Registers and Grilles
- Sprinkler Heads
- Ceiling Tile
- Doors and Hardware
- Carpet and Base
- Wood Paneling (first only)
- Wood Floor (first only)
- Bathrooms
- Finish Paint
- Finish Electric
- Test and Balance HVAC

Envelope
- Building Enclosure
- Roofing

Exterior Finishes
- Parking Lot
- Landscaping

Building Systems
- Electrical
- Plumbing
- Fire Protection
- Mechanical

Figure 5.2

Activity List - Means Office Building (High Detail)

Site Work
    Clear Site
    Grade Site
    Install U/G Utilities
        Storm Drain System
        Gas Service
        Water Service
        Sewage System
    Parking Lot
        Curb and Gutter
        Base
        Paving
        Striping
        Line Painting
        Wheel Stops
    Landscaping
        Sidewalks and Steps
        Irrigation System
        Lawn & Shrubs
Foundation
    Foundations
        Excavate for Foundations
        Form Footings - Continuous/Spread
        Reinforcing
        Place Footings
        Backfill
    Elevator Pit
        Excavating
        Forming
        Reinforcing
        Place and Finish Concrete
    Foundation Columns
        Form
        Place
    Foundation Walls
        Form Walls and Pilasters
        Reinforce Walls and Pilasters
        Place Concrete
        Finish Walls
    Foundation Drain
        Bituminous Coating
        Pipe Bedding
        French Drain System
    Slab on Grade
        Gravel Fill
        Form
        Welded Wire Fabric
        Place and Finish Concrete

Figure 5.3

Structure
   Masonry
      Basement
      Penthouse
   Waffle Slab
      Form Deck for Slab
      Reinforcing
      Place and Finish
      Curing
   Structural Steel
      Main Steel Structure
      Steel Decking
      Roof Trusses
      Penthouse Roof Structure
         Joists
         Decking
   Elevated Slabs
      Forming
      Reinforcing
      Place and Finish
      Curing
Rough-ins
   Rough Ductwork
   Studs and Framing
      Hollow Metal Door Frames
   Sprinkler Piping
   Rough Plumbing
   Rough Electrical
      Panels
      Conduit
      Wiring
   Insulation
   Rough Paint
Finishes
   Ceiling Grid
   Light Fixtures
   Registers and Grills
   Sprinkler Heads
   Ceiling Tile
   Doors and Hardware
   Carpet and Base
   Wood Paneling (first only)
   Wood Floor (first only)
   Bathrooms
      Vanities
      Plumbing Fixtures
      Toilet Partitions
      Bathroom Accessories

Figure 5.3 Cont.

                     Finish Paint
                     Finish Electric
                     Test and Balance HVAC
               Envelope
                     Building Enclosure
                           Curtain Wall
                           Store Front System at Front
                     Roofing
                           Sheet Metal and Roofing
               Exterior Finishes
                     Parking Lot
                           Base and Paving
                           Curb and Gutter
                           Line Painting
                           Wheel Stops
                     Landscaping
                           Irrigation System
                           Lawn
                           Shrubs and Trees
                           Sidewalks
               Building Systems
                     Electrical
                           Fixtures
                           Conduits
                           Wiring
                           Panels
                     Plumbing
                           Rough-ins - Piping and Stacks
                           Finishes - Fixtures
                     Fire Protection
                           Standpipes
                           Piping and Sprinklers
                     Mechanical
                           Ductwork
                           Diffusers and Registers
                           Penthouse Equipment
                                 Chillers
                                 Fan Coil Unit
                                 Cooling Tower
                           Piping for Equipment
                           Heating Equipment
                           Heating Piping
                           Piping Insulation
                           Balancing
                           Controls

Figure 5.3 Cont.

Establishing the Sequence of Work

After the activity list for the project has been developed, the scheduler or project manager must decide the order in which the activities will be performed, and communicate that information to those responsible for carrying them out. The construction plan is normally represented by a *Logic Diagram*, or *Network*, which is the basis for the CPM system of scheduling. The diagram is both a tool for making the scheduling decisions and a means of representing the outcome. The diagram will always evolve through a series of versions as the schedule develops and as the project proceeds.

Diagramming Systems

Two methods for representing job logic are in use today. They are commonly known as the *Precedence Diagramming Method (PDM)* and the *Arrow Diagramming Method (ADM)*. Either system can be used very effectively on construction projects. There is, however, some debate over the relative merits of these systems, as well as some misunderstanding about the nature of each. Of the two, the arrow system (ADM) is older, and many persons in the industry have used it for most of their careers. It is, however, being rapidly replaced by the precedence system (PDM), which has certain advantages. PDM offers ease of use and understanding, and the capacity to represent a wide variety of job situations. It is for these reasons that PDM is used for all presentations in this book. Most of the techniques for fully representing job logic using PDM are discussed in the text.

Diagramming Formats

Basically, any diagramming technique or format will work in the PDM system so long as it roughly resembles Figure 5.4, in which the activity being represented is shown as a node (typically a rectangle or circle), and the relationship between two or more activities is shown as an arrow between the activities, or nodes. For drawing rough diagrams, a wide range of formats can be used. One option is a work sheet that has pre-drawn nodes; only activity titles and arrows need to be added. The opposite extreme is a blank sheet of drafting paper. Refinement of the diagram as the plan develops typically results in better and more clearly drafted successive versions.

Key Questions to Ask When Establishing Logic

In order to develop the construction plan, the scheduler or manager need only take each activity in turn and answer the following questions about that activity and related work activities:

    1. What other work must be completed before the activity can begin?

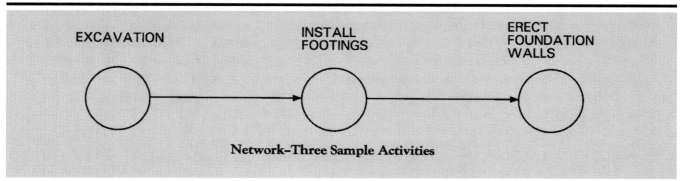

Network–Three Sample Activities

Figure 5.4

2. What other work cannot begin before the activity is completed?

3. What other work can be performed at the same time as the activity and not interfere with the activity?

To illustrate this concept, visualize the process of placing the foundation for the sample office building. The following general activities would be included:

- Excavate
- Install footings
- Erect foundation walls

The first activity, "excavate," is not preceded by any other activity. The next activity is "install footings." None of the other activities can take place at the same time as this one, and it must follow excavation since the footings are below grade. Looking ahead to "erect foundation walls," the scheduler could say that this activity must be preceded by "install footings," since the walls must rest on the footings. The simple relationships between these three activities are illustrated in Figure 5.4.

Priority of Relationships

For a scheduler developing the logic, it is helpful to think in terms of which activity relationships are most important. In addition to the obvious physical relationships between activities, there are others which should logically be considered. Among them are the order of use of various pieces of equipment, weather scheduling problems, and priorities of manpower. These factors involve more complex decision-making techniques. The general principle is that the relationships should be treated in order from the least to the most flexible. The following order of treatment has been proven a most effective approach.

1. Deal with the physical relationships first. These are by far the least flexible. For example, a column must rest on top of a footing if that is what the plan shows; the relationship between these two activities cannot be altered.

2. Deal with the contractual or external relationships next. If there are weather considerations or contractual obligations that must be reflected in the order of activities, these may be altered to some degree.

3. Deal with the managerial and equipment relationships last. Once the previous relationships between activities have been established, the manager can then start to make decisions about the order of equipment and manpower assignments to get the job done.

Complex Relationships Between Activities

As noted earlier in this chapter, the relationships between activities depend on what must be finished prior to starting an activity, and what may begin when an activity is complete. This basic idea is at the heart of the CPM concept. One of the advantages of the PDM system of notation is that it permits the construction manager to vary the relationship between activities in order to more fully represent the actual events on a job site.

To consider these advanced forms of activity relationships, a system of definitions must first be established. The standard relationship shown in all the figures of this chapter so far can be defined as a finish-to-start relationship. Finish-to-start is again illustrated in Figure 5.5 , showing the node notation format and a time-scaled bar chart of the relationship between "erect studs" and "hang drywall." Simply put, this standard relationship says that if erecting studs precedes the hanging of drywall, then the studs must be finished before drywall can start.

While this basic relationship applies to many, if not most, activities on a project, there are also many cases where more complex relationships exist, or where the construction manager scheduling the job may want to represent the relationship more realistically. For example, consider the case in which studs and drywall are being installed in a very large building, and there is no point in waiting until all studs are erected before hanging any drywall. It is quite often possible under these circumstances to erect some portion of the studs, say 20% or so, then begin the drywall while stud work proceeds.

This kind of relationship between activities can be shown as *lag relationships*, or *overlapping activities*. Instead of showing the relationship between studs and drywall as *finish-to-start (FS)*, it can be shown as a *start-to-start (SS Lag)*. A notation is typically made on the relationship arrow (see Figure 5.6, which also shows the time relationships between the studs and drywall). Another type of lag is the finish-to-finish relationship, sometimes called an *F-F lag*, or *FF relationship*. The F-F lag shows a relationship in the finishing times of activities (see Figure 5.7).

Lag relationships can be used anywhere in a network to represent all kinds of situations. It is even possible to have different kinds of lag relationships between the same two activities, if the construction situation requires this arrangement. The most common use of SS and FF relationships is in situations where crews are planned to proceed along a job at different rates of production. In this case, the lags are used to establish the correct starting times. The objective is to prevent too great of an initial spacing, which

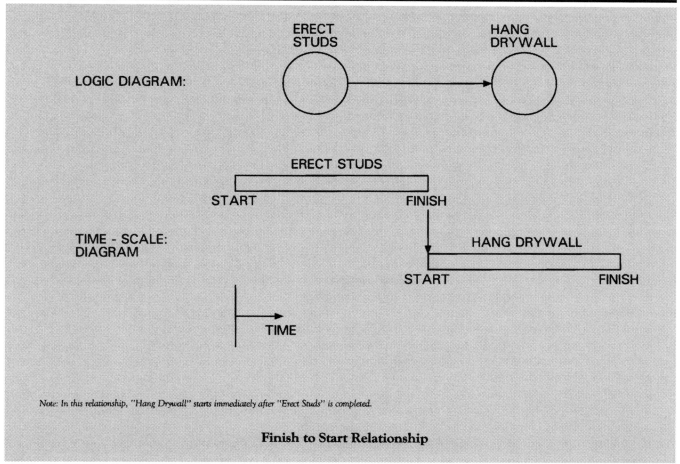

LOGIC DIAGRAM:

ERECT STUDS

HANG DRYWALL

TIME - SCALE: DIAGRAM

ERECT STUDS

START

FINISH

HANG DRYWALL

START

FINISH

TIME

Note: In this relationship, "Hang Drywall" starts immediately after "Erect Studs" is completed.

Finish to Start Relationship

Figure 5.5

would be inefficient, or overrunning of crews, which would cause interference. Specifically, SS lags are typically used where the succeeding activity is slower than the leading activity, and FF lags are used where the succeeding activity is faster than the leading activity. This point is illustrated in Figure 5.8 where different times are applied to erecting studs and hanging drywall. SS and FF lags are used to show the necessary spacing. In Case 1, it can be seen from the relative times of the two crews that the succeeding drywall crew proceeds more slowly than the stud crew. Consequently, there is no danger of the drywall crew catching up with the stud crew and causing interference. In Case 2, the succeeding drywall crew is faster than the stud crew, and there is a danger of interference if the drywall crew starts too soon. The effect of the FF lag is to delay the start of the drywall crew until such time as interference will not occur.

Tips for Establishing Work Sequences

The following tips may be helpful in working up an effective and realistic network.

1. Make absolutely sure that the plan reflects what the field construction managers want to do with the job. If the people who have to carry out the

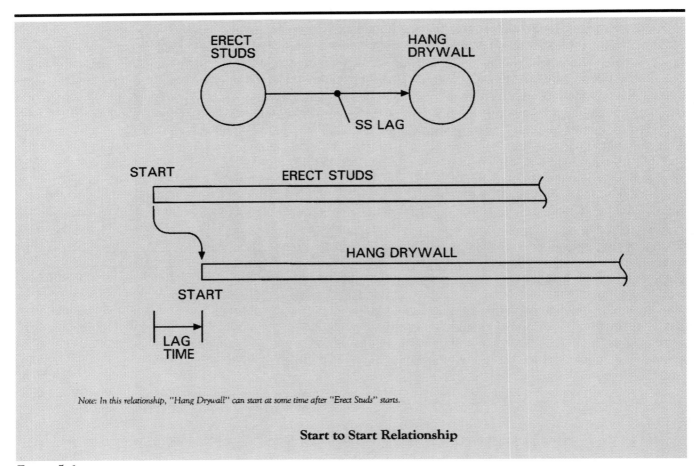

Note: In this relationship, "Hang Drywall" can start at some time after "Erect Studs" starts.

Start to Start Relationship

Figure 5.6

plan are not committed to it, the chances for success are minimal. Although it is probably best to have the actual managers develop the plan, it is not essential, so long as they are regularly consulted and their ideas are incorporated into the plan.

2. When developing the construction plan, or network, remember that the diagram only represents what is to be done on the job, and that the schedule is not an end in itself. Under no circumstances should scheduling or computer considerations ever dictate construction operations.

3. Remember that developing a construction plan is a creative process, and that the first pass is never the final solution. Be prepared to erase, re-draw, and use lots of paper if necessary.

4. There are no hard and fast rules about how the network should be drawn. Some schedulers claim that an arrow should never be drawn in a backwards direction, for example, a statement which is not really valid. What counts is that the diagram is understandable, and while neat drawings are more legible than sloppy ones, anything that works is acceptable practice.

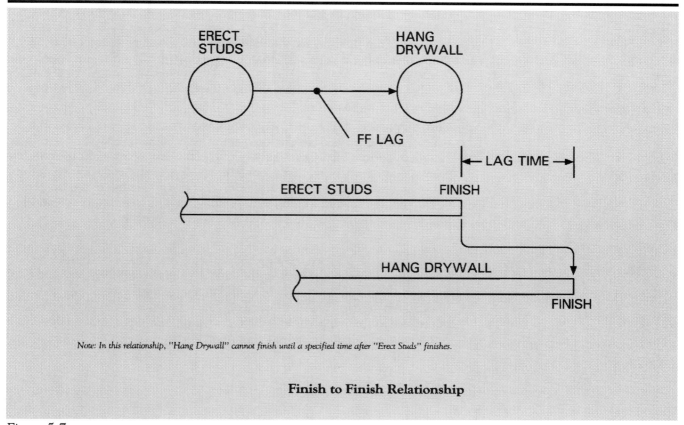

Note: In this relationship, "Hang Drywall" cannot finish until a specified time after "Erect Studs" finishes.

Finish to Finish Relationship

Figure 5.7

Also, some networks can be developed without sketching a logic diagram on paper by creating logic directly as one puts activities into a computer scheduling program. Realistically, however, this practice is probably limited to small networks, or to networks for projects which are quite similar to previous work.

Step-by-Step Development of the Overall Logic Diagram

Developing a logic diagram is a relatively simple task at one level, yet can be a very difficult task at another level. For example, most people can easily create logic diagrams for relatively small portions of a building, even if they have very little experience in formal scheduling. A superintendent can readily visualize the sequence for a set of footings, and perhaps even an entire foundation without much difficulty. A set of activities which would cover the work of the foundation on the sample office building might consist of less than two dozen individual activities, and is therefore quite easy to diagram.

Consider, however, the task of developing all the activities of the sample office building or larger structure. In this case, hundreds of activities may be required, and it is impossible for a scheduler or superintendent to visualize the entire sequence. Consequently, one of the major problems the scheduler must deal with is one of keeping the information in some kind of order and thus rendering a total schedule which can be used effectively.

The secret to handling this kind of situation lies in working in a manner opposite to that of developing the list of activities. In that case, the answer was to work from the general to the specific, i.e., going from large scale to small scale. To develop the logic diagram, we should proceed from small, manageable sub-units to larger and larger overall units of work. For example, consider again the foundation work.

The first step would be to look at an individual element of the work and its tasks. A good example would be the footing work. The construction tasks involved are as follows, and in the following order: *Form, Reinforce, Place, Strip*. These items can be strung together in a sequence recognized by all individuals experienced in the construction industry (as shown in Figure 5.9). Next, the similar tasks for walls could be strung together in a similar manner as shown in Figure 5.10. Columns work contains the same elements, but in slightly different order, as shown in Figure 5.11. In carrying out this development, the tasks necessary to build three physical elements of the building have been logically combined in small sub-networks, which can be carried to the next stage in the process.

Next, the physical elements of footings, walls, and columns can be combined with Building Excavation, and brought together in a larger diagram, shown in Figure 5.12. The result is an overall diagram which represents the work necessary for the complete phase of Foundations work. If we continue this process, subsequently developing the sub-units of work and combining them with other elements in the appropriate phases, we then have larger units (phases) which we can then link together into an overall logic diagram. The results of this process are shown in Appendix B.

Summary   In this chapter, we have seen how a scheduler or project manager can develop an overall plan for a project by breaking the job down into its component parts and tasks, and then working out a sequence best suited to completing the job quickly and efficiently. In the next chapter, we will look at how the results of this process of analysis can be used to determine how long each activity will take to perform, and then determine the likely overall time for the project as a whole.

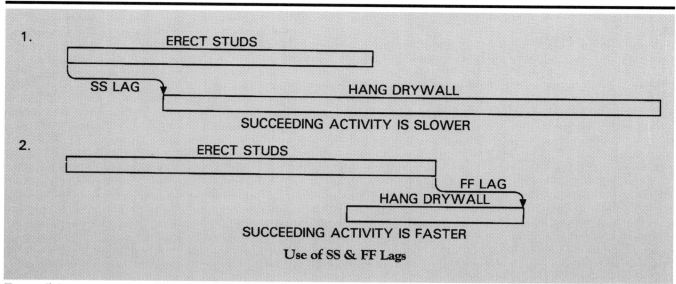

Figure 5.8

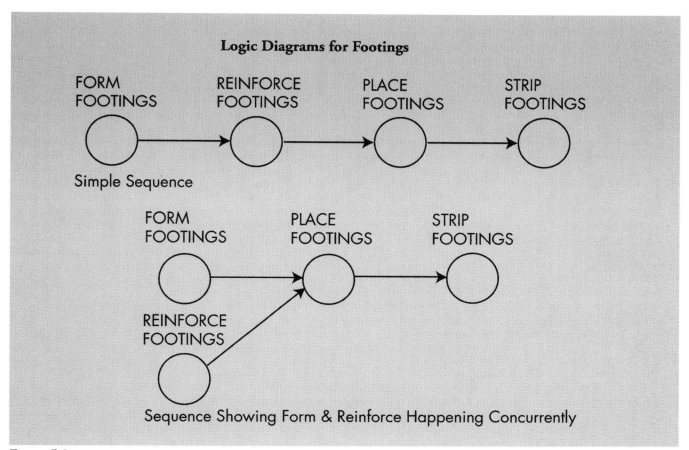

Figure 5.9

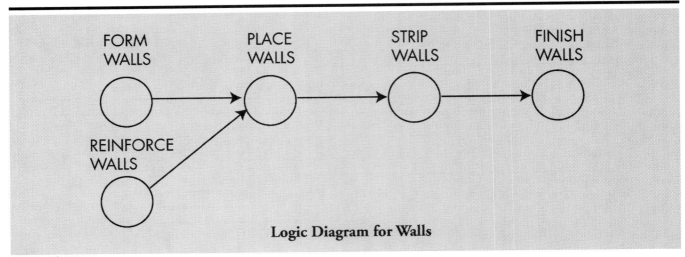

Logic Diagram for Walls

Figure 5.10

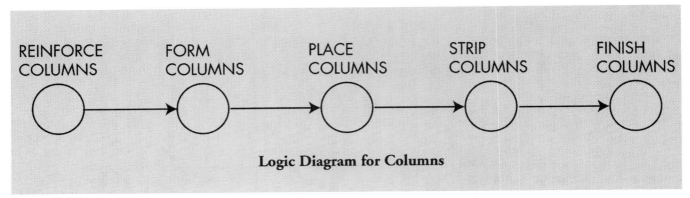

Logic Diagram for Columns

Figure 5.11

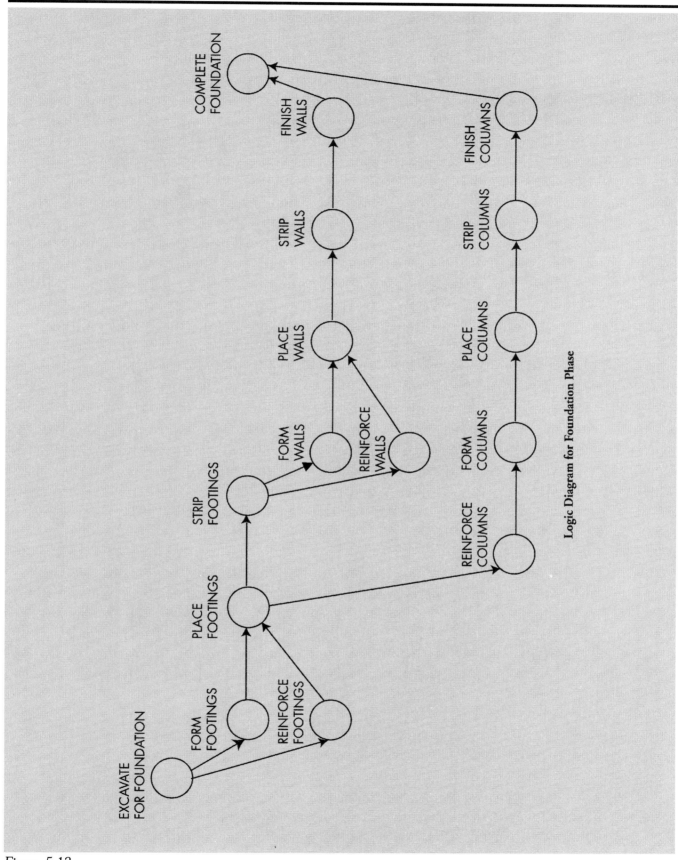

Figure 5.12

Logic Diagram for Foundation Phase

77

6

Scheduling the Project

6

Scheduling the Project

The previous chapter provides guidelines for initial job planning. Included are the processes of breaking the project down into workable sub-parts, or activities, and then determining the sequence of work that will be used to accomplish those activities. Once these two tasks are complete, the project manager has created some "tools" to help finish the job. This organized approach must be carried further, however, since no time information has yet been developed. This chapter addresses time issues, specifically:

1. estimating the times of individual activities, and
2. calculating the length of the job as a whole.

We will describe techniques for accomplishing these two tasks and for relating work times to calendar times.

Estimating Durations

A number of specific methods can be used to arrive at reasonably accurate estimates of the time required to perform a given activity or piece of work on a job. Before getting into the details of these methods, however, some general rules should be noted. These rules can help to arrive at realistic times and avoid serious errors, and should be observed by anyone developing a construction schedule.

1. Assume Each Activity Will Be Done Normally

First, the time estimates should initially assume a normal or ideal set of working conditions. The reason for using this assumption can be seen in Figure 6.1, which relates efficiency, or unit cost, to activity time. For most activities, there is a most efficient rate of production which results in the lowest possible unit cost. Because all jobs vary somewhat, this rate of production is not a precise figure. Instead, it represents a range of production rates, which, experience has shown, result in the lowest unit cost. Figure 6.1 also shows that if the production rate is significantly higher or lower, the unit cost changes accordingly.

In the best of all possible worlds, a construction manager would expect all the activities on a job to be carried out at a rate close to the ideal. In the real world, the ideal rate is actually possible for most activities. However, those that do not proceed on schedule may be critical to the job, or hold up the progress of other activities in some way. The best procedure, therefore, is to plan all activities initially in terms of ideal time, and then change only those that must be changed for valid reasons, such as overall time.

2. Evaluate Each Activity Independently

In addition to assuming initially an ideal time for each activity, the scheduler should compute individual activity times as if no other work existed. Clearly, this is not realistic in the long run; but practice has shown that much of the work of a project does in fact proceed without being affected very much by other work. It is also true that if a person drawing up a schedule tries at the start to consider every constraint affecting an activity, the number of variables may rapidly become overwhelming. Further, many of the factors that will affect a given activity cannot be known until the overall project time has been determined. Thus, it is better to plan each activity independently, and then account for constraints as necessary and as they become known in the scheduling process.

3. Use Consistent Time Units

Throughout this book, the time units used to describe activity and project durations are *work days*. These work days are converted to calendar days through the calendar definition process, covered later in this chapter. Days are by far the most common unit of time measure in the construction industry, although hours or weeks can be used appropriately in many circumstances.

Regardless of the time unit used, it is important to be consistent in order to prevent confusion and misunderstanding over the scheduled times for various parts of the job. Calculated times for work activities are usually in work days; the quoted times for delivery of materials are often in calendar days. The person preparing the schedule must be certain that one is converted, if necessary, to be consistent with the other.

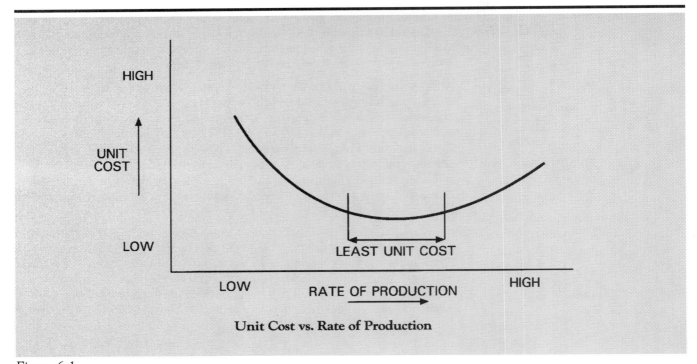

Unit Cost vs. Rate of Production

Figure 6.1

4. Keep Good Records as the Schedule is Developed

It is often helpful during the schedule development process to be able to refer to previous assumptions, calculations, and "trial balloons." For example, in trying to decide how much to speed up various activities, it is helpful if one knows what is the assumed normal rate. With this information, it is possible to gauge the effect of one activity's acceleration on the various other activities, so as to decide on the most efficient mix. Toward this end, most good schedulers maintain analysis and record sheets on each activity as the schedule develops. Figure 6.2 is a sample sheet used for this purpose.

Typically, any given activity may have several sheets worked out over the course of the job. Dating and keeping each subsequent sheet in order is important. The sheets might be kept in a loose-leaf notebook, catalogued by a classification system, such as the CSI MasterFormat. An organized approach makes referring back to previous data much easier.

Actual Calculation of Activity Durations

Several methods can be used for determining an accurate activity duration, depending on the situation. The emphasis in this book is on *labor-hour* (or "man-hour") *productivity*, or *daily production rate-based* methods. These methods have proven to be the most flexible and have the additional advantage that they are based on readily available data from a variety of sources. Possible sources include a company's own historical data, or published information such as *Means Productivity Standards*.

Our sample office building project is used to illustrate the productivity-based techniques and methods. The calculations examples are from the network for the foundation of the sample office building (developed in the previous chapter). An activity list, logic diagram, and summary of all activity durations for the foundation are shown in Figures 6.3 through 6.5.

Labor-hour Productivity Method

Traditionally, cost and productivity data within the construction industry have been collected and recorded using the *basic dollars per unit of work in place* (e.g., $/S.F., $/C.Y.) method. However, there has been a growing trend toward the use of labor-hours per unit of work placed (e.g., L.H./S.F., L.H./C.Y.) as a basis for cost estimating and work planning. There are several reasons for this change, including the fact that payroll systems must collect data on a labor-hour basis anyway, and inflation has made the traditional use of dollars per unit less reliable and subject to frequent change. The *labor-hours per unit measure approach* has proven in practice to be easier to use and more accurate—in both estimating and work planning.

Basic Calculations

The use of labor-hour productivity data in estimating activity duration is based on the following formulas:

1. Total labor-hours required for an activity = Labor-hours/unit × units of work for the activity; which can be stated mathematically as:
   Total Labor-hours = Labor-hours/Unit × No. of Units

2. Total days required to finish an activity =
   Total labor-hours/labor-hours worked per day; which can be stated mathematically as:

$$\text{Total Days} = \frac{\text{Total Labor-hours}}{\text{Labor-hours/day}}$$

For the standard eight-hour workday, the above formula can be restated as:

$$\text{Total Days} = \frac{\text{Total Labor-hours}}{\text{Crew Size} \times 8 \text{ hrs/day}}$$

To show how these formulas work, we will use the wall footing activity of the sample foundation network. The total number of square feet of contact area in the wall footings is 4213, a figure that would typically be obtained from the company's estimate. Looking

Activity Analysis Sheet

Activity No.:_____ CSI Number: _____

Estimate Page Number:_____

Date:_____

Revision Number:_____

Activity Definition:

Action:_____

Object:_____

Location:_____

General Description:_____

_____

Codes Involved:

Cost Code:_____

Schedule Code:_____

Limiting Factors:_____

Total Units of Work:_____

Productivity: LH/Unit:_____   EH/Unit:_____

Calculations:

$$\frac{LH}{Units} \ x \ \underline{\hspace{1cm}} \ Total \ Units = \underline{\hspace{1cm}} Total \ LH$$

$$\frac{Total \ LH}{LH/Crew \ Day} = \underline{\hspace{1cm}} Total \ Days$$

Equipment Used: Type:_____Qty:_____

_____

_____

Crew Description:_____

_____

_____

Comments and Assumptions:_____

_____

_____

Figure 6.2

at *Means Building Construction Cost Data*, line number 031-158-0150 (Figure 6.6), it can be seen that the labor-hour productivity for continuous footings of the type called for in the hotel is .066 labor-hours per SFCA installed. Applying these numbers to the basic formulas, we obtain the following results.

Total Labor-hours = 4213 SFCA × .066 Labor- hours/SFCA = 278 Total Labor-hours

Total days = 278 ÷ 32 ((3 CARPS + 1 CLAB)× 8hrs) = 8.7 days

This calculated time of 8.7 days can then be used in work planning, and in the later calculation of overall project time.

Daily Production Rate Method

In addition to keeping production information in a labor-hour/unit format, many companies have traditionally kept the information in the form of a daily rate of production for a given crew. Publications such as *Means Building Construction Cost Data* also provide this kind of information. The daily crew productivity method is somewhat simpler than using the labor-hour productivity method, but it is probably not as flexible, particularly when it comes to varying the crew size by a few workers either way in order to adjust times. The following example is based on the same sample activity used to illustrate the labor-hour productivity method.

Basic Calculations

The use of daily output or production rate data in estimating activity times is based on this simple formula:

Total Days Required for an Activity = Units of Work for the Activity/Daily Output or, stated mathematically:

$$\text{Total Days} = \frac{\text{Total Units}}{\text{Daily Output}}$$

To illustrate this method, we will again use the first activity of the foundation. The total number of square feet of contact area is 4213. Looking at *Means Building Construction Cost Data* line number 031-158-0150 (Figure 6.6), it can be seen that the daily output for the type of footing called for is 485 SFCA per day for a C-1 crew

Activity List		
Sample Office Foundation		
Excavate Footings	Reinforce Walls	Form Columns
Form Footings	Place Walls	Place Columns
Reinforce Footings	Strip Walls	Strip Columns
Place Footings	Finish Walls	Finish Columns
Strip Footings	Reinforce Columns	Complete Foundation
Form Walls		

Figure 6.3

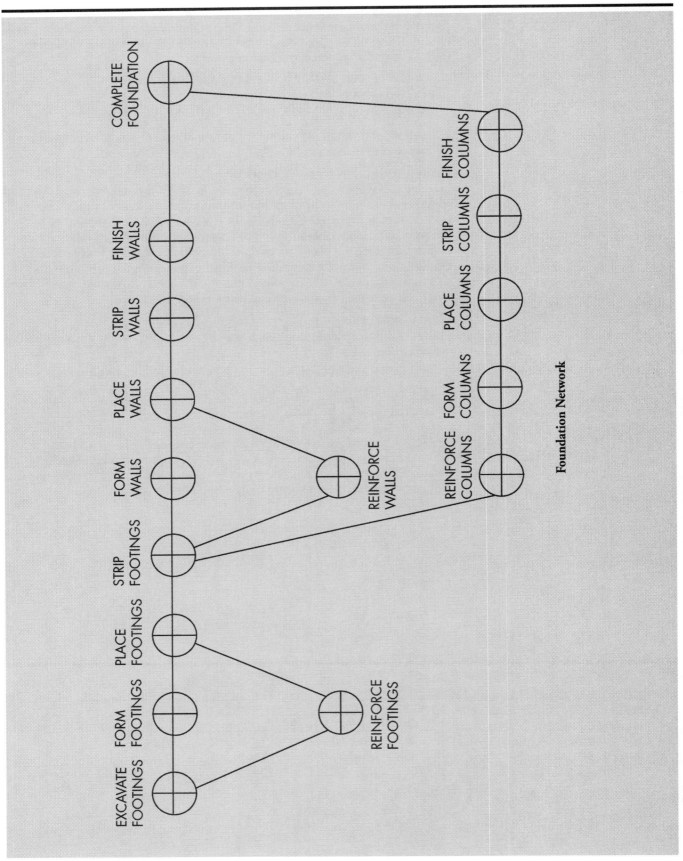

Foundation Network

Figure 6.4

(Figure 6.7), which consists of three carpenters and one laborer. With these numbers applied to the basic formula, the following results are obtained:

$$\text{Total Days} = \frac{4213 \text{ SFCA}}{485 \text{ SFCA per day}} = 8.7 \text{ days}$$

This time figure is the same as was calculated using the labor-hour productivity method, which is to be expected. By examining the relationship between the two methods, one can see why the results are the same. Crew C-1 consists of four individuals, which means that 4×8 labor-hours = 32 labor-hours/day are invested in accomplishing the work. Dividing 32 labor-hours by 485 SFCA installed per day means that the labor-hours/SFCA is .066, which coincides with the value used in the labor-hour productivity method.

Adjustment of Calculated Times

While the two calculation methods just presented are the best basis for finding accurate times, we must recognize that productivity numbers usually reflect average or ideal conditions and as such, may not apply to our specific project. We should therefore adjust our calculated times, if necessary, to reflect the complexity and peculiarities of our own situation. There are many factors involved in these adjustments; some examples follow.

Foundation Network Time Calculations								
Activity		Qty	Unit	LH/Unit	Total LH Req'd	Typical Crew Size	Calc. Days Req'd	Rounded Days Req'd
Excavate:	Footings	390	CY	0.08	31	1.5	2.6	3
Form:	Footings	4213	SFCA	0.041	173	4	5.4	6
	Walls and Pilasters	11185	SFCA	0.096	1074	12	11.2	12
	Columns	93	LF	0.192	18	4	0.6	1
Reinforce:	Footings	5.75	Tn	15.240	88	3	3.7	4
	Walls and Pilasters	9.49	Tn	10.670	101	3	4.2	5
	Columns	9.43	Tn	13.910	131	3	5.5	9
Place:	Footings	232	CY	0.400	93	8	1.5	6
	Walls and Pilasters	253	CY	0.580	147	8	2.3	3
	Columns	18	CY	0.460	8	8	0.1	1
Strip:	Footings	4213	SFCA	0.014	59	4	1.8	2
	Walls and Pilasters	11185	SFCA	0.032	385	4	11.2	12
	Columns	93	SFCA	0.064	6	4	0.2	1
Finish:	Walls and Pilasters	6793	SF	0.015	102	2	6.4	7
	Columns	730	SF	0.030	22	2	1.4	2

Figure 6.5

031 | Concrete Formwork

031 100 | Struct C.I.P. Formwork

			CREW	DAILY OUTPUT	LABOR-HOURS	UNIT	MAT.	LABOR	EQUIP.	TOTAL	TOTAL INCL O&P	
150	6200	Bulkhead forms for slab, w/keyway expanded metal	R031 -020									**150**
	6210	In lieu of 2 piece form		C-1	1,100	.029	L.F.	1.23	.73		1.96	2.50	
	6215	In lieu of 3 piece form	R031 -050		960	.033		1.23	.83		2.06	2.66	
	6220	6" high, 4 uses			1,100	.029		1.48	.73		2.21	2.77	
	6500	Curb forms, wood, 6" to 12" high, on elevated slabs, 1 use	R031 -060		180	.178	SFCA	1.53	4.44		5.97	8.70	
	6550	2 use			205	.156		1.23	3.90		5.13	7.50	
	6600	3 use			220	.145		.89	3.64		4.53	6.75	
	6650	4 use			225	.142		.73	3.56		4.29	6.40	
	7000	Edge forms to 6" high, on elevated slab, 4 use			500	.064	L.F.	.37	1.60		1.97	2.92	
	7100	Alternate pricing, 1 use			350	.091	SFCA	.43	2.29		2.72	4.08	
	7500	Depressed area forms to 12" high, 4 use			300	.107	L.F.	.68	2.67		3.35	4.95	
	7550	12" to 24" high, 4 use			175	.183		.93	4.57		5.50	8.20	
	8000	Perimeter deck and rail for elevated slabs, straight			90	.356		9.15	8.90		18.05	24	
	8050	Curved			65	.492		12.55	12.30		24.85	33	
	8500	Void forms, round fiber, 3" diameter			450	.071		.46	1.78		2.24	3.31	
	8550	4" diameter			425	.075		.46	1.88		2.34	3.47	
	8600	6" diameter			400	.080		.81	2		2.81	4.04	
	8650	8" diameter			375	.085		1.32	2.13		3.45	4.81	
	8700	10" diameter			350	.091		2.23	2.29		4.52	6.05	
	8750	12" diameter			300	.107		2.89	2.67		5.56	7.40	
	8800	Metal end closures, loose, minimum					C	29.50			29.50	32.50	
	8850	Maximum					"	152			152	167	
154	0010	**FORMS IN PLACE, EQUIPMENT FOUNDATIONS** 1 use		C-2	160	.300	SFCA	2.41	7.75		10.16	14.85	**154**
	0050	2 use			190	.253		1.33	6.50		7.83	11.70	
	0100	3 use			200	.240		.96	6.20		7.16	10.80	
	0150	4 use			205	.234		.79	6.05		6.84	10.35	
158	0010	**FORMS IN PLACE, FOOTINGS** Continuous wall, plywood, 1 use	R031 -050	C-1	375	.085	SFCA	2.39	2.13		4.52	6	**158**
	0050	2 use			440	.073		1.31	1.82		3.13	4.30	
	0100	3 use	R031 -060		470	.068		.95	1.70		2.65	3.73	
	0150	4 use			485	.066		.78	1.65		2.43	3.46	
	0500	Dowel supports for footings or beams, 1 use			500	.064	L.F.	.64	1.60		2.24	3.22	
	1000	Integral starter wall, to 4" high, 1 use			400	.080		1.20	2		3.20	4.47	
	1500	Keyway, 4 use, tapered wood, 2" x 4"		1 Carp	530	.015		.21	.40		.61	.86	
	1550	2" x 6"			500	.016		.27	.42		.69	.97	
	2000	Tapered plastic, 2" x 3"			530	.015		.47	.40		.87	1.15	
	2050	2" x 4"			500	.016		.62	.42		1.04	1.35	
	2250	For keyway hung from supports, add			150	.053		.82	1.41		2.23	3.12	
	3000	Pile cap, square or rectangular, plywood, 1 use		C-1	290	.110	SFCA	1.90	2.76		4.66	6.45	
	3050	2 use			346	.092		1.05	2.31		3.36	4.79	
	3100	3 use			371	.086		.76	2.16		2.92	4.23	
	3150	4 use			383	.084		.62	2.09		2.71	3.97	
	4000	Triangular or hexagonal caps, plywood, 1 use			225	.142		2.25	3.56		5.81	8.05	
	4050	2 use			280	.114		1.24	2.86		4.10	5.85	
	4100	3 use			305	.105		.90	2.62		3.52	5.10	
	4150	4 use			315	.102		.73	2.54		3.27	4.80	
	5000	Spread footings, plywood, 1 use			305	.105		1.70	2.62		4.32	6	
	5050	2 use			371	.086		.94	2.16		3.10	4.42	
	5100	3 use			401	.080		.68	2		2.68	3.89	
	5150	4 use			414	.077		.55	1.93		2.48	3.65	
	6000	Supports for dowels, plinths or templates, 2' x 2'			25	1.280	Ea.	3.15	32		35.15	54	
	6050	4' x 4' footing			22	1.455		6.60	36.50		43.10	65	
	6100	8' x 8' footing			20	1.600		13.50	40		53.50	78	
	6150	12' x 12' footing			17	1.882		22	47		69	98	
	7000	Plinths, 1 use			250	.128	SFCA	2.45	3.20		5.65	7.75	
	7100	4 use			270	.119	"	.75	2.96		3.71	5.50	

Figure 6.6

Crews

Crew B-90

Crew No.	Bare Costs Hr.	Bare Costs Daily	Incl. Subs O & P Hr.	Incl. Subs O & P Daily	Cost Per Labor-Hour Bare Costs	Cost Per Labor-Hour Incl. O&P
1 Labor Foreman (outside)	$22.65	$181.20	$35.65	$285.20	$22.58	$34.97
3 Laborers	20.65	495.60	32.50	780.00		
2 Equip. Oper. (light)	26.30	420.80	40.00	640.00		
2 Truck Drivers (heavy)	21.70	347.20	33.30	532.80		
1 Road Mixer, 310 H.P.		986.40		1085.05		
1 Dist. Truck, 2000 Gal.		328.55		361.40	20.55	22.60
64 L.H., Daily Totals		$2759.75		$3684.45	$43.13	$57.57

Crew B-90A

	Hr.	Daily	Hr.	Daily	Bare Costs	Incl. O&P
1 Labor Foreman	$22.65	$181.20	$35.65	$285.20	$24.88	$38.32
2 Laborers	20.65	330.40	32.50	520.00		
4 Equip. Oper. (medium)	27.55	881.60	41.90	1340.80		
2 Graders, 30,000 Lbs.		1116.80		1228.50		
1 Roller, Steel Wheel		238.00		261.80		
1 Roller, Pneumatic Wheel		237.20		260.90	28.43	31.27
56 L.H., Daily Totals		$2985.20		$3897.20	$53.31	$69.59

Crew B-90B

	Hr.	Daily	Hr.	Daily	Bare Costs	Incl. O&P
1 Labor Foreman	$22.65	$181.20	$35.65	$285.20	$24.43	$37.73
2 Laborers	20.65	330.40	32.50	520.00		
3 Equip. Oper. (medium)	27.55	661.20	41.90	1005.60		
1 Roller, Steel Wheel		238.00		261.80		
1 Roller, Pneumatic Wheel		237.20		260.90		
1 Road Mixer, 310 H.P.		986.40		1085.05	30.45	33.50
48 L.H., Daily Totals		$2634.40		$3418.55	$54.88	$71.23

Crew B-91

	Hr.	Daily	Hr.	Daily	Bare Costs	Incl. O&P
1 Labor Foreman (outside)	$22.65	$181.20	$35.65	$285.20	$24.48	$37.69
2 Laborers	20.65	330.40	32.50	520.00		
4 Equip. Oper. (med.)	27.55	881.60	41.90	1340.80		
1 Truck Driver (heavy)	21.70	173.60	33.30	266.40		
1 Dist. Truck, 3000 Gal.		353.05		388.35		
1 Aggreg. Spreader, S.P.		615.20		676.70		
1 Roller, Pneu. Tire, 12 Ton		237.20		260.90		
1 Roller, Steel, 10 Ton		238.00		261.80	22.55	24.81
64 L.H., Daily Totals		$3010.25		$4000.15	$47.03	$62.50

Crew B-92

	Hr.	Daily	Hr.	Daily	Bare Costs	Incl. O&P
1 Labor Foreman (outside)	$22.65	$181.20	$35.65	$285.20	$21.15	$33.29
3 Laborers	20.65	495.60	32.50	780.00		
1 Crack Cleaner, 25 H.P.		72.40		79.65		
1 Air Compressor		74.00		81.40		
1 Tar Kettle, T.M.		21.80		24.00		
1 Flatbed Truck, 3 Ton		174.80		192.30	10.72	11.79
32 L.H., Daily Totals		$1019.80		$1442.55	$31.87	$45.08

Crew B-93

	Hr.	Daily	Hr.	Daily	Bare Costs	Incl. O&P
1 Equip. Oper. (med.)	$27.55	$220.40	$41.90	$335.20	$27.55	$41.90
1 Feller Buncher, 50 H.P.		377.60		415.35	47.20	51.92
8 L.H., Daily Totals		$598.00		$750.55	$74.75	$93.82

Crew B-94A

	Hr.	Daily	Hr.	Daily	Bare Costs	Incl. O&P
1 Laborer	$20.65	$165.20	$32.50	$260.00	$20.65	$32.50
1 Diaph. Water Pump, 2"		28.00		30.80		
1-20 Ft. Suction Hose, 2"		6.50		7.15		
2-50 Ft. Disch. Hoses, 2"		8.80		9.70	5.41	5.95
8 L.H., Daily Totals		$208.50		$307.65	$26.06	$38.45

Crew B-94B

	Hr.	Daily	Hr.	Daily	Bare Costs	Incl. O&P
1 Laborer	$20.65	$165.20	$32.50	$260.00	$20.65	$32.50
1 Diaph. Water Pump, 4"		62.00		68.20		
1-20 Ft. Suction Hose, 4"		12.50		13.75		
2-50 Ft. Disch. Hoses, 4"		17.00		18.70	11.44	12.58
8 L.H., Daily Totals		$256.70		$360.65	$32.09	$45.08

Crew B-94C

	Hr.	Daily	Hr.	Daily	Bare Costs	Incl. O&P
1 Laborer	$20.65	$165.20	$32.50	$260.00	$20.65	$32.50
1 Centr. Water Pump, 3"		36.60		40.25		
1-20 Ft. Suction Hose, 3"		9.50		10.45		
2-50 Ft. Disch. Hoses, 3"		10.80		11.90	7.11	7.82
8 L.H., Daily Totals		$222.10		$322.60	$27.76	$40.32

Crew B-94D

	Hr.	Daily	Hr.	Daily	Bare Costs	Incl. O&P
1 Laborer	$20.65	$165.20	$32.50	$260.00	$20.65	$32.50
1 Centr. Water Pump, 6"		155.20		170.70		
1-20 Ft. Suction Hose, 6"		20.50		22.55		
2-50 Ft. Disch. Hoses, 6"		37.00		40.70	26.59	29.25
8 L.H., Daily Totals		$377.90		$493.95	$47.24	$61.75

Crew B-95

	Hr.	Daily	Hr.	Daily	Bare Costs	Incl. O&P
1 Equip. Oper. (crane)	$28.60	$228.80	$43.50	$348.00	$24.63	$38.00
1 Laborer	20.65	165.20	32.50	260.00		
16 L.H., Daily Totals		$394.00		$608.00	$24.63	$38.00

Crew B-95A

	Hr.	Daily	Hr.	Daily	Bare Costs	Incl. O&P
1 Equip. Oper. (crane)	$28.60	$228.80	$43.50	$348.00	$24.63	$38.00
1 Laborer	20.65	165.20	32.50	260.00		
1 Hyd. Excavator, 5/8 C.Y.		395.65		435.20	24.73	27.20
16 L.H., Daily Totals		$789.65		$1043.20	$49.36	$65.20

Crew B-95B

	Hr.	Daily	Hr.	Daily	Bare Costs	Incl. O&P
1 Equip. Oper. (crane)	$28.60	$228.80	$43.50	$348.00	$24.63	$38.00
1 Laborer	20.65	165.20	32.50	260.00		
1 Hyd. Excavator, 1.5 C.Y.		706.55		777.20	44.16	48.58
16 L.H., Daily Totals		$1100.55		$1385.20	$68.79	$86.58

Crew B-95C

	Hr.	Daily	Hr.	Daily	Bare Costs	Incl. O&P
1 Equip. Oper. (crane)	$28.60	$228.80	$43.50	$348.00	$24.63	$38.00
1 Laborer	20.65	165.20	32.50	260.00		
1 Hyd. Excavator, 2.5 C.Y.		1681.00		1849.10	105.06	115.57
16 L.H., Daily Totals		$2075.00		$2457.10	$129.69	$153.57

Crew C-1

	Hr.	Daily	Hr.	Daily	Bare Costs	Incl. O&P
3 Carpenters	$26.45	$634.80	$41.65	$999.60	$25.00	$39.36
1 Laborer	20.65	165.20	32.50	260.00		
32 L.H., Daily Totals		$800.00		$1259.60	$25.00	$39.36

Crew C-2

	Hr.	Daily	Hr.	Daily	Bare Costs	Incl. O&P
1 Carpenter Foreman (out)	$28.45	$227.60	$44.80	$358.40	$25.82	$40.65
4 Carpenters	26.45	846.40	41.65	1332.80		
1 Laborer	20.65	165.20	32.50	260.00		
48 L.H., Daily Totals		$1239.20		$1951.20	$25.82	$40.65

Crew C-2A

	Hr.	Daily	Hr.	Daily	Bare Costs	Incl. O&P
1 Carpenter Foreman	$28.45	$227.60	$44.80	$358.40	$25.64	$40.03
3 Carpenters	26.45	634.80	41.65	999.60		
1 Cement Finisher	25.40	203.20	37.90	303.20		
1 Laborer	20.65	165.20	32.50	260.00		
48 L.H., Daily Totals		$1230.80		$1921.20	$25.64	$40.03

Figure 6.7

Rounding Up All Times

First of all, it should be a standard rule to never use optimistic times in a schedule. In practice, always round up at least to the next higher number of days. For example, if we calculated a time of 4.2 days for a set of footings, we should put a figure of 5 days into the schedule. The reality of doing work in the field is that we must always set up the work, get up to speed with our technique, do the actual work, and then take down the equipment. Providing the small cushion of rounding up will help accommodate these necessities.

Ensuring Productivity Data is Used Correctly and Appropriately

To illustrate this point, consider the case of forming wall footings for the sample office building. First, looking at the various lines which refer to continuous wall footings in Figure 6.6, we can see that line number 031-158-0010 refers to using the formwork material only once. We know from the size of the sample office building and from common industry practice that we are unlikely to use a piece of formwork lumber only once, especially considering its cost. If we look farther down, we can see that line number 031-158-0150 refers to using the formwork 4 times, which is much more likely in our situation. Also, we can see that the productivities for the two lines are quite different, .085 Labor-hours/SFCA vs. .066 Labor hours/SFCA. The labor-hours required for single use formwork is some 30% higher, and if we used the inappropriate figure, we would introduce a significant error.

Also, if we were planning a schedule with a high level of detail, the installation might be broken down into forming, reinforcing, placing, and stripping, rather than simply forming. The two formwork activities—forming and stripping—would be separate. Looking at the data from *Means Building Construction Cost Data*, section 031-158-0150 (Figure 6.6), we can see that the line refers to "Forms in place." When using any data from a reference source, it pays to determine exactly what that data includes by consulting the explanatory section to ensure that the data does in fact fit our specific situation. In this case, the explanation is provided in the rear of the cost book, under Reference Number R031-060 (Figure 6.8). In this reference section, we can see that the labor-hour productivity of .066 Labor-hours/SFCA includes erecting, stripping, cleaning and moving.

Since the activities in the sample list are broken down into forming (erecting) and stripping, the .066 Labor-hours/SFCA should not be applied by itself to either task alone. It must be divided appropriately between the two tasks if our activity times are to be as accurate as possible. One technique might be to use a 75/25 rule of thumb for time distribution of forming and stripping. The productivity time for forming alone can be calculated as: .066 Labor-hours/SFCA × 75% = .049 Labor-hours/SFCA. The productivity for stripping can be calculated as: .066 MH/SFCA × 25% = .017.

In any case, in selecting any time data for application, it is better to err on the side of being conservative rather than over-optimistic. There is a definite practical and psychological value to building small amounts of "cushion time" into schedules.

More Than One Type of Work in the Activity

Not all productivity reference materials contain data in exactly the same format as the work breakdown in the scheduler's activity list. As an example, the installation of bathroom accessories in the sample office building is included as a single activity for each floor, in part because listing every single towel bar and soap dispenser is not a practical level of detail, and because it is logical to assign all the items in a bathroom to one carpenter anyway. However, if we look at major classification 108-204 in *Means Building Construction Cost Data* (Figure 6.9), we can see that there is no listing for accessories in an entire bathroom. Rather, the items are listed individually. So to determine the overall activity time, we simply lump the total calculated labor-hours together and calculate the work based on how long it would take a single carpenter to install all the items. The total in this case can be built up by simply multiplying the

R031-060 Formwork Labor Hours

Item	Unit	Hours Required			Total Hours	Multiple Use		
		Fabricate	Erect & Strip	Clean & Move	1 Use	2 Use	3 Use	4 Use
Beam and Girder, interior beams, 12" wide	100 S.F.	6.4	8.3	1.3	16.0	13.3	12.4	12.0
Hung from steel beams		5.8	7.7	1.3	14.8	12.4	11.6	11.2
Beam sides only, 36" high		5.8	7.2	1.3	14.3	11.9	11.1	10.7
Beam bottoms only, 24" wide		6.6	13.0	1.3	20.9	18.1	17.2	16.7
Box out for openings		9.9	10.0	1.1	21.0	16.6	15.1	14.3
Buttress forms, to 8' high		6.0	6.5	1.2	13.7	11.2	10.4	10.0
Centering, steel, 3/4" rib lath			1.0		1.0			
3/8" rib lath or slab form	▼		0.9		0.9			
Chamfer strip or keyway	100 L.F.		1.5		1.5	1.5	1.5	1.5
Columns, fiber tube 8" diameter			20.6		20.6			
12"			21.3		21.3			
16"			22.9		22.9			
20"			23.7		23.7			
24"			24.6		24.6			
30"	▼		25.6		25.6			
Round Steel, 12" diameter			22.0		22.0	22.0	22.0	22.0
16"			25.6		25.6	25.6	25.6	25.6
20"			30.5		30.5	30.5	30.5	30.5
24"	▼		37.7	▼	37.7	37.7	37.7	37.7
Plywood 8" x 8"	100 S.F.	7.0	11.0	1.2	19.2	16.2	15.2	14.7
12" x 12"		6.0	10.5	1.2	17.7	15.2	14.4	14.0
16" x 16"		5.9	10.0	1.2	17.1	14.7	13.8	13.4
24" x 24"		5.8	9.8	1.2	16.8	14.4	13.6	13.2
Steel framed plywood 8" x 8"			10.0	1.0	11.0	11.0	11.0	11.0
12" x 12"			9.3	1.0	10.3	10.3	10.3	10.3
16" x 16"			8.5	1.0	9.5	9.5	9.5	9.5
24" x 24"			7.8	1.0	8.8	8.8	8.8	8.8
Drop head forms, plywood		9.0	12.5	1.5	23.0	19.0	17.7	17.0
Coping forms		8.5	15.0	1.5	25.0	21.3	20.0	19.4
Culvert, box			14.5	4.3	18.8	18.8	18.8	18.8
Curb forms, 6" to 12" high, on grade	▼	5.0	8.5	1.2	14.7	12.7	12.1	11.7
On elevated slabs		6.0	10.8	1.2	18.0	15.5	14.7	14.3
Edge forms to 6" high, on grade	100 L.F.	2.0	3.5	0.6	6.1	5.6	5.4	5.3
7" to 12" high	100 S.F.	2.5	5.0	1.0	8.5	7.8	7.5	7.4
Equipment foundations		10.0	18.0	2.0	30.0	25.5	24.0	23.3
Flat slabs, including drops		3.5	6.0	1.2	10.7	9.5	9.0	8.8
Hung from steel		3.0	5.5	1.2	9.7	8.7	8.4	8.2
Closed deck for domes		3.0	5.8	1.2	10.0	9.0	8.7	8.5
Open deck for pans		2.2	5.3	1.0	8.5	7.9	7.7	7.6
Footings, continuous, 12" high		3.5	3.5	1.5	8.5	7.3	6.8	6.6
Spread, 12" high		4.7	4.2	1.6	10.5	8.7	8.0	7.7
Pile caps, square or rectangular		4.5	5.0	1.5	11.0	9.3	8.7	8.4
Grade beams, 24" deep		2.5	5.3	1.2	9.0	8.3	8.0	7.9
Lintel or Sill forms		8.0	17.0	2.0	27.0	23.5	22.3	21.8
Spandrel beams, 12" wide		9.0	11.2	1.3	21.5	17.5	16.2	15.5
Stairs			25.0	4.0	29.0	29.0	29.0	29.0
Trench forms in floor		4.5	14.0	1.5	20.0	18.3	17.7	17.4
Walls, Plywood, at grade, to 8' high		5.0	6.5	1.5	13.0	11.0	9.7	9.5
8' to 16'		7.5	8.0	1.5	17.0	13.8	12.7	12.1
16' to 20'		9.0	10.0	1.5	20.5	16.5	15.2	14.5
Foundation walls, to 8' high		4.5	6.5	1.0	12.0	10.3	9.7	9.4
8' to 16' high		5.5	7.5	1.0	14.0	11.8	11.0	10.6
Retaining wall to 12' high, battered		6.0	8.5	1.5	16.0	13.5	12.7	12.3
Radial walls to 12' high, smooth		8.0	9.5	2.0	19.5	16.0	14.8	14.3
But in 2' chords		7.0	8.0	1.5	16.5	13.5	12.5	12.0
Prefabricated modular, to 8' high		—	4.3	1.0	5.3	5.3	5.3	5.3
Steel, to 8' high		—	6.8	1.2	8.0	8.0	8.0	8.0
8' to 16' high		—	9.1	1.5	10.6	10.3	10.2	10.2
Steel framed plywood to 8' high		—	6.8	1.2	8.0	7.5	7.3	7.2
8' to 16' high	▼	—	9.3	1.2	10.5	9.5	9.2	9.0

Figure 6.8

108 200	Bath Accessories	CREW	DAILY OUTPUT	LABOR-HOURS	UNIT	MAT.	LABOR	EQUIP.	TOTAL	TOTAL INCL O&P
0010	**BATH ACCESSORIES**									
0200	Curtain rod, stainless steel, 5' long, 1" diameter	1 Carp	13	.615	Ea.	27.50	16.30		43.80	55.50
0300	1-1/4" diameter	"	13	.615	"	29.50	16.30		45.80	58
0500	Dispenser units, combined soap & towel dispensers,									
0510	mirror and shelf, flush mounted	1 Carp	10	.800	Ea.	262	21		283	320
0600	Towel dispenser and waste receptacle,									
0610	18 gallon capacity	1 Carp	10	.800	Ea.	274	21		295	335
0800	Grab bar, straight, 1-1/4" diameter, stainless steel, 18" long		24	.333		35.50	8.80		44.30	53
0900	24" long		23	.348		38.50	9.20		47.70	56.50
1000	30" long		22	.364		41	9.60		50.60	60.50
1100	36" long		20	.400		44.50	10.60		55.10	65.50
1200	1-1/2" diameter, 24" long		23	.348		41	9.20		50.20	59.50
1300	36" long		20	.400		48	10.60		58.60	69
1500	Tub bar, 1-1/4" diameter, 24" x 36"	↓	14	.571	↓	89	15.10		104.10	122
1600	Plus vertical arm	1 Carp	12	.667	Ea.	71	17.65		88.65	106
1900	End tub bar, 1" diameter, 90° angle, 16" x 32"		12	.667		100	17.65		117.65	138
2300	Hand dryer, surface mounted, electric, 115 volt, 20 amp		4	2		460	53		513	590
2400	230 volt, 10 amp		4	2		460	53		513	590
2600	Hat and coat strip, stainless steel, 4 hook, 36" long		24	.333		43	8.80		51.80	61.50
2700	6 hook, 60" long		20	.400		67	10.60		77.60	90
3000	Mirror, with stainless steel 3/4" square frame, 18" x 24"		20	.400		63	10.60		73.60	85.50
3100	36" x 24"		15	.533		163	14.10		177.10	201
3200	48" x 24"		10	.800		203	21		224	257
3300	72" x 24"		6	1.333		291	35.50		326.50	375
4100	Mop holder strip, stainless steel, 5 holders, 48" long		20	.400		55	10.60		65.60	77
4200	Napkin/tampon dispenser, recessed		15	.533		360	14.10		374.10	415
4300	Robe hook, single, regular		36	.222		11	5.90		16.90	21.50
4400	Heavy duty, concealed mounting		36	.222		13.60	5.90		19.50	24
4600	Soap dispenser, chrome, surface mounted, liquid		20	.400		38.50	10.60		49.10	59
4700	Powder		20	.400		70	10.60		80.60	93.50
5000	Recessed stainless steel, liquid		10	.800		71.50	21		92.50	113
5100	Powder		10	.800		248	21		269	305
5300	Soap tank, stainless steel, 1 gallon		10	.800		125	21		146	171
5400	5 gallon		5	1.600		200	42.50		242.50	287
5600	Shelf, stainless steel, 5" wide, 18 ga., 24" long		24	.333		35	8.80		43.80	53
5700	48" long		16	.500		60.50	13.25		73.75	87.50
5800	8" wide shelf, 18 ga., 24" long		22	.364		44	9.60		53.60	63.50
5900	48" long		14	.571		78.50	15.10		93.60	111
6000	Toilet seat cover dispenser, stainless steel, recessed		20	.400		97	10.60		107.60	124
6050	Surface mounted		15	.533		30	14.10		44.10	55
6100	Toilet tissue dispenser, surface mounted, SS, single roll		30	.267		9.60	7.05		16.65	21.50
6200	Double roll		24	.333		14.65	8.80		23.45	30
6400	Towel bar, stainless steel, 18" long		23	.348		27.50	9.20		36.70	44.50
6500	30" long		21	.381		31.50	10.10		41.60	50.50
6700	Towel dispenser, stainless steel, surface mounted		16	.500		41	13.25		54.25	66
6800	Flush mounted, recessed		10	.800		133	21		154	180
7000	Towel holder, hotel type, 2 guest size		20	.400		11.90	10.60		22.50	30
7200	Towel shelf, stainless steel, 24" long, 8" wide		20	.400		47	10.60		57.60	68
7400	Tumbler holder, tumbler only		30	.267		19.25	7.05		26.30	32
7500	Soap, tumbler & toothbrush		30	.267		19.30	7.05		26.35	32
7700	Wall urn ash receiver, surface mount, 11" long		12	.667		97	17.65		114.65	134
7800	7-1/2", long		18	.444		69	11.75		80.75	94.50
8000	Waste receptacles, stainless steel, with top, 13 gallon		10	.800		180	21		201	231
8100	36 gallon	↓	8	1	↓	284	26.50		310.50	350

Figure 6.9

unit labor-hours times the quantity of each item, then adding the total number of labor-hours as shown in the table in Figure 6.10.

After calculating the total number of labor-hours, it is an easy task to determine the time needed for one carpenter to complete this work on each floor by dividing the number of labor-hours by 8 to get 1.375 days, and we then round up to 2 days per floor.

Not All Scheduled Work Time Is Production Time

Looking at the activity in the sample office building for gypsum wallboard installation, we can see that hanging, taping, and drying are included. The labor-hour productivity is .017 LH/SF (Figure 6.11). The time required to install the wallboard is:

$$\frac{883 \text{ Labor-hours}}{3 \text{ crews} \times 2 \text{ people} \times 8 \text{ hours/day}} = 18.4 \text{ days}$$

The allowance does not, however, take into account time required to dry the mud used in the taping process. This drying time will not show up in any references on labor-hour productivity, as it does not involve actual work, but it must be added by the scheduler when the overall activity time is established. In this case, it would be reasonable to add three days of drying time, resulting in a total activity time of 22 days. This figure would be used as the scheduled time.

Labor-Hour Productivity Does Not Govern Activity Time

Some types of work are not purely a function of the number of labor-hours required per unit of work. This fact must be taken into account when scheduling extra crews or workers. This point can be illustrated in the previous example of installing bathroom accessories. Increasing the number of carpenters decreases the activity time proportionally. In this case, one carpenter is essentially independent of the others and works proceeds according to the basic productivity rate. Not all types of work fit this situation. An example that does not fit is spraying the fireproofing on the structural steel. Looking at the line number in *Means Building Construction Cost Data* for fireproofing structural steel (Figure 6.12), we can see that the crew used (G-2) consists of 3 craft workers and one piece of grouting equipment (Figure 6.13). Experience tells us that the rate of production is dependent on the machine rather than the number of workers. Adding one person to the crew is unlikely to speed up the rate at which the machine sprays. Changes in scheduled time would have to be planned on the basis of adding whole crews of three persons each, rather than individual workers, as was the case with bathroom accessories. To vary the scheduled time, a project manager would need to go up to six workers and two machines, or up to nine workers and three machines.

Taking Learning Curves into Account

Frequently, work is scheduled as a series of similar activities. For example, the waffle slab in the sample office building could easily be scheduled as a series of placements, each containing approximately two column bays of slab. If this were the case, crews assigned to forming the slab would probably produce the last segment more efficiently than they would the first. This rising productivity or production rate, i.e., the learning curve, should be reflected in the times provided by establishing slower times for the earlier activities and shorter times for the later activities which are performed more quickly.

Determining Subcontractor Activity Times

Frequently, a scheduler or project manager is faced with the task of having to put together a schedule with little or no information on some of the activities. A prime example is when a general contractor is building a schedule that contains a lot of mechanical or electrical work, yet there is little or no expertise within the general contractor's firm in these fields. Under these conditions, the general contractor should take the following actions.

First, consult the subcontractors in question as soon and as often as possible. The subcontractor should be encouraged to supply activity time determinations based on the same methodology used by the general contractor to determine time for other activities. Obtaining such information from subcontractors helps the scheduler set a more accurate activity time, providing information on the manning levels needed by the subcontractors to complete the work.

Secondly, the general contractor must look at the role of each subcontractor in the overall picture. As the calculations for the project are developed, the mechanical and electrical will have to be assigned even if the subcontractor has not calculated them. These times must be based on average times for other activities, and sound assumption that the mechanical and electrical subs must fit the overall sequence like everyone else. In this situation, it is a common and effective practice to determine an overall timing for each phase based on experience and judgment, then go to the subs and say, "This is the sequence and these are the time limits we all must meet; can you do it, and what will it take?" The emphasis must be on consultation and cooperation with all parties if the schedule is to work effectively in a real job environment.

Applying Experience to the Final Result
When all is said and done, and activities times have been calculated "rationally," a final step remains. All activities times should be checked by experienced field personnel, (superintendents and foremen), preferably those who will actually manage the work in the field, to see if the times are in fact reasonable for the work and conditions expected. Historical data can be misapplied, calculation mistakes can be made, and a good field supervisor can often catch these mistakes in work and judgment. This step also serves to further involve and gain the acceptance of the superintendent and others in the CPM schedule development process.

Calculating Overall Job Duration

After the times have been calculated for the individual activities, the scheduler or project manager is then in a position to determine how long the entire project should take to accomplish. This is done by applying the times or durations for the activities to the logic diagram, which determines the order in which the activities are performed. We will use the sample foundation network to illustrate this procedure. Included are activities from the beginning of *Excavate Footings* to *Complete Foundation*. See Figure 6.14.

Summation of Labor-Hours Required for Complete Bathroom				
Qty.	Line No.	Description of Item	LH/Ea.	Total
3	108-204-0610	Bathroom accessories, towel disp. and waste receptacle, 18 gallon cap	0.8	2.4
2	108-204-1100	Bathroom accessories, grab bar, straight, 1-1/4" dia., SS, 36" long	0.4	0.8
1	108-204-3000	Bathroom accessories, mirror, w/SS 3/4" sq. ft. 18" x 24"	0.4	0.4
2	108-204-4200	Bathroom accessories, napkin/tampon dispenser, recessed	0.533	1.1
5	108-204-4600	Bathroom accessories, soap disp., chrome, surf. mounted, liquid	0.4	2.0
2	108-204-5700	Bathroom accessories, shelf, SS, 5' wide, 18 ga., 48" long	0.5	1.0
6	108-204-6100	Bathroom accessories, toilet tissue disp., surf. mounted, SS, single roll	0.267	1.6
4	108-204-7800	Bathroom accessories, wall urn ash rcvr., surface mount, 7-1/2", long	0.444	1.8
		Total Number of Labor-Hours for Each Floor		11

Figure 6.10

092 | Lath, Plaster & Gypsum Board

092 600 | Gypsum Board Systems

		CREW	DAILY OUTPUT	LABOR-HOURS	UNIT	1998 BARE COSTS				TOTAL INCL O&P	
						MAT.	LABOR	EQUIP.	TOTAL		
608	0250	On beams, columns, or soffits, no finish included	2 Carp	675	.024	S.F.	.17	.63		.80	1.18	**608**
	0300	1/2" thick, on walls, standard, no finish included **CN**		2,000	.008		.15	.21		.36	.49	
	0350	Taped and finished		965	.017		.24	.44		.68	.95	
	0400	Fire resistant, no finish included		2,000	.008		.21	.21		.42	.56	
	0450	Taped and finished		965	.017		.30	.44		.74	1.02	
	0500	Water resistant, no finish included		2,000	.008		.23	.21		.44	.58	
	0550	Taped and finished		965	.017		.32	.44		.76	1.04	
	0600	Prefinished, vinyl, clipped to studs		900	.018		.54	.47		1.01	1.33	
	1000	On ceilings, standard, no finish included		1,800	.009		.15	.24		.39	.53	
	1050	Taped and finished		765	.021		.24	.55		.79	1.13	
	1100	Fire resistant, no finish included		1,800	.009		.21	.24		.45	.60	
	1150	Taped and finished		765	.021		.30	.55		.85	1.20	
	1200	Water resistant, no finish included		1,800	.009		.23	.24		.47	.62	
	1250	Taped and finished		765	.021		.32	.55		.87	1.22	
	1500	On beams, columns, or soffits, standard, no finish included		675	.024		.17	.63		.80	1.18	
	1550	Taped and finished		475	.034		.28	.89		1.17	1.70	
	1600	Fire resistant, no finish included		675	.024		.24	.63		.87	1.26	
	1650	Taped and finished		475	.034		.35	.89		1.24	1.78	
	1700	Water resistant, no finish included		675	.024		.26	.63		.89	1.28	
	1750	Taped and finished		475	.034		.37	.89		1.26	1.80	
	2000	5/8" thick, on walls, standard, no finish included		2,000	.008		.20	.21		.41	.55	
	2050	Taped and finished		965	.017		.29	.44		.73	1.01	
	2100	Fire resistant, no finish included		2,000	.008		.21	.21		.42	.56	
	2150	Taped and finished		965	.017		.30	.44		.74	1.02	
	2200	Water resistant, no finish included		2,000	.008		.25	.21		.46	.61	
	2250	Taped and finished		965	.017		.34	.44		.78	1.06	
	2300	Prefinished, vinyl, clipped to studs		900	.018		.62	.47		1.09	1.42	
	3000	On ceilings, standard, no finish included		1,800	.009		.20	.24		.44	.59	
	3050	Taped and finished		765	.021		.29	.55		.84	1.19	
	3100	Fire resistant, no finish included		1,800	.009		.21	.24		.45	.60	
	3150	Taped and finished		765	.021		.30	.55		.85	1.20	
	3200	Water resistant, no finish included		1,800	.009		.25	.24		.49	.65	
	3250	Taped and finished		765	.021		.34	.55		.89	1.24	
	3500	On beams, columns, or soffits, no finish included		675	.024		.23	.63		.86	1.25	
	3550	Taped and finished		475	.034		.34	.89		1.23	1.77	
	3600	Fire resistant, no finish included		675	.024		.24	.63		.87	1.26	
	3650	Taped and finished		475	.034		.35	.89		1.24	1.78	
	3700	Water resistant, no finish included		675	.024		.29	.63		.92	1.31	
	3750	Taped and finished		475	.034		.39	.89		1.28	1.83	
	4000	Fireproofing, beams or columns, 2 layers, 1/2" thick, incl finish		330	.048		.51	1.28		1.79	2.58	
	4050	5/8" thick		300	.053		.60	1.41		2.01	2.88	
	4100	3 layers, 1/2" thick		225	.071		.90	1.88		2.78	3.95	
	4150	5/8" thick		210	.076		.90	2.02		2.92	4.16	
	5050	For 1" thick coreboard on columns		480	.033		.52	.88		1.40	1.96	
	5100	For foil-backed board, add					.07			.07	.08	
	5200	For high ceilings, over 8' high, add	2 Carp	3,060	.005		.09	.14		.23	.32	
	5270	For textured spray, add	2 Lath	1,600	.010		.12	.26		.38	.52	
	5300	For over 3 stories high, add per story	2 Carp	6,100	.003		.05	.07		.12	.17	
	5350	For finishing corners, inside or outside, add	"	1,100	.015	L.F.	.06	.38		.44	.68	
	5500	For acoustical sealant, add per bead	1 Carp	500	.016	"	.03	.42		.45	.70	
	5550	Sealant, 1 quart tube				Ea.	4.64			4.64	5.10	
	5600	Sound deadening board, 1/4" gypsum	2 Carp	1,800	.009	S.F.	.15	.24		.39	.54	
	5650	1/2" wood fiber	"	1,800	.009	"	.26	.24		.50	.66	
612	0010	**METAL STUDS, DRYWALL** Partitions, 10' high, with runners R092 -610										**612**
	0050	See also Studding, division 051-230										

Figure 6.11

It should also be noted that the scheduling procedures are fairly straightforward and can be performed manually. The calculations can, however, be tedious, and it is easy to make detail errors. It is therefore recommended that anyone involved in scheduling construction projects understand the calculation procedures and perform them using a good CPM computer scheduling program.

Goals of the Project Calculation Procedure

The last of the basic steps in the planning and scheduling process is determining several facts about the upcoming work, based on the assumptions and plans built into the logic diagram and activity times. These goals are:

1. To determine the desired or possible starting times for each of the activities which have been identified and established as necessary for getting the whole job done.

2. To determine the finishing times for these activities.

3. To determine how much flexibility is possible in these start and finish times, given the constraints which have been identified as affecting the project.

4. To determine the activities which are crucial to the success of on-time performance, i.e., the Critical Path.

Once the above information is known, the project management team can effectively control the work of all the parties to get the entire job done.

072 | Insulation & Fireproofing

		072 500	Fireproofing	CREW	DAILY OUTPUT	LABOR-HOURS	UNIT	1998 BARE COSTS				TOTAL INCL O&P	
								MAT.	LABOR	EQUIP.	TOTAL		
554	0400		Beams	G-2	1,500	.016	S.F.	.41	.36	.15	.92	1.17	554
	0500		Corrugated or fluted decks		1,250	.019		.62	.43	.18	1.23	1.54	
	0700		Columns, 1-1/8" thick		1,100	.022		.46	.49	.21	1.16	1.49	
	0800		2-3/16" thick		700	.034		.86	.76	.33	1.95	2.49	
	0850		For tamping, add						10%				
	0900		For canvas protection, add	G-2	5,000	.005	S.F.	.06	.11	.05	.22	.29	
	1000		Acoustical sprayed, 1" thick, finished, straight work, minimum		520	.046		.43	1.03	.44	1.90	2.54	
	1100		Maximum		200	.120		.46	2.67	1.14	4.27	5.90	
	1300		Difficult access, minimum		225	.107		.46	2.38	1.02	3.86	5.30	
	1400		Maximum		130	.185		.50	4.11	1.76	6.37	8.85	
	1500		Intumescent epoxy fireproofing on wire mesh, 3/16" thick										
	1550		1 hour rating, exterior use	G-2	136	.176	S.F.	5.30	3.93	1.68	10.91	13.75	
	1600		Magnesium oxychloride, 35# to 40# density, 1/4" thick		3,000	.008		1.12	.18	.08	1.38	1.59	
	1650		1/2" thick		2,000	.012		2.24	.27	.11	2.62	3	
	1700		60# to 70# density, 1/4" thick		3,000	.008		1.47	.18	.08	1.73	1.98	
	1750		1/2" thick		2,000	.012		2.97	.27	.11	3.35	3.81	
	2000		Vermiculite cement, troweled or sprayed, 1/4" thick		3,000	.008		1.01	.18	.08	1.27	1.47	
	2050		1/2" thick		2,000	.012		2	.27	.11	2.38	2.74	

Figure 6.12

Crews

Crew F-2A

Crew No.	Bare Costs Hr.	Bare Costs Daily	Incl. Subs O&P Hr.	Incl. Subs O&P Daily	Cost Per Labor-Hour Bare Costs	Cost Per Labor-Hour Incl. O&P
2 Carpenters	$26.45	$423.20	$41.65	$666.40	$26.45	$41.65
16 L.H., Daily Totals		$423.20		$666.40	$26.45	$41.65

Crew F-3

Crew No.	Hr.	Daily	Hr.	Daily	Bare Costs	Incl. O&P
4 Carpenters	$26.45	$846.40	$41.65	$1332.80	$26.88	$42.02
1 Equip. Oper. (crane)	28.60	228.80	43.50	348.00		
1 Hyd. Crane, 12 Ton		438.10		481.90	10.95	12.05
40 L.H., Daily Totals		$1513.30		$2162.70	$37.83	$54.07

Crew F-4

Crew No.	Hr.	Daily	Hr.	Daily	Bare Costs	Incl. O&P
4 Carpenters	$26.45	$846.40	$41.65	$1332.80	$26.31	$40.96
1 Equip. Oper. (crane)	28.60	228.80	43.50	348.00		
1 Equip. Oper. Oiler	23.45	187.60	35.65	285.20		
1 Hyd. Crane, 55 Ton		785.20		863.70	16.36	17.99
48 L.H., Daily Totals		$2048.00		$2829.70	$42.67	$58.95

Crew F-5

Crew No.	Hr.	Daily	Hr.	Daily	Bare Costs	Incl. O&P
1 Carpenter Foreman	$28.45	$227.60	$44.80	$358.40	$26.95	$42.44
3 Carpenters	26.45	634.80	41.65	999.60		
32 L.H., Daily Totals		$862.40		$1358.00	$26.95	$42.44

Crew F-6

Crew No.	Hr.	Daily	Hr.	Daily	Bare Costs	Incl. O&P
2 Carpenters	$26.45	$423.20	$41.65	$666.40	$24.56	$38.36
2 Building Laborers	20.65	330.40	32.50	520.00		
1 Equip. Oper. (crane)	28.60	228.80	43.50	348.00		
1 Hyd. Crane, 12 Ton		438.10		481.90	10.95	12.05
40 L.H., Daily Totals		$1420.50		$2016.30	$35.51	$50.41

Crew F-7

Crew No.	Hr.	Daily	Hr.	Daily	Bare Costs	Incl. O&P
2 Carpenters	$26.45	$423.20	$41.65	$666.40	$23.55	$37.08
2 Building Laborers	20.65	330.40	32.50	520.00		
32 L.H., Daily Totals		$753.60		$1186.40	$23.55	$37.08

Crew G-1

Crew No.	Hr.	Daily	Hr.	Daily	Bare Costs	Incl. O&P
1 Roofer Foreman	$25.50	$204.00	$44.05	$352.40	$21.97	$37.95
4 Roofers, Composition	23.50	752.00	40.60	1299.20		
2 Roofer Helpers	17.15	274.40	29.60	473.60		
1 Application Equipment		164.80		181.30		
1 Tar Kettle/Pot		43.85		48.25		
1 Crew Truck		191.35		210.50	7.14	7.86
56 L.H., Daily Totals		$1630.40		$2565.25	$29.11	$45.81

Crew G-2

Crew No.	Hr.	Daily	Hr.	Daily	Bare Costs	Incl. O&P
1 Plasterer	$25.10	$200.80	$38.45	$307.60	$22.27	$34.40
1 Plasterer Helper	21.05	168.40	32.25	258.00		
1 Building Laborer	20.65	165.20	32.50	260.00		
1 Grouting Equipment		228.80		251.70	9.53	10.49
24 L.H., Daily Totals		$763.20		$1077.30	$31.80	$44.89

Crew G-3

Crew No.	Hr.	Daily	Hr.	Daily	Bare Costs	Incl. O&P
2 Sheet Metal Workers	$30.50	$488.00	$47.35	$757.60	$25.58	$39.92
2 Building Laborers	20.65	330.40	32.50	520.00		
32 L.H., Daily Totals		$818.40		$1277.60	$25.58	$39.92

Crew G-4

Crew No.	Hr.	Daily	Hr.	Daily	Bare Costs	Incl. O&P
1 Labor Foreman (outside)	$22.65	$181.20	$35.65	$285.20	$21.32	$33.55
2 Building Laborers	20.65	330.40	32.50	520.00		
1 Light Truck, 1.5 Ton		167.40		184.15		
1 Air Compr., 160 C.F.M.		94.80		104.30	10.93	12.02
24 L.H., Daily Totals		$773.80		$1093.65	$32.25	$45.57

Crew G-5

Crew No.	Hr.	Daily	Hr.	Daily	Bare Costs	Incl. O&P
1 Roofer Foreman	$25.50	$204.00	$44.05	$352.40	$21.36	$36.89
2 Roofers, Composition	23.50	376.00	40.60	649.60		
2 Roofer Helpers	17.15	274.40	29.60	473.60		
1 Application Equipment		164.80		181.30	4.12	4.53
40 L.H., Daily Totals		$1019.20		$1656.90	$25.48	$41.42

Crew G-6A

Crew No.	Hr.	Daily	Hr.	Daily	Bare Costs	Incl. O&P
2 Roofers Composition	$23.50	$376.00	$40.60	$649.60	$23.50	$40.60
1 Small Compressor		20.95		23.05		
2 Pneumatic Nailers		37.90		41.70	3.68	4.05
16 L.H., Daily Totals		$434.85		$714.35	$27.18	$44.65

Crew G-7

Crew No.	Hr.	Daily	Hr.	Daily	Bare Costs	Incl. O&P
1 Carpenter	$26.45	$211.60	$41.65	$333.20	$26.45	$41.65
1 Small Compressor		20.95		23.05		
1 Pneumatic Nailer		18.95		20.85	4.99	5.49
8 L.H., Daily Totals		$251.50		$377.10	$31.44	$47.14

Crew H-1

Crew No.	Hr.	Daily	Hr.	Daily	Bare Costs	Incl. O&P
2 Glaziers	$25.80	$412.80	$39.30	$628.80	$27.77	$46.88
2 Struc. Steel Workers	29.75	476.00	54.45	871.20		
32 L.H., Daily Totals		$888.80		$1500.00	$27.77	$46.88

Crew H-2

Crew No.	Hr.	Daily	Hr.	Daily	Bare Costs	Incl. O&P
2 Glaziers	$25.80	$412.80	$39.30	$628.80	$24.08	$37.03
1 Building Laborer	20.65	165.20	32.50	260.00		
24 L.H., Daily Totals		$578.00		$888.80	$24.08	$37.03

Crew H-3

Crew No.	Hr.	Daily	Hr.	Daily	Bare Costs	Incl. O&P
1 Glazier	$25.80	$206.40	$39.30	$314.40	$22.98	$35.50
1 Helper	20.15	161.20	31.70	253.60		
16 L.H., Daily Totals		$367.60		$568.00	$22.98	$35.50

Crew J-1

Crew No.	Hr.	Daily	Hr.	Daily	Bare Costs	Incl. O&P
3 Plasterers	$25.10	$602.40	$38.45	$922.80	$23.48	$35.97
2 Plasterer Helpers	21.05	336.80	32.25	516.00		
1 Mixing Machine, 6 C.F.		41.20		45.30	1.03	1.13
40 L.H., Daily Totals		$980.40		$1484.10	$24.51	$37.10

Crew J-2

Crew No.	Hr.	Daily	Hr.	Daily	Bare Costs	Incl. O&P
3 Plasterers	$25.10	$602.40	$38.45	$922.80	$23.93	$36.50
2 Plasterer Helpers	21.05	336.80	32.25	516.00		
1 Lather	26.15	209.20	39.15	313.20		
1 Mixing Machine, 6 C.F.		41.20		45.30	.86	.94
48 L.H., Daily Totals		$1189.60		$1797.30	$24.79	$37.44

Crew J-3

Crew No.	Hr.	Daily	Hr.	Daily	Bare Costs	Incl. O&P
1 Terrazzo Worker	$26.20	$209.60	$38.70	$309.60	$23.88	$35.28
1 Terrazzo Helper	21.55	172.40	31.85	254.80		
1 Terrazzo Grinder, Electric		44.00		48.40		
1 Terrazzo Mixer		62.40		68.65	6.65	7.32
16 L.H., Daily Totals		$488.40		$681.45	$30.53	$42.60

Crew J-4

Crew No.	Hr.	Daily	Hr.	Daily	Bare Costs	Incl. O&P
1 Tile Layer	$26.10	$208.80	$38.60	$308.80	$23.55	$34.83
1 Tile Layer Helper	21.00	168.00	31.05	248.40		
16 L.H., Daily Totals		$376.80		$557.20	$23.55	$34.83

Figure 6.13

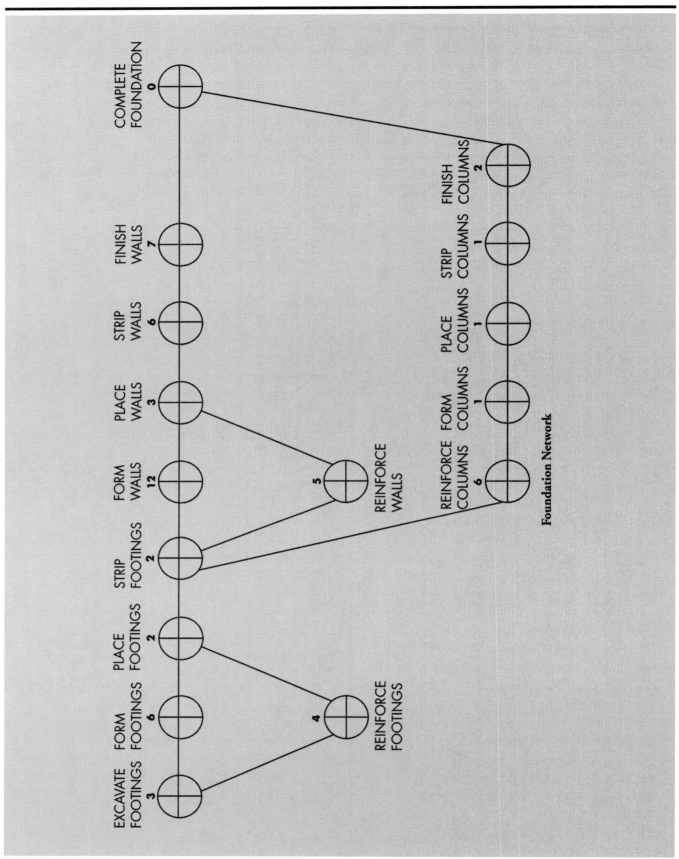

Foundation Network

Figure 6.14

Definitions

To determine the above information, it is necessary to understand the following terms which are commonly used in the calculation process.

Succeeding Activity/Preceding Activity: Activity A precedes Activity B. Activity B is the succeeding activity. In logic terms, a preceding activity must be completed before a succeeding activity can begin.

Duration (DUR): The calculated or estimated time for an individual activity (determined in the previous section of this chapter).

Early Start (ES): The earliest possible time an activity can start, assuming all previous activities have been completed. The early start of an activity is also the early finish of the preceding activity.

Early Finish (EF): The earliest possible time an activity can be completed, assuming again that all previous work has been completed. In practice, the EF is equal to the activity time added to the early start time.

Late Finish (LF): The latest time an activity can finish, and still not delay the completion of the project as a whole. The late finish of an activity is equal to the late start of the succeeding activity.

Late Start (LS): The latest time an activity can begin, and still not delay the final completion. In practice, LS is equal to the activity time subtracted from the late finish.

Total Float (TF): The difference between the early and late times on an activity; it is the allowable delay in starting the activity.

Critical Path (CP): The set of activities, or path in which the early times are equal to their late times, i.e., total float equals 0. In other words, Critical Path represents the group of activities that must start on time in order to keep the project as a whole on time.

Milestone Activity: An activity with zero duration, which marks the end of a particular phase of work.

The Actual Calculation Procedure

The actual process used to determine early times, late times, and floats consists of three individual steps, which must proceed in order. None of the steps can be bypassed in order to obtain the information on the next one, as each depends upon its predecessor. Working through these steps can be tedious, but each is essential. Specifically, they are:

1. *Forward Pass:* The procedure whereby the early times for a project are calculated. It is called the *forward pass* because it proceeds "forward" along the logic diagram from left to right.

2. *Backward Pass:* The procedure in which the late times of a project are determined. It is called the *backward pass* because it proceeds "backward" along the logic diagram from right to left.

3. *Calculation of Floats and Critical Path:* The procedure in which the difference between the allowable starting times is calculated and the activities which have no slack are identified.

Demonstration of the Actual Procedure

The entire project calculation procedure is demonstrated step-by-step in the following figures. The various times for each activity are shown using the notations system in Figure 6.15.

Forward Pass

The forward pass is illustrated in Figure 6.16. It begins on the left side of the sample logic diagram, in this case with the initial activity of *Excavate Footings*. Normal practice is to begin any network with a single starting activity. This is not absolutely necessary, but it simplifies the hand calculation procedure considerably.

To start the process, *Excavate Footings* is assigned an early start time of Day 0. The early finish of this activity can then be calculated as ES + DUR = EF, 0 + 3 = 3. These numbers are then written in the appropriate quadrants of the node, according to the notation system shown in Figure 6.15.

If we define early start times as the earliest time any activity can begin assuming all previous work has been completed, it can be deduced that the early start time for the next activity, *Form Footings*, is *Day 3*. In other words, forming for footings cannot begin until the footings have been excavated. The same is true for *Reinforce Footings*, shown immediately under *Form Footings*.

Using the same logic as that applied to excavating, it can be seen that *Form Footings* can finish on Day 9 (3 + 6 = 9). Further, *Reinforcing Footings* can finish on Day 7 (3 + 4 = 7). It should be noted that both forming footings and reinforce footings can start on the same day, but finish on different days because their durations are different.

Looking ahead to *Place Footings*, it can be seen that this activity is dependent on (i.e., preceded by) two activities. Each of these activities has a different early finish time, so the question arises, what is the earliest possible time *Place footings* can begin? The answer lies in the definition of early start—the earliest possible time an activity can begin assuming all previous work has been completed. Under this definition, *Place Footings* cannot begin until form footings has been completed, i.e., Day 9. *Place Footings* cannot begin on Day 7, because at that time, *Form Footings* is still under way, with 2 more days to go, and to start it early would violate the rule that all previous work must be completed.

A simple rule for dealing with multiple preceding activities is to take the early start as the latest or last early finish of all preceding activities. Using this rule, the choices are 7 and 9. The early start of *Place Footings* becomes 9, since it is that last of the preceding activities to finish.

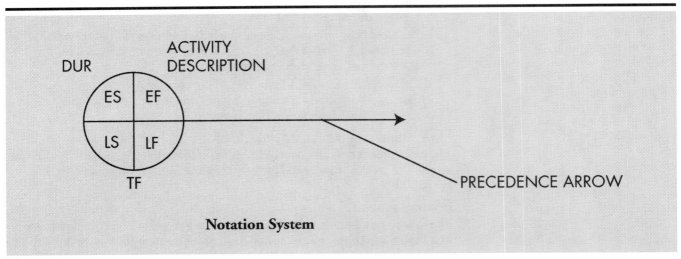

Notation System

Figure 6.15

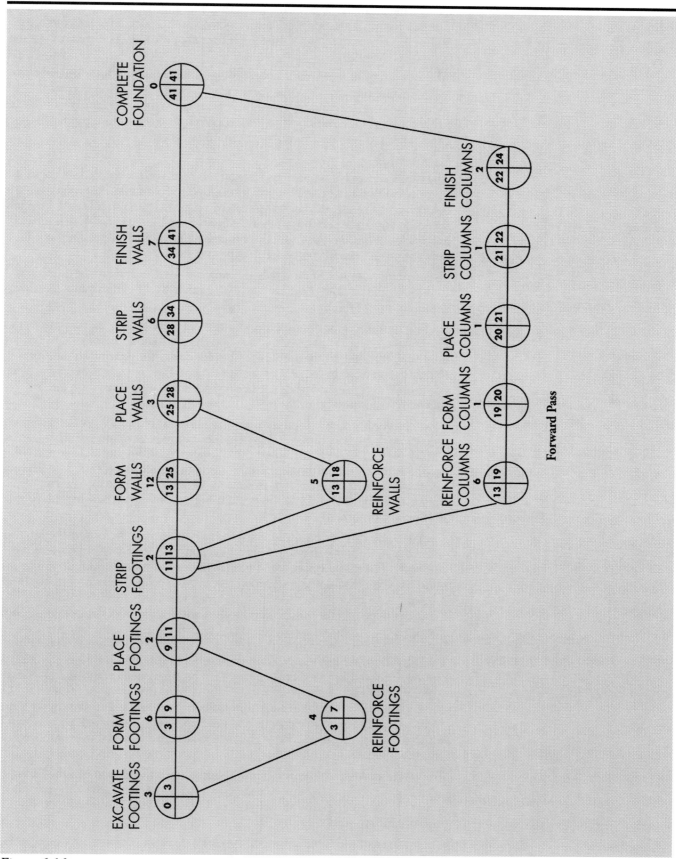

Figure 6.16

Continuing across the diagram in the same manner, it can be seen that the last activity, *Complete Foundation*, which is a milestone activity with a duration of zero, can occur on Day 41. This means that for this sample diagram, the earliest possible finish for the "project" is Day 41.

At this point, the forward pass is complete, and all activities have had their early start and finish times calculated. While the calculation process is by no means complete, the diagram does have value at this point. For example, if the excavation of footings had just begun, it would be possible to tell the concrete placement contractor that his crews would probably need to be on the job 9 days hence.

Backward Pass

The backward pass is illustrated in Figure 6.17. It begins on the right side of the logic diagram, in this case with the last activity of *Complete Foundation*. Following the definition of late finish, this last activity can be assigned a late finish of Day 41. Logically, this judgment is based on the fact that if it finishes any later than day 41, the project as a whole finishes late. A simple rule of thumb is that in the single ending node for a network, the late finish must be equal to the early finish.

To determine the late start for *Complete Foundation*, we refer again to the definitions. In this case, the late start of the last activity is equal to the late finish minus the activity duration $(41 - 0 = 41)$.

Looking back across the diagram, the activities that precede *Complete Foundation* are *Finish Walls* and *Finish Columns*. The question arises as to how late these activities can finish and still not delay the start of the *Complete Foundation* activity. The answer is that they must finish by the time of the latest start of the *Complete Foundation* activity, i.e., Day 41. The rule for establishing late finishes is that they are equal to the late start of the following activity.

Again, proceeding leftward and calculating the late start of *Finish Walls* is a matter of subtracting the activity time of 7 days from the late finish, establishing the late start as Day 34. $(41 - 7 = 34)$. Looking farther to the left, the late finishes and late starts of each activity can be calculated in the same way, until the late start of *Place Walls* has been calculated as Day 25, the late start of *Reinforce Walls* is Day 20 and the late start of *Reinforce Columns* is Day 30. At this point, it is apparent that one activity, *Strip Footings* is influenced by these 3 activities.

The next questions involve determining the latest possible finish for *Strip Footings* that will not delay the start of any following activities in a way which will delay the project as a whole. The answer can be found again in the logic of previous definitions. The late finish must be a time at which strip footings can be completed without delaying the following activities beyond their late start times, which were already calculated. To illustrate this point, take the late start for *Reinforce Walls*, and ask the question, if *Strip Footings* is completed on Day 23, what happens to the start of subsequent activities? To answer the question, consider the effect on *Form Walls*. If *Strip Footings* is not finished until Day 23, then *Form Walls* could not start until Day 23, which is 10 days past its already calculated late start time of Day 13. The same question can also be asked regarding *Reinforce Columns*. In this case, if the finish of strip footings is delayed to Day 30, then the start of *Reinforce Columns* would be delayed past its late start date of Day 13. It is clear that in no case can the finish of *Strip Footings* be delayed beyond Day 13 without delaying the start of one of the subsequent activities, and thus delaying the project as a whole.

The simplest rule in dealing with multiple succeeding activities is to take the lowest, or earliest late start among the succeeding activities as the late finish for the preceding activity. In this case, it is the late start of Day 13, which is the lowest of the three succeeding activities.

Continuing to the left on the diagram, the backward pass is completed at the beginning node with a late start (for *Excavate Footings*) of Day 0. This determination is consistent

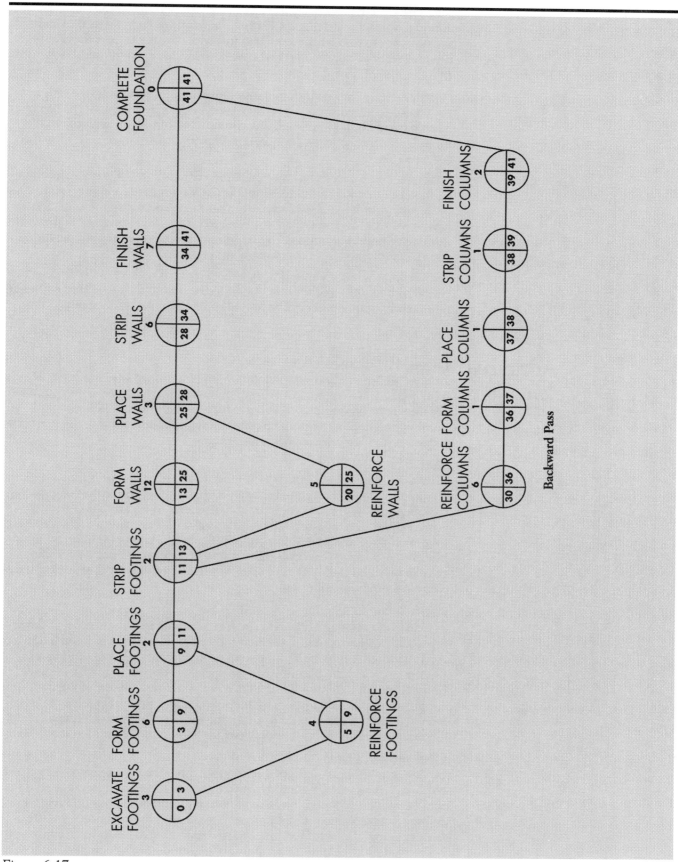

Figure 6.17

Backward Pass

103

with the logic that the late start is the latest time that the activity can begin without delaying any other activity. In fact, in networks with single beginning and ending nodes and no advanced calculations techniques involved, the calculation of the backward pass must result in a late start of 0; otherwise there is an error in the calculation.

Floats and Critical Path

Now that the forward and backward passes have been completed, and the early and late times determined, the total float for all activities can be calculated. This part of the procedure is much simpler than the last two steps and consists of simply subtracting the early start time from the late start time (or early finish from late finish) for each activity in turn.

Looking at Figure 6.18, it can be seen that the TF (total float) for excavate footing is $0 - 0 = 0$; for form footings, it is $9 - 9 = 0$. Looking at *Reinforce Footings*, however, it can be seen the value is $9 - 7 = 2$. A value of more than 0 means that these activities have some "slack" or permissible delay, built into the times they can start. In other words, *Reinforce Footings* has a "window" of Day 3 to Day 5; it can start any time during this period and still meet the requirements for the project as a whole.

Further, it can be seen that the activities which have a float value of 0 constitute the critical path for the project. These activities must start at their scheduled early start times, otherwise the project will be delayed beyond the calculated completion time of Day 41.

Advanced Calculations

Lagged Relationships

As noted earlier, the basic relationship between activities is the *finish to start* or *FS*, relationship. This relationship is by far the most common type used in networks, and was used in the previous section covering basic forward pass and backward pass calculations. The other relationships, *start to start (SS)* and *finish to finish (FF)*, are also very valuable. Their calculation is as follows.

Start to Start

In calculating the SS relationship, rather than basing the start time of the succeeding activity on the finish of the preceding one, each start time is based on the start time of the preceding activity. This concept is best shown in Figure 6.19, which also shows the notation system and time scale of this relationship. In this diagram, two activities, A&B, have times of 10 days and 20 days respectively, and are connected by an SS 5 relationship. In order to calculate the start time of the succeeding activity B, the lag value of 5 is added to the start time of 0 for the preceding activity A, to arrive at a start time of 5 for the succeeding activity B.

Finish to Finish

The calculation of the FF (Finish to Finish) relationship is similar in concept, though it is slightly more complex. To illustrate this point, Figure 6.20 shows two activities A&B, which have times of 20 and 15 days respectively, and are connected by an FF5 relationship. In order to calculate the starting time for B, the early finish for A must first be determined; it is $0 + 20 = 20$. The finish time for B can then be calculated by adding the lag value of 5 to the finish time of A, or $20 + 5 = 25$. Now that the finish time of B has been determined to be 25, the early start of B can be determined by subtracting the duration of Activity B from the finish time of B, or $25 - 15 = 10$.

Constrained Dates

In addition to showing overlapping relationships, the scheduler is often faced with the problem of showing or factoring in events or circumstances which are outside the actual construction process. For example, it is very common in construction to have delivery dates determined by factors completely outside the job site, such as manufacturing schedules. In another typical circumstance, a portion of the site may not be available until a given date, or an owner may impose a required finish date on all or part of the project. In these cases, it is common practice to use what are known as

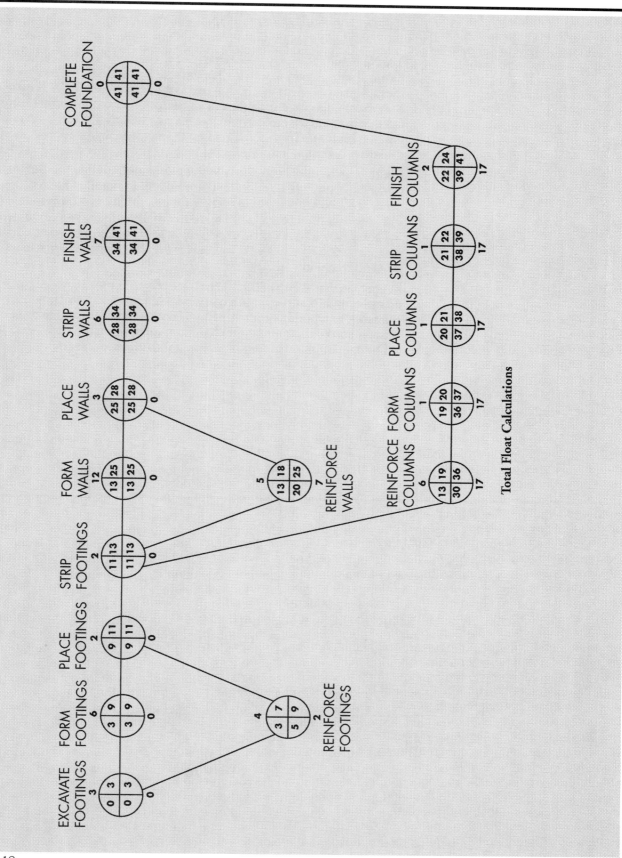

Figure 6.18

105

constrained dates, or as they are sometimes known, *plugged dates*. These constraints are classified as *no later than (NLT)* or *No Earlier Than (NET)* dates, and each affects the schedule calculations differently.

The NET date affects only the forward pass. To illustrate the point, Figure 6.21 shows the small sample network with a constraint added. Specifically, the constraint is that the gypsum wallboard cannot be delivered to the job site until Day 25. Logic tells us that the gypsum wallboard installation cannot take place before the material arrives; a fact that must be considered in the calculations. This situation leads to what is known as a *Start No Earlier Than (SNET)* of Day 25 for gypsum wallboard. The SNET is determined by simply imposing the constraint of Day 25 over the calculated day of 20.

Continuing the calculations for the rest of the forward pass shows an early finish for gypsum wallboard of 34, and ES/EF (Early Start/Early Finish) of 34 and 40 for rough paint. This schedule puts the completion of the project at Day 40, which is five days later than originally planned, and equal to the five day delay in the start of the gypsum wallboard caused by the delay in delivery. It must be noted, however, that if the constraint was a SNET Day 18, it would have no effect, since the gypsum wallboard could not start until Day 20 anyway.

By contrast, the NLT (Not Later Than) date affects only the backward pass. As an example, Figure 6.22 points out a case in which, for some external reason, the rough paint must be finished no later than Day 32 (FNLT Day 32). In this case, the constraint is simply imposed over the late finish of rough paint, which becomes Day 32 instead of Day 35. The backward pass calculation is then carried out as before.

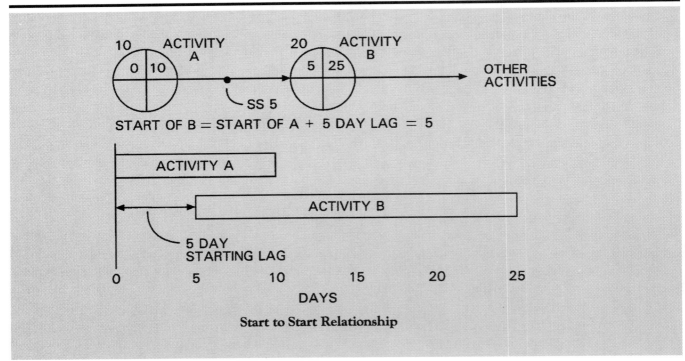

Figure 6.19

Note that at this point, the late start time for hollow metal door frames is now −3. This is not an error; the reason for this figure can be shown if the float calculations are carried out. The floats now show a critical path with floats all equal to −3. This float is now what is known as *Negative Float*. It tells the project manager that this project is three days behind before it even starts, if the constraint of finishing no later than day 32 is to be met. It means that somewhere along the critical path, some times must be reduced in order to meet the schedule requirement. Finally, as with the SNET constraint, it should be noted that the constraint would not affect any other activities.

It is possible to have *finish no earlier than* constraints, and *start no later than* constraints, but these situations do not commonly occur. In any case, the effect on calculations is the same.

Calendars

Basic Calendars

As noted earlier in this chapter, the calculations are done in work days. There are very good reasons for using work days as a time unit when calculating scheduled times. However, the use of work days raises some problems in the use of schedules by workers and managers in the field. Information must be communicated to the persons who must execute the work. Unfortunately for the person who calculated the schedule in work days, no one in the real world thinks in these terms. To say to a superintendent that form walls must start on Day 13 tells him nothing. The calculated work schedule must be converted to calendar dates to be useful.

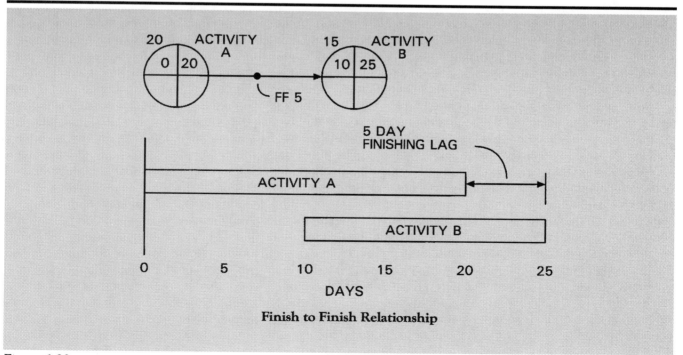

Finish to Finish Relationship

Figure 6.20

It is possible to convert calculated work days to calendar days by hand, but in this day and age, there is absolutely no reason to do so. This task can be easily computerized, which is what is typically done. All available CPM computer systems are designed to allow establishment of at least one basic calendar which takes into account all holidays, the number of days in a work week, and other factors. These programs take the basic logic of the schedule and the activity durations, use them to calculate starts and finishes, and then display the resulting times as calendar days. Many systems also allow the creation of multiple calendars, some with varying holidays, and permit the assignment of different activities to different calendars to suit the more complex requirements of some projects. The availability of these features provides yet another strong argument for

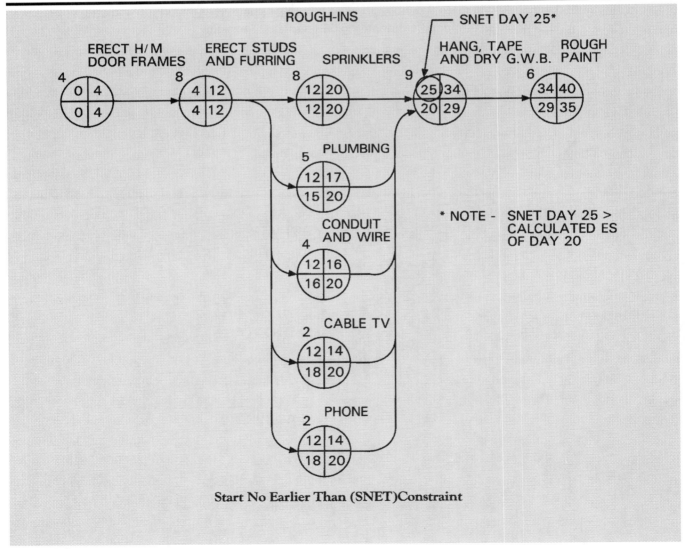

Figure 6.21

purchase and application of computer software for scheduling. An example of what the sample foundation network would look like when calculated and converted using SureTrak ® is shown in Figure 6.23.

Dealing with the Effect of Weather on Project Calendars

There are several ways to deal with the weather factor when scheduling construction jobs. The first principle is that only those activities that are affected by weather should be adjusted or adapted. For example, weather clearly has an effect on excavation, but has no impact on the installation of bathroom tile. Also, some activities can be performed as quickly in poor weather as in good if the proper precautions are taken. Concreting is an example for which weather becomes a cost concern, but not necessarily a schedule concern. The key is to treat each activity individually according to its particular requirements.

There are two methods for dealing with the effect of weather on activity duration; these are:

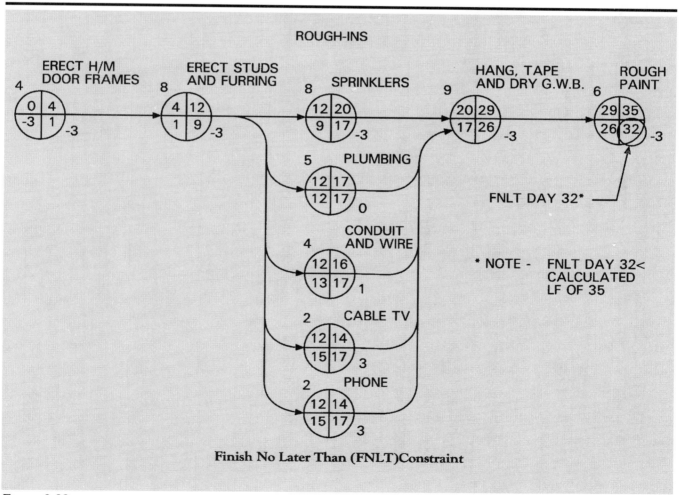

Figure 6.22

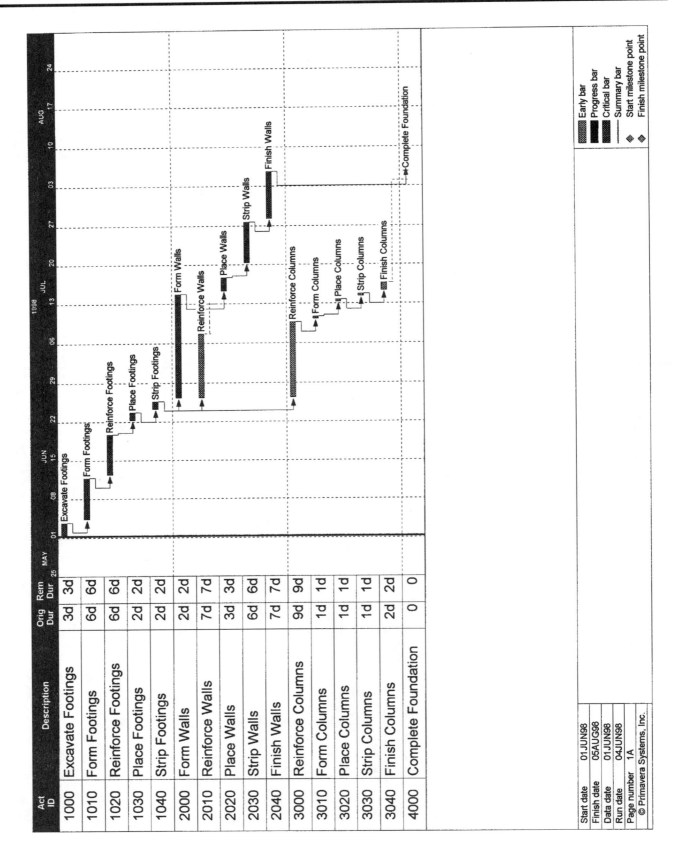

Figure 6.23

110

- add time to the activity to compensate, or
- schedule fewer working days within the calendar period.

To illustrate the point, consider an excavation activity which is scheduled to take 20 days. If records show that it rains an average of 25 of the days in the season and location specified, then the activity length can be increased to 25 days. The alternative is to schedule the activity on the basis of four-day rather than five-day weeks. In either case, the activity is effectively "stretched" by 25, thus providing extra time to make up for those days when no excavation work can be performed. Lengthening the activity time is the simpler of the two methods, though it will not work in certain circumstances. In such cases, multiple calendars may be needed to reflect the differing effects of weather on various activities. This multiple calendar approach would be needed when it is determined that no work of a certain type could be performed during a certain season, or seasons. A specific example might be the erection of structural steel in Wyoming, which may be impossible during the months of December, January, and February. A calendar would have to be established to accommodate the steel erection during the appropriate season(s).

Summary

In this chapter, we built on the techniques discussed in Chapter 5 to develop ways the scheduler or project manager can develop activity times and duration for the entire project. When these calculations have been completed, the schedule is then ready for use in the field. It is often true, however, that schedules have many activities and are full of detail which may be difficult to use. The next chapter is therefore devoted to the task of organizing and displaying the schedule information for the project in the clearest way possible so that the project managers can attack the key problems on the job and not spend time worrying about tasks which do not need attention.

7

Organizing and Displaying Project Information

Organizing and Displaying Project Information

Scheduling using CPM techniques can involve a considerable amount of detail work. As projects grow larger, the number of activities increases, and a high level of detail becomes almost inevitable. As a result, managers can become overwhelmed by the amount of data, finding it difficult to obtain the information they need for the task at hand. This chapter describes how to use a schedule efficiently even when large amounts of detail are involved. The tasks required to organize and effectively use the schedule may seem too complicated to be worthwhile. In fact, quite the opposite is true. A moderate amount of effort and time invested in organizing the schedule early in the project can yield enormous dividends later by making the right information accessible at the right time, thus helping the managers in their decision-making.

Key Questions To Ask

First, we must ask, *Who will use the information?* We must recognize that not all managers need the same information. For instance, a vice president requires very different information from that needed by the project manager. Likewise, the superintendent requires a different set of data from that which is useful to the VP and the PM. If the schedule is not designed to handle these differing needs, then the VP is forced to wade through information intended for the PM and superintendent, and vice versa. Simply put, different managers need different kinds of information.

Our second question is, *What will they need to know?* To avoid confusion, the schedule must be organized in such a way that only the important and relevant elements are presented to each party at the proper time. The manager must not be presented with information concerning portions of the job that are not currently relevant. For example, when the sample office building is in the structural stage, a project manager cannot afford to be concerned with future activities like roofing or the third floor interior work.

Our third question is, *How can we design the schedule to provide the proper information at the right time?* To accomplish this task, we must design "intelligence" into the schedule activities so that we can easily and efficiently find the right information elements from among a mass of otherwise irrelevant information, then arrange and display it in such a way that it is easily understood by the parties who need it. Once we have found the correct information, we must then arrange it in such a way that it is clear and easily understood by all users. Fortunately, most modern scheduling software systems provide the tools necessary to do that job.

Tasks That Must Be Performed in Order to Provide the Right Information

So far, we have described the need to organize the schedule information. The question that remains is how to do it. Specifically, the schedule must be organized in such a way that these three key tasks can be accomplished:

1. **Selection:** First, it is necessary to separate certain information from all other information. For example, if the superintendent wants information about the forming of footing line A alone, then our schedule system must allow us to identify each element of footing line A separate from all other work in the job. Or, the superintendent may wish to look only at forming of footings, and ignore placement, reinforcement, etc. Similarly, the schedule should be designed to permit that kind of selection.

2. **Sorting:** In addition to selecting, we must also be able to sort and present the data in an order that has some meaning to the people reviewing it. In the case of footing line A, the superintendent would probably want to list each element in the order in which it is supposed to occur.

3. **Summation:** For example: If the project manager needs to check on the progress of the footings in general, but does not wish to see the detail, then the system must be capable of summarizing all footing activities into a single activity for display.

Finally, it is important to be able to accomplish all of these tasks at one time. For instance, if the vice president wants information about the foundation as a whole, and does not want to see information about the structure above or other elements, then the schedule must permit selection of foundation activities (excluding all others), **and** a summary of that set of activities. If the foundation is presented relative to other work, then sorting is also necessary.

This detailed process of selecting, sorting, and summarizing may at first glance seem like a formidable task. Fortunately, this is not the case. All up-to-date computerized schedule systems are designed with these tasks in mind. The key lies in the coding of activities, using the schemes provided by the systems. In reality, very little work is required to create a well organized, useful schedule, as we shall see.

Types of Coding Schemes

The following coding schemes from the sample office building and other building types are examples of types of coding that allow the project scheduler to provide information in a number of different ways. These schemes are not the only ones that could be used, nor must a coding scheme be as complex as these in order to be useful or effective. They are intended only as representative types of schemes.

Coding by Project Phases
Most construction projects are carried out in logical phases, with certain milestones marking the end of each phase. For example, a simple house schedule might use the following phases:

- Foundation
- Framing and roof
- Dry-in
- Rough-ins
- Finishes
- Site work and landscaping

Similarly, a schedule for the sample office building might be broken down into the following phases:

- Site work
- Foundation
- Structure
- Penthouse
- Building envelope

- Basement
- Interiors – 1st floor
- Interiors – 2nd floor
- Interiors – 3rd floor
- Finish site work
- Closeout

Coding by Project Level or Area

High rise or multi-level projects benefit from schemes that allow the project manager to review work taking place at different levels. A typical scheme for the same office building might be as follows:

- Basement
- 1st Floor
- 2nd Floor
- 3rd Floor
- Roof and penthouse

Similarly, projects spread over large areas typically use codes to denote horizontal location. For example, oil refineries often use a grid reference system to denote location of specific work.

Coding by Trade

It is often helpful to be able to view the sequence of operations of a particular trade or crew without regard to building level. For example, if the general contractor building the sample hotel elects to do all concrete using his company's employees, then it would be a great help to the project manager if he could selectively display the activities involving the contractor's own employees or crews, while ignoring activities involving subcontractors or other trades. This type of code is also helpful in identifying overlaps in scheduling crews, and for allocating labor.

Coding by Contractor or Subcontractor

In addition to reviewing activities involving one particular trade, it may also be helpful for the project manager to see the sequence of an individual subcontractor's work separate from all other work. In fact, subcontractors are usually eager for as much information as is available regarding the dates when they will be required to work, and they are apt to be more cooperative when they are better informed.

Other Coding Possibilities

While the above-mentioned coding schemes are generally useful on commercial building projects, other types are more appropriate for other kinds of work. For example, a contractor who does roadwork may wish to schedule and control bridgework separately from earthwork or paving. A contractor who builds large industrial plants may need to identify work on a horizontal or "geographic" basis. Home builders who construct large subdivisions might want to see or schedule work based on separate streets or by individual houses or groups of houses.

Ways to Arrange the Information

Once we have selected the information from the overall schedule, we must then think of how to arrange the information in ways that are clear to the user. Usually, this means three basic sorting schemes:

1. by identifier
2. by time, e.g., early start
3. by degree of importance, e.g., total float

The first case, by *activity identifier*, is frequently used by schedulers who must work with large lists of data. For example, if a preliminary schedule has been created and a scheduler must then work with a list of activities to add further information, the information would be sorted and displayed on a worksheet in identifier order so the scheduler can easily find the appropriate activity. Activity identifiers can also be used to select information for schedules for field personnel, especially if intelligence is built into the activity identifier numbers. This approach is less common, but this idea has been built into the schedule for the sample office building. As the reader can see, the site work activity identifiers are in the 1000 series, the foundation is in the 2000 series, and so on.

The second sorting schedule, by time, is much more commonly used. Most people in the construction industry think of time in a "left to right" representation, and many schedules are therefore presented in what is known as an "early start" sort. This creates a form of chart, known as a *Bar chart* or *Gantt chart*, which is intuitively and readily understood by most people in the construction field. Most of the example schedule reports at the end of this chapter are sorted "ES," and the reader can easily see the clarity of the information presented.

The last sorting device, by degree of importance, can be used to emphasize activities that must receive more emphasis than others. For example, a bar chart can be sorted by total float, so that the critical activities, or those with the least float, will be displayed at the top of the list of work to be done. An example of this type of bar chart is also shown at the end of this chapter.

Sample Reports: Office Building

Figures 7.1 through 7.5 are samples of typical schedule reports that might be generated for use by managers constructing an office building. All of these samples have been created using SureTrak scheduling software, by Primavera Systems, Bala Cynwyd, PA.

Summary Schedule by Phase: An example of information about the project as a whole. There are only 11 activities shown in this report as seen in Figure 7.1. The chart gives the scheduled start and finish dates of only the major phases such as Site Work, Foundation, etc. None of the specific work is shown.

Schedule for a Single Phase: Within each phase of the project, there are details of the actual work to be done. Figure 7.2 shows the activities required to complete the foundation.

Schedule for a Single Sub: In addition to details of a phase, it is sometimes necessary to show the work of a single subcontractor or superintendent. In Figure 7.3 all concrete work is shown, which spans two phases, Foundation and Structure.

Schedule for a Single Floor: Different parts of the building can be assigned to different superintendents. In this case, the interior work for a single floor (the first floor) is shown in Figure 7.4. Later reports could show work for Floors 2 and 3 if necessary.

By Time Window: Sometimes it is desirable to show only the work that happens in the very near future. This report, Figure 7.5 shows only the activities which are due to start within the first four weeks of the job.

Summary

In this chapter, we covered one of the most important parts of the scheduling process, i.e., displaying the information developed during the planning process and beyond. One key point is that the value of the schedule to the Project Manager can be enhanced considerably if it is displayed in a form which is easily understood by all. Good schedule information helps superintendents and foremen plan their work well, and contributes to a smooth and efficient job. Conversely, if it is displayed poorly, its value is lost, and much effort can be wasted, not to mention the project may go badly and no one will know. The next chapter deals with the next step after the project is planned and started, i.e., monitoring and controlling the work as it proceeds and the inevitable unexpected problems start to surface.

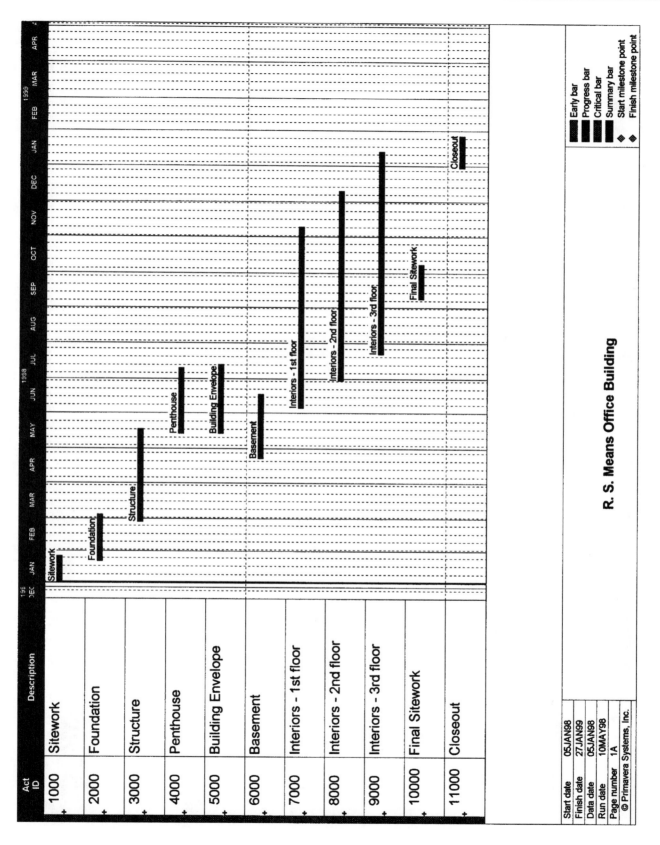

Figure 7.1

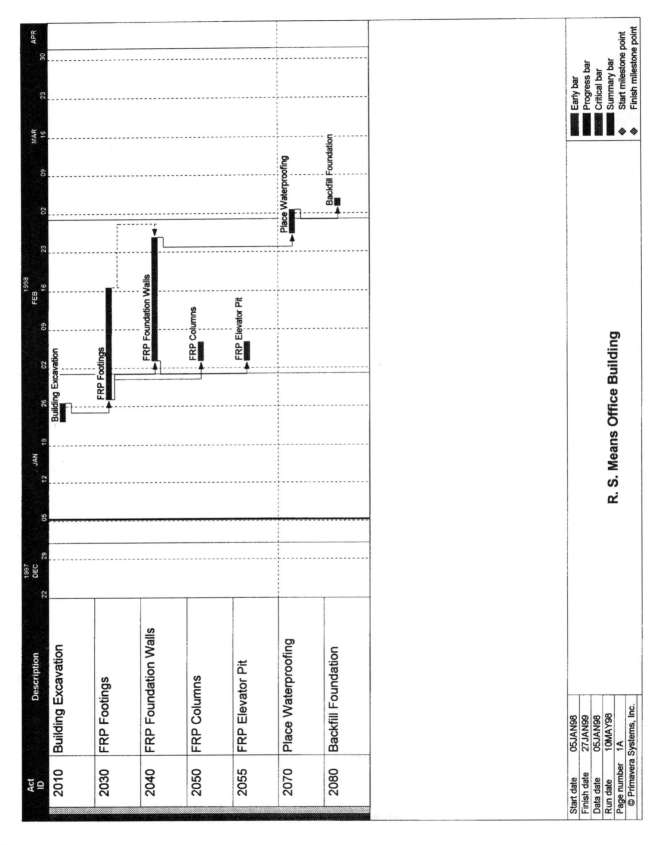

Figure 7.2

120

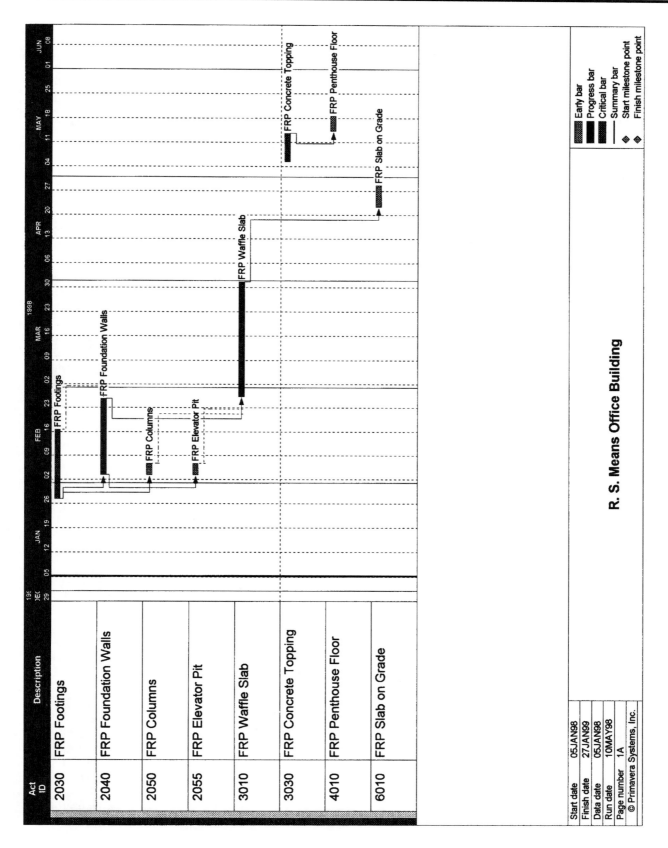

Figure 7.3

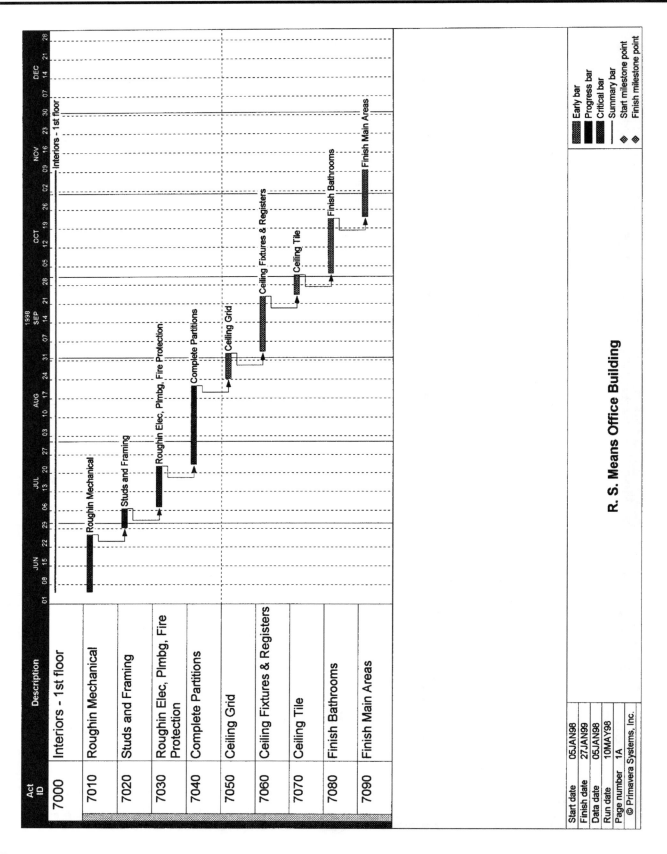

Figure 7.4

122

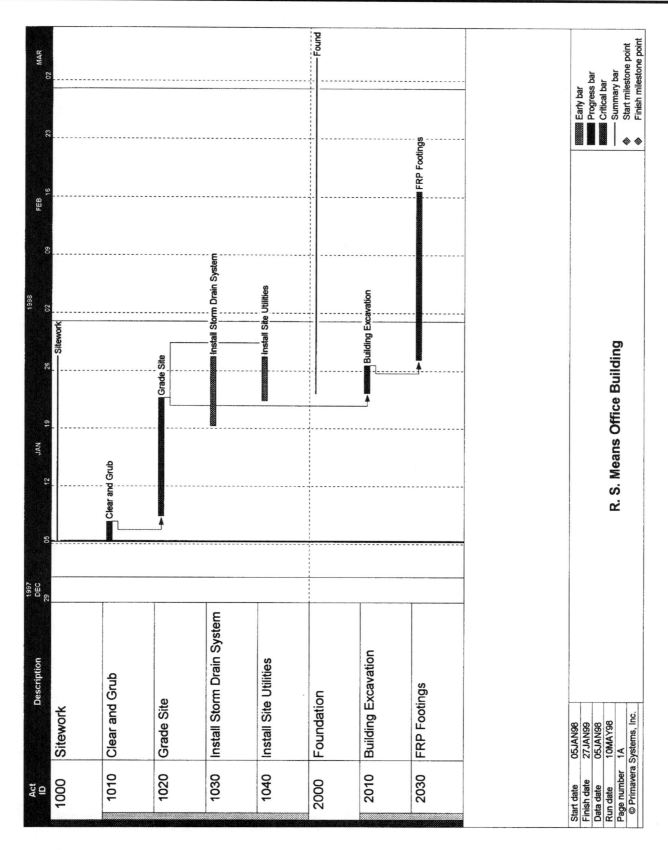

Figure 7.5

123

Monitoring and Controlling the Project

Monitoring and Controlling the Project

The Monitoring Process

While a good initial plan is essential, it is not enough to ensure a successful project. During the course of construction, uncontrollable events are bound to alter the original plan. The project manager must have a means of monitoring the effects of these outside factors. Once the deviations have been detected and measured, the project team must be mobilized to bring the project back on schedule. The monitoring process consists of the following steps.

1. **Monitoring Progress.** This step is frequently called *progress measurement, or updating the schedule*. It is primarily a process of collecting detailed data on the work, then processing it in a computer or manual system to arrive at an accurate representation of the current job status. Monitoring progress corresponds with Steps 3 and 4 of the Project Control Cycle (see Chapter 2 for a definition and illustration of the Project Control Cycle).

2. **Comparing Progress to Goals.** The actual progress on the job is compared to the progress planned in the original schedule. This is Step 5 of the Project Control Cycle, and consists of displaying the data collected in the updating step. The project team uses this information to make decisions regarding future actions.

3. **Taking Corrective Action.** In this final stage, the project manager corrects any schedule problems based on all of the available information. Personnel and equipment are mobilized to carry out a new plan for finishing the job.

The Key Element of Communication

First of all, the controlling function depends on good communication at the construction site. A project manager who thoroughly monitors and compares, and then decides on a course of action to correct deficiencies, but does this without the participation of the subcontractors, superintendents, and other members of the project team, may find that his measures are doomed to failure. First, it is almost impossible to determine the status of the project without talking to the people who are actually carrying out the work. As good as they are, CPM systems have real limitations, and will not provide all of the details needed to get an accurate picture of where the job stands. CPM may provide a warning system indicating where a problem is occurring, but it does not diagnose the problem. Secondly, the project manager depends on the project team (subcontractors, superintendents, and others) to carry out whatever corrective action is needed. Members of the project team may not be highly motivated to solve problems unless they are involved in the decision-making process. In any case, if the team members are not competent to participate in the problem solving process, they probably should not be on the team in the first place.

Controlling is like the planning and scheduling processes that precede it in that the first vital step is to bring all pertinent parties into the process. Effective communication requires the following.

1. **Consulting personnel** during the monitoring process, since they are the best source of data regarding the individual parts of the job. This chapter covers the specific procedures for updating the schedule, but it must be recognized that the basic source of input is the project team.

2. **Displaying the information obtained in the clearest possible way.** This means using simple, straightforward, graphic displays which are understandable to everyone. As a general rule, the best means of communication are time-scaled bar charts developed from the CPM schedule. It is best to provide only the information that is pertinent to the tasks or activities being dealt with at that moment, thereby avoiding information overload. Fortunately, most of today's computer systems have the capacity to selectively organize and display information.

3. **Communicating regularly** with all parties in order to determine what corrective actions need to be taken. A project manager should hold regularly scheduled meetings that include all of the parties working on a job at that time. The following elements should be included in such meetings.

   - Attendance at the meeting should be required (preferably by contract) for all subcontractors and superintendents whose work is either under way or due to begin in the near future.

   - Every attendee should be given a photocopy of the schedule, showing progress during the last reporting period, and what is anticipated for the next two reporting periods. For example, if the meetings were held weekly, the schedule would show a three-week time span. Provisions would also be made to project the schedule on an overhead or schedule board of some kind so that all parties can see the changes as they are made.

   - The meeting must be conducted in such a way that all parties can comment on what has happened thus far and what is being planned. By encouraging this kind of participation, an atmosphere is created which fosters public commitment to schedule performance. These kinds of commitments tend to be honored more faithfully than private ones, since reputation among one's peers can be a strong motivater. It is not necessarily critical to reach an absolute consensus on every decision, but it is important not to dictate to subs or superintendents without consultation.

   - The decisions that result from the meeting should immediately be published and distributed to all parties.

   - Finally, the meetings must be held without fail on a regular basis, and the decisions followed up on by the project manager.

Monitoring Progress

The goal of updating is to determine the present status of the job. In the simplest terms, is the job behind, on time, or ahead of schedule? It is also necessary to know which specific aspects of the job are behind. Thus, details of individual activities are also important. In order to perform updates, it is necessary to establish the start and finish times of activities, and if possible, their production rates.

In addition to recognizing currently active parts of the job, it is important to know how the present work status affects future work. This factor is known as the *downstream impact*. For example, it is possible to be approximately on schedule at a given time, but—if the correct details are not observed—to end up behind later on in the job—without realizing that the schedule is not going to be met. The capacity to measure such downstream effect is one of the most important aspects of the CPM technique, and serves as a very useful tool in planning recovery when behind schedule. It is also necessary to record the progress of the job for legal purposes. Good schedule records serve as the basis for claims, and as a defense against them.

Steps in Updating

To determine the present status of the job, a two-step process is necessary and must be taken in order. Bypassing one to get to the other leads to inaccuracy at best, and can be dangerous at worst. The two steps are:

1. Measure the progress of each activity individually. The updating need not occur in the order that the activities occur, especially since updating is often done sometime after the actual work is performed. It is important to update all activities before attempting to update the job as a whole.

2. Measure the impact of the activity progress on the job as a whole. This is done by using the information derived from the individual activities to recalculate the forward pass and backward pass, and then determining a new overall job duration.

How Often to Update?

How often should the monitoring process be carried out? In the industry, it is not performed frequently enough, as a general practice. The value of a construction management system is in direct proportion to the timeliness of the information it provides. If the controlling process is not carried out often enough, or on a regular basis, the benefits are likely to be lost.

To be more specific, once a month should probably be the maximum period between updates and schedule meetings. Many construction jobs can be run with meetings held at monthly intervals, but in most cases, weekly meetings and updates are advisable. In fact, if the situation warrants, daily schedule updates may be necessary. An example of such a situation is where the potential for lost revenues from a facility being built is extremely high relative to the value of the construction on the facility. In any case, the benefits of updating by carrying out the control cycle must be measured against the costs. The benefits are difficult to measure precisely, but considering the costs of schedule delays, it is usually better to err on the side of too many schedule updates rather than too few.

Updating the Individual Activities

The status of individual activities can fall into several different categories, depending on how much progress has been made at the time the update occurs. Progress is reported on the basis of the concepts illustrated in Figure 8.1.

Each reporting cycle covers a predetermined time period; the status of each activity is reported from the perspective of a "time now" date, usually called a *data date*. As can be seen in Figure 8.1, the data date represents the end of the chosen reporting period. (In this case, a monthly reporting period is used.) The status of individual activities relative to the data date, or "time now" point, falls into one of the following cases, or a variation thereof.

Case 1 in Figure 8.1 is an activity that was started and completed prior to the data date. In this circumstance, the activity simply has an actual start (AS), and an actual finish (AF) reported.

Case 2 is more complex. The activity was started prior to the data date, but has not yet finished. The start is reported as an actual start (AS). The problem is determining present status and subsequent expected finish (ExF). It is important to be as accurate as possible so that the expected finish has the proper effect on the downstream impact calculations. The three methods for determining present status and expected finish are listed below.

1. **Percent Complete (PC):** This method involves determining how much of the total work is complete, calculating a rate of progress per day, and then

extending this value to determine an expected finish. To establish a percent complete, a project team member must calculate—in the field—the percentage of work that has been accomplished as of the data date. The actual finish date is subtracted from the data date in order to determine the number of days worked. The percent complete is then divided by the number of days in order to arrive at a rate of progress per day. The remainder of the work can be divided by the rate per day to determine how many work days remain for this activity. This number is then added to the data date to determine the expected finish. This procedure is illustrated in the following formulas.

% per day = % done/days worked, or

% per day = % done/DD (Data Date) − AS (Actual Start) then,

DD + (% remaining/% per day) = ExF (Expected Finish)

Using a computerized scheduling system, the percent complete number is simply input and the calculations carried out automatically.

2. **Remaining Duration (RD):** Using this procedure, the number of remaining work days is estimated and this figure added to the data date in order to determine the expected finish. The following formula is used.

DD + RD = ExF

The estimate of the remaining duration can be anything from an educated guess to a carefully calculated figure based on field data.

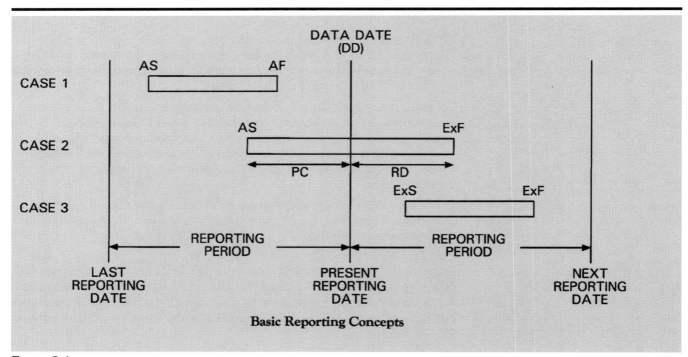

Basic Reporting Concepts

Figure 8.1

3. **Expected Finish (ExF):** For this procedure, the expected completion date is entered as a value. It is an appropriate method where the project manager has good reason to believe an activity will finish at a specific time and wishes to display that fact in the update reports.

Problems with the Various Update Methods

All three of these methods have limitations and, therefore, should be used judiciously to ensure an accurate update. The problem with the use of actual starts and finishes is that this information is usually gathered long after the fact. Ideally, all job activity should be recorded on a daily job log. Unfortunately, entries are sometimes sporadic or incomplete. The person who reviews the reports at the end of the month often has to read between the lines to get a picture of the actual work done. Inadequate record keeping is a problem that also affects the percent complete method, since the actual starts may be missing as well.

The percent complete method tends to fall short primarily because detailed, accurate determinations are very seldom made for the actual work done. Usually, the percent complete is simply estimated, typically in 10% increments. As a result, the calculated expected finish may be even more inaccurate. Even when fairly accurate calculations are made, the production rate is often variable, or may be affected by stops and starts.

Finally, the expected finish method is often inaccurate because it depends on the prediction of a future event. This is especially difficult where both an expected start and expected finish are involved. Also, the further the expected event is into the future, the more likely it is to be inaccurate.

So, the practical question remains—how to get the best possible information on the individual activities. The good judgment of the scheduler helps, but procedures can also be set up which will contribute to more accurate input and updates.

How and Where to Find Information about Activity Progress

The previous section covered how to calculate progress on individual activities, and how to predict completion dates on activities using such pieces of information as Percent Complete, Remaining Duration, and the like. When entered into a scheduling software program, the figures will provide a reasonably accurate calculation of the status of a project. However, scheduling software systems is like any other program; the rule of "garbage in, garbage out" applies. If the percent complete figures and other information about individual activity status are not accurate, then the information provided by the updated schedule will not be accurate either. With this in mind, the following section describes some of the methods that can be used to gather accurate information.

Measure Actual Work Done

The best of all possible methods is to physically count or calculate work done, then translate that count to a percent complete or remaining duration figure. Calculating actual work accomplished is generally easier said than done, however. Construction is not like manufacturing, where the number of units coming off an assembly line can be easily and accurately determined.

In some cases, the task is relatively simple. Consider for example, the case of calculating the work done in a single concrete activity: "Place Footing Concrete." The scheduler can simply observe which footings are complete, calculate the cubic yardage in each footing, add the totals, and then calculate the percentage of the whole task of placing concrete in footings. This kind of calculation is probably fairly accurate. The same kind of thing can be done with other kinds of work where it is relatively easy to see where one unit of the building has been completed, and others have not.

Other kinds of activities are much more difficult. Consider the difficulty in calculating how much work has been done in an activity called "Form Footings." The problem in measuring formwork effort is that often a great deal of work is done before any footings are actually erected or placed. Fabrication of the formwork takes place long before any actual panels are erected, and this effort would go unmeasured if the scheduler relied on simple observation of work in place.

Other examples might include installation of piping, erection of stud walls, and other highly detailed tasks that take place in a variety of places which makes physical observation and measurement difficult. In these cases, a scheduler is often forced to rely on a superintendent's judgment call, which may or may not be accurate, depending on the degree of the superintendent's optimism or pessimism.

Daily Job Logs

Quite often, superintendents are required by company policy to keep a log of their daily activities and of the work done on a job. These records are often dictated by legal considerations, but they can also be useful tools for the scheduler trying to figure out where a specific activity stands in its progress. The quality of these records can be a mixed bag. Some superintendents keep quite detailed records, in which they note precisely where work took place, how many laborers were working, and what delays were experienced. Others provide a lot less. Where one superintendent will note, "placed footing concrete—column line A," another may record no more than, "placed footing concrete," worse yet, "placed concrete." Given this tendency, information obtained from these logs must often be supplemented with that obtained from direct interviews.

Interviewing Field Personnel

Quite often, a scheduler is reduced to simply asking a superintendent or project manager what work was performed or completed in the last reporting period. While this can be reliable, more often than not, it is not. Problems include the usual limits and inaccuracies of human memory, the reluctance of an action-oriented field person to sit still for detailed questioning, and the constant telephone interruptions that invariably occur during such meetings. Still, there are times when interviews are the only way to gather data. In such cases, it is better to update more often so that memories are fresher and presumably more accurate.

Job Records

Many types of job records can be useful for gathering information on job progress. Typical examples include time cards, purchase orders, and other accounting records, or in many cases, test results and other records of work action. Better still, however, are the minutes of job meetings that most architects, superintendents and project managers use to memorialize the discussions and other aspects of job site meetings. These meetings often occur weekly and begin with a review of progress for the most recent period. If recorded in sufficient detail, the minutes can provide a highly accurate and useful source of data.

Other Areas to Check

In addition to the actual field activities, there are other influences that affect the schedule. These, too, must be checked. Following are examples.

1. **Changes in contractual dates.** Any change in contract dates, such as an extension of time, must be entered. These dates are typically recorded as constraints or "plugged dates."

2. **Changes in work sequences by field personnel.** It is not uncommon for field superintendents to perform work out of sequence without informing the project manager or scheduler of the changes. Work done out of sequence may not affect the schedule, but if the changes are major, they should be reflected in the update in the form of logic changes. This is particularly true if more work of the same type remains to be done.

3. **Changes in material delivery dates.** This is an area that can have a tremendous impact on projects, yet this information can be difficult to track. Ideally, a company should have some sort of a system for recording these changes. Unfortunately, this is often not the case. Gathering all the

information about materials usually means consulting a variety of sources, such as telephone logs or submittal data logs, or interviewing purchasing agents or other individuals who are responsible for buying. At the very least, there should be a log of purchase orders and a correspondence file for each vendor on the job site. These files should contain all of the most recent information.

Measuring Progress on the Entire Job

Once the progress of all the individual activities has been determined, the progress of the entire job can be assessed. This task is relatively simple in concept, but can unfortunately be fairly cumbersome in practice.

To determine the progress of the job as a whole, information from the update of individual activities is used, and a new set of dates and times is calculated. This is done using the same calculation techniques shown in Chapter 6. The process of carrying out the forward and backward passes is no different at this point than it was for the original schedule, except that the actual and expected dates become fixed in both passes.

Because updating the entire job can be a cumbersome task, use of a computer CPM system offers a great advantage. A computer system is not foolproof, however, and care must be taken to avoid input errors. Also, it may be necessary to do several computer runs to ensure that the information is accurate before proceeding to the next step.

Comparing Progress to Goals

After the status of each activity has been established and the impact on the entire project has been determined by performing a new forward and backward pass, the project manager can then determine whether or not corrective action is necessary. To do this, it is necessary for the Project Manager to compare the progress on the schedule to date to the planned schedule and determine if a significant variation exists, i.e., is the project behind schedule.

Setting the Target Schedule

The first step in this process is the establishment of a standard against which progress can be measured. This standard is known as a **Target Schedule**, or in some cases, a **Baseline Schedule**. It reflects the original plan of attack for completing the job, and serves as the reference point for determining whether or not the plan is being executed adequately.

Establishing the target schedule is a relatively simple task. The project manager does, however, have certain options in drawing it up, and making the correct choices is important to the long-run success of the project. The following paragraphs describe some of the approaches that the Project Manager can use to ensure the overall effectiveness of the scheduling process.

- The initial schedule contains both early and late times. It is generally best to set the target schedule based on early rather than late times, since this approach fosters an "earliest possible" perspective, and does not allow putting off an activity until the latest possible start time. The idea is to promote an attitude that encourages getting on and off the job with each item of work as rapidly as possible.
- Some activities will be critical, while others will have float and can therefore be started at various times. It is best not to display or consider the float as part of the target schedule, since this approach defeats the sense of urgency created by the use of early start dates in the target schedule.
- It is important to note that there are sometimes legitimate reasons for changing the target schedule times. For example, the weather or delayed delivery of owner-furnished materials may both be grounds for an extension of time for the project. If an extension is necessary, a new target

schedule should be worked out and used. This new schedule must be clearly communicated to project personnel, and the reasons for the change explained thoroughly.

- The project manager may also decide to delay the start of certain activities in order to use manpower or equipment more efficiently. The target schedule should be changed to reflect this kind of modification. Once again, the change and the reasons behind it should be clearly explained to project personnel.

Setting target schedules can be accomplished easily with most up-to-date computer CPM systems. The initial schedule or any updated versions can be designated as the target schedule. This plan can be stored and remain unaltered until the decision is made to change it. CPM systems are programmed to allow display of the target and the current schedule alongside of one another, thereby making the comparison process much simpler.

Displaying the Results

Normally, the comparison between Target and Actual Progress is done using a bar chart or other display which will place the planned activity beside the actual outcome so that any differences are readily apparent. Typical of these kinds of reports are Target Bar Charts or Variance reports, some examples of which are shown in the sample update at the end of this chapter.

Preventing Information Overload

It is important to direct the project's decision-makers to the major issues of a job at the time that these events are occurring. One of the computer's assets—the ability to store vast amounts of data—can actually present problems in that having this much information can make it difficult to zero in on the most critical issues. It, therefore, becomes important to abstract or sort out information for display, to highlight that which is pertinent, and ignore—for the moment—all other data.

To highlight the most pressing issues, the computer can be directed to display only *exception information*. Exception information pertains to situations that are not going according to plan. As long as there are only a few activities, it is not difficult for the manager to pick out the ones that are behind schedule. However, if there are 100 activities, then it is very important to have a method for singling out the late ones and flagging them for attention. The display created for the regularly scheduled meetings should clearly identify and separate the activities that need attention.

When displaying the schedule, only those parts that are currently being worked on should be shown. It serves no purpose, for example, to display schedule information pertaining to work completed three months ago, or work that will be performed four months in the future.

Finally, the experienced judgment of the scheduler or Project Manager plays a key role in deciding what information to display. It is important to remember that the schedule is only a tool, used to gather and display information that is needed to build the job. Rigid rules about how to run or display the schedule are completely inappropriate, and certainly unnecessary given the flexibility that modern CPM systems offer. It is often helpful to people in the field to see information in a familiar format. The schedule system should be used to accommodate personnel in this way, and not to force them into predetermined, unfamiliar procedures.

What to Look for in Project Reports

In reviewing update information, it is important to look beyond the job status as simply ahead or behind schedule. Other areas to be examined are:

1. What caused the job or parts of the job to fall behind schedule?
2. What events that have occurred thus far are likely to continue downstream as the job proceeds?

Answering the first question is important because knowing causes is essential to finding effective corrective actions. The answer to the second question is also key to the prevention of further delays. These questions are among the most typical. However, to get a complete picture of the job situation, the project manager and scheduler should look beyond the overall schedule results to other general points, including the following items:

Status of Critical Activities: By definition, the critical path is the list of activities that must be started and completed on time in order for the job to be finished on time. This group of activities should immediately be examined to determine their status since failure to keep them on schedule will delay the project as a whole.

Non-critical Activities That Are Late in Starting: The problem with activities that start late is that they are more likely to finish late. This is true for reasons other than the obvious. The problem is that late-starting activities also tend to progress more slowly than they should. It is quite common to see activities that start before the late start date, which is acceptable, but then end up finishing beyond the late finish date. This puts them on the critical path. It is best to prevent this occurrence by detecting the problem at the start.

Activities with Low Production Rates: A related problem is activities that start on time, but are proceeding more slowly than planned. Early on, their progress may seem fine, but their duration may be extended, undetected, until an overly late finish.

Delays in Resource Delivery: This element is one of the most difficult to deal with in construction. As any experienced construction manager knows, material suppliers frequently move delivery dates back. Much effort is spent trying to compensate for the delays. Fortunately, most delivery delays are grounds for extensions of contract time. Nevertheless, the fact of the delay must be recorded and its effects shown in the schedule. Most schedules use constrained dates to reflect material deliveries, or use a separate chain of activities for each major item. It is therefore good practice to check every constrained date or major material item on the project at the time of each update and control cycle.

Activities with More Downstream: Any activity that either starts late or shows a low rate of progress must be carefully watched. This is particularly true if there are more activities of the same type occurring later in the project. It may then be necessary to change the durations of the similar activities downstream, so that the schedule is realistic.

Changes in Outside Factors: Quite often, a scheduler concentrates on the field work, while ignoring the outside factors that also influence the schedule. For example, if a time extension has been granted, and the finish-no-later-than date for the project is not changed, then the calculated floats will be inaccurate. If the date has been moved back, the floats will be too large, and the field will be working with less flexibility than they actually have.

How to Find Out Why the Job Is Behind

Usually a scheduling system informs the Project Manager only about the parts of a job that are behind. It does not provide the reasons why. To truly know the condition of the job, the project manager must get out of the office and trailer and deal with the people in the field. While the schedule information points the way to where the problems lie, there is no substitute for face-to-face interviews with those responsible for the actual work.

The project manager must carry out the information-gathering interviews in a non-threatening manner. A superintendent or other supervisor who perceives that a Project Manager is out to "hang the guilty party" is more likely to provide self-serving information. As a result, the true causes of the job-site problems may go unnoticed, and the job continues in trouble. A far better approach is to encourage open communication and to involve the field supervisors in solving the problem. Most construction superintendents and foremen are quite proud of their achievements and want to do everything possible to maintain their reputations. This includes working toward an effective solution when problems arise.

Taking Corrective Action

The feedback loop is not complete until corrective action has been taken to bring the project back in line with the original plan. There are several points worth considering in this last part of the process.

The Necessity for Follow-Up

Follow-up frequently does not occur. It is all too common for a construction company or Project Manager to set up a good general plan for completing a job, then fail to properly monitor and control it. Effective follow-up requires a methodical and organized approach. Otherwise, it is all too easy to bypass problems in the rush of daily concerns. Follow-up can be challenging in that it requires regular meetings, and many people in construction tend to regard meetings as an unproductive waste of time.

A positive attitude ("we will run this job, it is not going to run us") is also important. Too often, managers say that events inevitably come along which make a schedule useless, when what they should be saying is that a way will be found to meet the schedule, regardless of circumstances. This constructive approach is particularly important since those who choose to simply react to events almost guarantee failure on a construction job.

Types of Corrective Actions

It is impossible to cover all of the possible actions that a project manager can take to bring a schedule back in line. Nevertheless, there are some basic, sound measures which can be grouped into general categories, as follows.

Apply More Resources: The classic first response to schedule delay involves getting more people on the job, going to overtime, or mobilizing more equipment. Any of these responses may be appropriate under certain circumstances, but each must be considered carefully. For example, there is almost always an additional cost associated with speeding up work. The problem is that it is difficult to determine whether or not the costs of speeding up are less than the cost of a schedule overrun. It is clear that additional resources should be applied only to those activities that are on the critical path. Speeding up activities with float simply buys more float, which is of no value in completing the job earlier. Applying more resources can be a difficult decision. However, there are techniques available to assist the project manager in making these choices. These techniques are covered in Chapters 9 and 10.

Re-examine the Job Logic: In addition to applying more resources, the project manager also has the option of revising the sequence of activities on the job. For example, if the original job logic was done conservatively and used mainly finish-to-start lags, it is usually possible to go through the logic diagram and overlap activities more than was originally called for. Usually this is a better solution than applying additional resources. It does, however, call for closer control as the job progresses. It is, of course, possible to completely revise the sequence of operations to reflect an entirely new approach. This more drastic method would probably not be justified except in cases of extreme delay and penalties.

Example Update Problem

The following example illustrates the principles described in this chapter, the following example is shown.

In this case, the project is assumed to have started on time (January 5), and the update is being performed at the end of the first month of work. Figure 8.2 shows the work that would probably occur in the first few months of the job. Note that the work scheduled for the first month includes the following activities: *Clear and Grub, Grade Site, Install Storm Drains, Install Site Utilities, Building Excavation,* and *FRP Footings.*

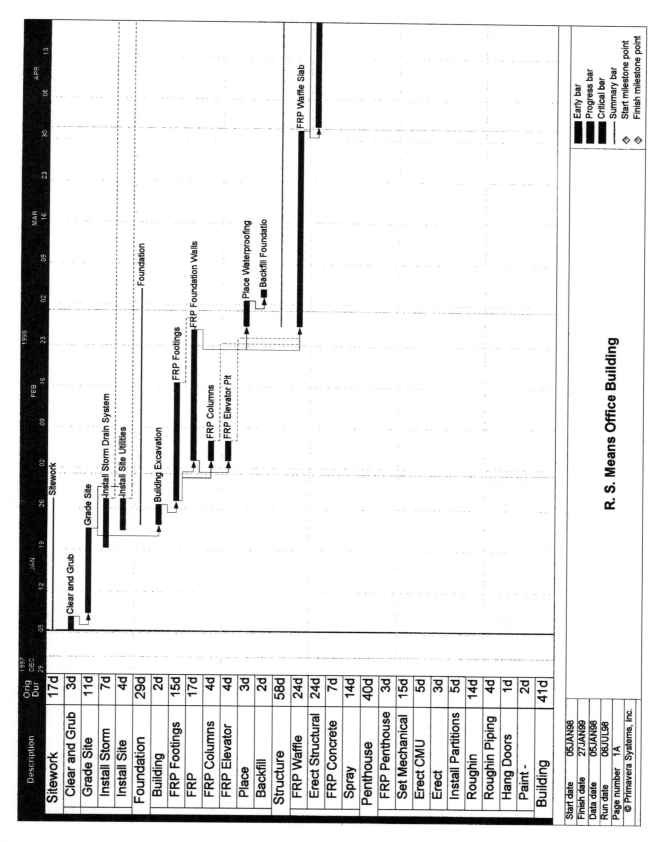

Figure 8.2

137

Typical information from the field might have yielded the following information on activity progress:

Clear and Grub: started and completed on time.

Grade Site: started on time right after Clear and Grub, but rain occurred for 4 days (Jan. 13 through Jan. 16) delaying completion until Jan. 28.

Install Storm Drains: started late due to delays on Grading Site. As of end of the month (Data Date), there are 2 days of work remaining. Expected completion date—February 3.

Install Site Utilities: no work yet.

Building Excavation: started late due to prior activity delays. Completion was on Jan. 30.

FRP Footings: no work yet.

If we establish a data date of February 2 and apply this information to the project, it provides us with a bar chart as shown in Figure 8.3. Further, we can see that *Clear and Grub, Grade Site* and *Building Excavation* have been completed, some work has been done on *Install Storm Drain System,* but no work has been done on *Site Utilities* or *FRP Footings.* While this information is probably useful to some degree, it does not indicate whether or not the project is on schedule.

To answer this question, we must look at a bar chart or other display that compares actual to planned. This concept is shown in a Target Bar Chart. (Figure 8.4).

This bar chart clearly shows some key pieces of information. Reviewing actual progress on each activity in turn against its planned time, we can see the following:

Clear and Grub: started and completed on time.

Grade Site: started on time, but completed nearly a week late, which would be expected in light of the rains encountered.

Install Storm Drain Systems: started over a week late, and still not complete.

Install Site Utilities: still not started, in spite of a delay of 1-1/2 weeks.

Building Excavation: started a week late, but completed more quickly.

FRP Footing: still has not started in spite of being a week late.

Given these comparisons, it is apparent that some delay has occurred. The only way to be sure how much is to look at those activities on the critical path. Doing that comparison shows us that the project is about one week behind overall. In the beginning of a project that has a duration of over one year, this is not a significant period of time, and there are no doubt many activities downstream that could be speeded up to recover the time. However, without the information shown in these basic reports, a Project Manager would have no way to even know that a problem existed.

Summary

In this chapter, we have just discussed the important process and techniques of monitoring and controlling a project. In Chapters 1 and 2, we also discussed how critical these steps can be to the final success of a project. However, in the hectic real world of project management, these monitoring steps are all too often forgotten or given short shrift. This is understandable in a way, since managing construction can seem like one long series of crises, and it is difficult to pay enough attention to the routine tasks like updating and holding regular scheduling conferences. But, we know that attention to these tasks pays dividends in the long run. Experience has shown us that if a project manager can establish and maintain an effective and regular monitoring process, the number of problems that are caught and solved early goes up, and the number of nasty surprises tends to go down.

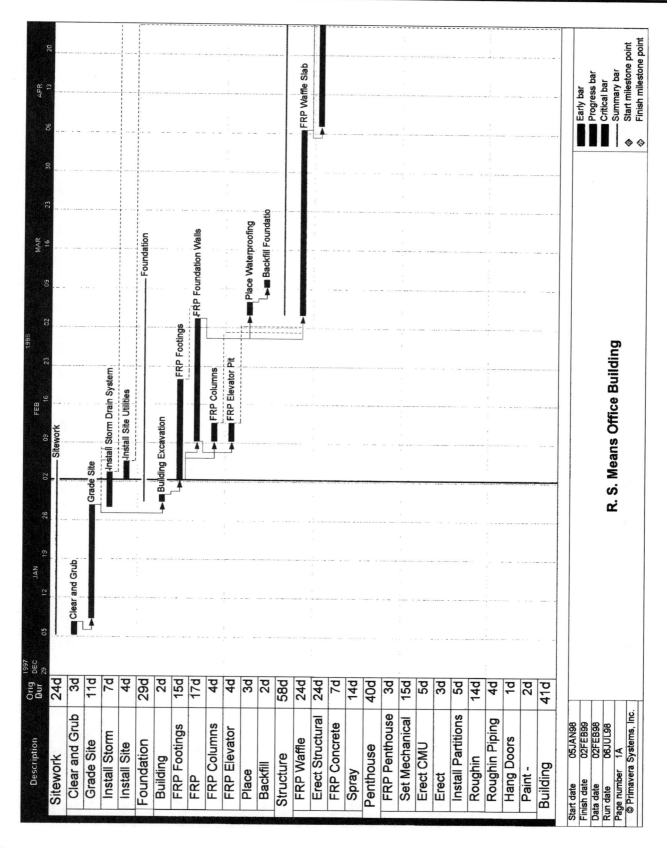

Figure 8.3

139

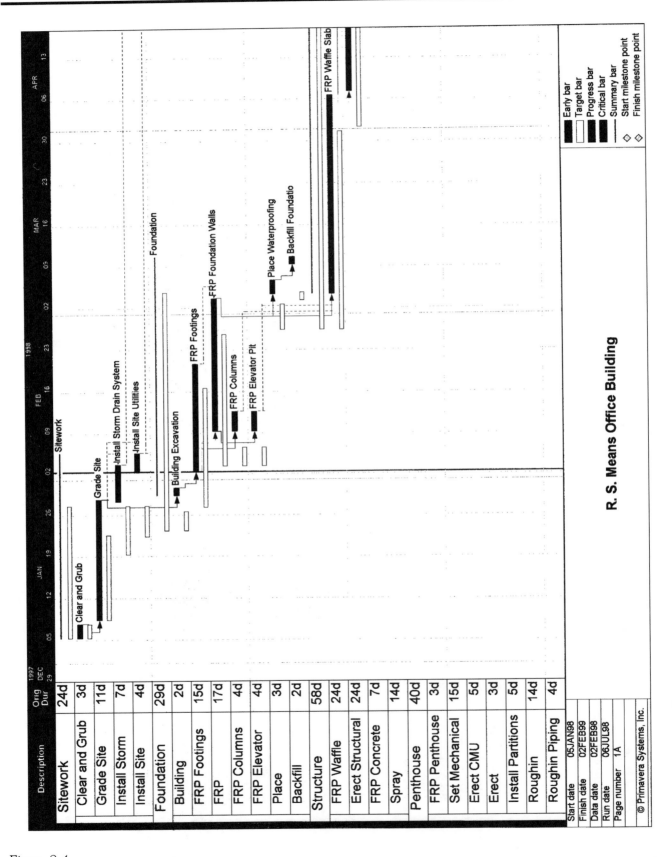

Figure 8.4

140

9

Resource Management

9
Resource
Management

One of the project manager's most important jobs is ensuring that all the resources necessary to build the project are available at the right time and place. While submittal data and procurement of material are important aspects of project management, they are not the only issues. Adequate labor of the right type or trade must also be available, as well as proper equipment for the trades to perform their work. Furthermore, the right amount of money has to be available at the right times to pay for resources of all types. This chapter deals with the techniques of ensuring the correct amount and timing of these three resources—material, equipment, and labor.

Management of Resources

The process of managing resources therefore has two key aspects: first, ensuring that enough of the right resource is available at the right time, and second, ensuring that the resource is used efficiently.

To address the first aspect, adequate and timely resources must be supplied in order to keep the work flowing so the project will be completed on time. Any shortage of resources will inevitably lead to delays, first in the activity in question, and then in the project as a whole. Consider the case of a Project Manager trying to decide how much labor to hire for a particular phase of the project. The project manager can, of course, use the estimate to find out how much total labor of a given type will be needed for the total activity. As we have seen, that information must be used in the calculation of how long an activity will take. However, the estimate seldom if ever addresses the issue of *when* the labor will be needed. Nor does it indicate how much labor will be needed on a daily or weekly basis. The estimate also cannot provide any information about conflicting demands for resources, e.g., when two activities of like type are scheduled to occur at the same time, and therefore need the same labor. This kind of information can only be derived by consulting the schedule.

The second case key aspect, efficient use of resources, can be promoted on a project by observing several principles. First, the rate and flow of work should be as orderly and even as possible. The PM should try to schedule crews so that hiring is smooth and even from the beginning of the job, and that the overall size of the work force remains as constant as possible. Extreme peaks of demand should also be avoided. Crews should be kept together, working on similar work for longer periods of time. It is very disrupting for skilled labor to have to jump around between different tasks, and to be alternatively laid off and rehired. Productivity invariably suffers when these conditions occur. The ideal pattern for a given trade should look something like Figure 9.1, which shows an even buildup of labor, then a constant period for the middle of the project where most of the work gets done, followed by a smooth reduction of labor at the end of the job.

While it can be difficult to create a perfectly smooth labor utilization pattern, or to predict exactly when and how much of a resource will be needed, a Project Manager can apply the techniques in this chapter to obtain better information than would be available by consulting the estimate alone.

The Resource Management Process

Resource management is the decision-making process in which activities are prioritized and scheduled so that the expenditure of labor and/or equipment occurs in a desirable way. The best time to begin this process is early in the project. If resources are handled properly from the start, the project's chances of falling behind are minimized and there is no need to play "catch-up."

The logical starting point for resource management is the critical path schedule as calculated for the project. In the beginning, this schedule is based on physical logic. It typically has an uneven pattern of resource expenditure, but serves as the starting point for the resource management analysis and refinement.

To perform the analysis, the project manager must be able to project the pattern of expenditure for a particular resource. There are two basic views of this pattern:

1. The *Resource Profile* (sometimes called a response histogram): a compilation of the demand by time period for a given resource for a particular schedule. (See Figure 9.2 for a typical Resource Profile).

2. The *Resource Summary Curve* (sometimes called an "S" curve): the sum of the resource expenditures over time. (See Figure 9.2)

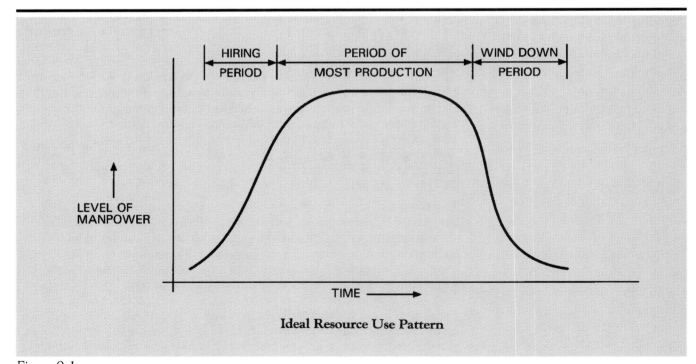

Ideal Resource Use Pattern

Figure 9.1

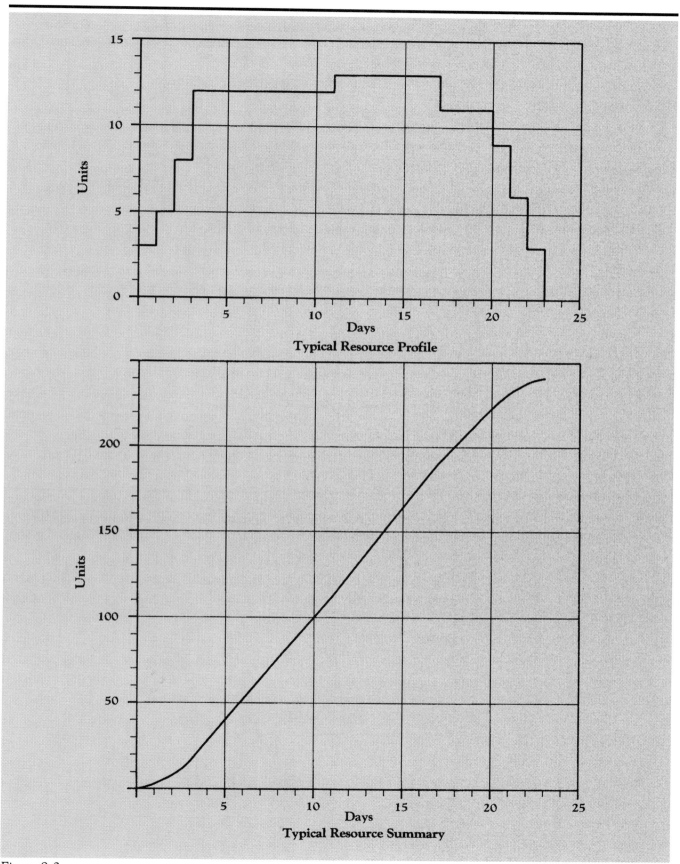

Typical Resource Profile

Typical Resource Summary

Figure 9.2

Development of the Resource Profile

The development of the resource profile is a four-step process, illustrated in Figures 9.3 and 9.4. The sample used for this illustration is the building of the foundation up through the foundation walls. The resource being plotted for analysis is *formwork carpenters*, used for the forming and stripping work.

Step 1 — Calculation of Required Resources

This initial step is shown in Figure 9.3, a listing of each activity in the hypothetical network with quantities of work, labor-hours per unit required, total labor-hours, crew size, and number of days required. All of this information can be obtained from the estimate and/or a published source such as *Means Building Construction Cost Data*. The key numbers here are the total labor-hours and crew size.

Step 2 — Distribution of Resources Across Activities

The next task is to assign the required resources to the appropriate activities. There are two methods for assigning resources. They may be based on:

1. a rate of expenditure per day, or
2. a total amount of resources for the entire activity.

The two methods are basically interchangeable. For example, if the number of carpenter labor-hours assigned per day is 4 men × 8 hours per day, the total number of carpenter labor-hours for a six-day activity is:

6 days × 32 = 192 labor-hours for the activity.

Foundation Network Time Calculations							
	Quan.	Unit	LH/ Unit	Total LH Req'd.	Typ. Crew Size	Calc. Days Req'd.	Rounded Days Req'd.
Mass Excavation	9,100	CY	.008	73	1.5	6.1	7
Trench Excavation — Walls	116	CY	.107	12	3	.5	1
Trench Excavation — Columns	42	CY	.107	4	3	.2	1
Formwork: Wall Footings	1,962	SFCA	.050	98	4	3.1	4
Column Footings	1,578	SFCA	.058	92	4	2.9	3
Walls	11,172	SFCA	.092	1,028	12	10.7	11
Concrete: Wall Footings	31	CY	.640	20	8	.3	1
Column Footings	40	CY	1.280	51	8	.8	1
Walls	132	CY	.750	99	8	1.5	2
Reinf: Wall Footings	.8	TNS	15.250	12	2	.8	1
Column Footings	1.0	TNS	15.250	15	2	1.0	1
Walls	2.6	TNS	10.670	28	2	1.7	2
Stripping: Wall Footings	1,962	SFCA	.019	37	4	1.2	2
Column Footings	1,578	SFCA	.017	27	4	.8	1
Walls	11,172	SFCA	.030	335	4	10.5	11

Figure 9.3

Alternately, the activity might have an assigned 192 labor-hours, which can be translated back to four workers per day.

192 labor-hours/6 days = 32 labor-hours per day, and
32 labor-hours per day/8 hours per worker = 4 workers per day.

Both methods have advantages. If the time of the activity is likely to be varied, and the number of workers adjusted up or down to vary the rate of progress, then it is probably better to assign total labor-hours. If the number of workers is to be fixed and the time of the activity is less definite, then assignment of number of workers per day is preferable. In the case of the sample problem, the formwork carpenters are assigned by number of workers per day, since it is much simpler to calculate by hand. It can be seen in Figure 9.4 that the number of carpenters assigned per day to *form wall footings* is four, for *form column footings*, four, and so on.

It should be noted that any unit of measure can be used for the resource. In this case, labor-hours is used, but work-days are equally valid. In analyzing another resource, such as bulldozers, the unit of measure might be *equipment hours* or *equipment days*. It is best if the unit of measure remains consistent for all resources where possible in order to prevent confusion.

The schedule across which the resources are spread can be *early start*, *late start*, or a combination of both. The most commonly used schedule is *early start*, since it represents the desired schedule of most project managers.

Step 3 — Summarize Resource Expenditure by Time Period
This task is performed by totalling the figures (downward) at the end of each day of the job. In the sample problem (See Figure 9.4), it can be seen that the number of carpenters required per day for the first day is four, but for the second day the number required rises to eight, and stays at that level until the fifth day, at which point it drops to zero. This process is carried out across the project schedule until the end of the last carpenter activity, *strip basement walls*.

Step 4 — Plot the Resulting Profile
The tabular data arrived at in the previous step, while accurate, is not very useful to a project manager, who is better served by converting this information to a graphic representation. Figure 9.5, the resource profile, shows more clearly the periods of demand for formwork carpenters on the foundation.

Adjusting the Schedule to Improve the Resource Expenditures

The pattern of resource expenditure is important in that it has a very real effect on efficiency and productivity. For example, it is apparent that the gap in the profile at about March 7 would call for the laying off of some carpenters for several days or reassigning them to other parts of the job. Laying off carpenters for such a short period is not very good for morale, and is not a desirable alternative. Thus, the project manager must find another area in which they can work productively in the interim, until it is time to strip the basement wall forms.

Fortunately, once a diagram is created showing the pattern of expenditure for the resource, there is a way to determine how best to alter the schedule. The project manager has several options. The goal is to alter the schedule so that the pattern of use is as close as possible to the curve shown in Figure 9.1. To achieve this goal, the Project Manager should try first to adjust noncritical activities within their float range to move peak periods of need into gaps in the diagram. This can be accomplished by delaying the start, extending the time, or working at varying rates to smooth out the flow. If the manipulation of noncritical activities does not work, then the project manager must begin altering the critical activities. A critical activity will probably have to be lengthened, and therefore the job as a whole is extended. This situation presents the project manager with one of his biggest challenges; trade-off decisions must be made between the value of smooth work flow and delay to the job.

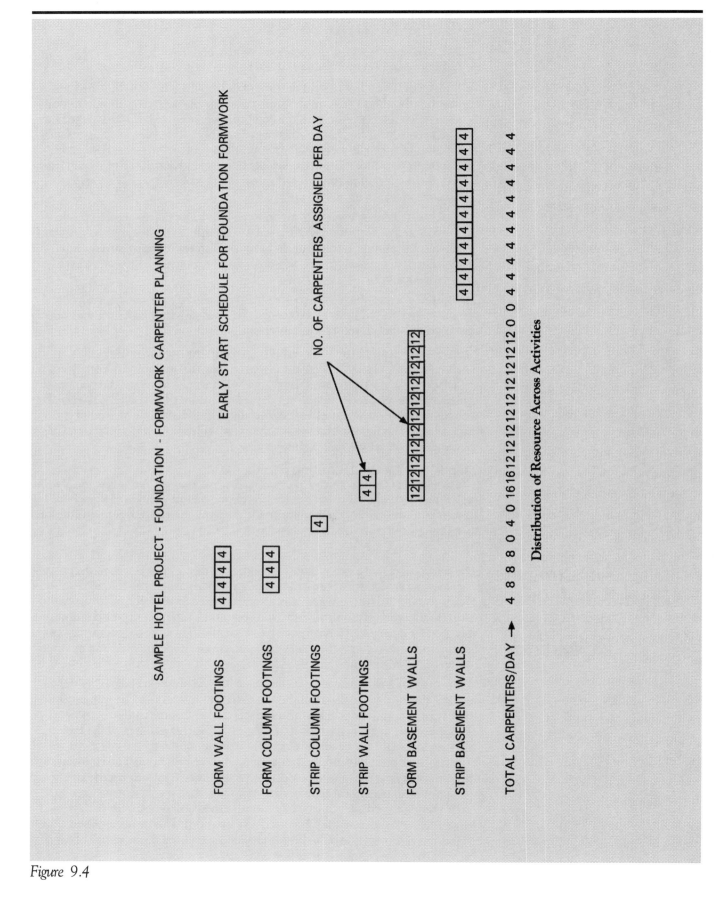

Figure 9.4

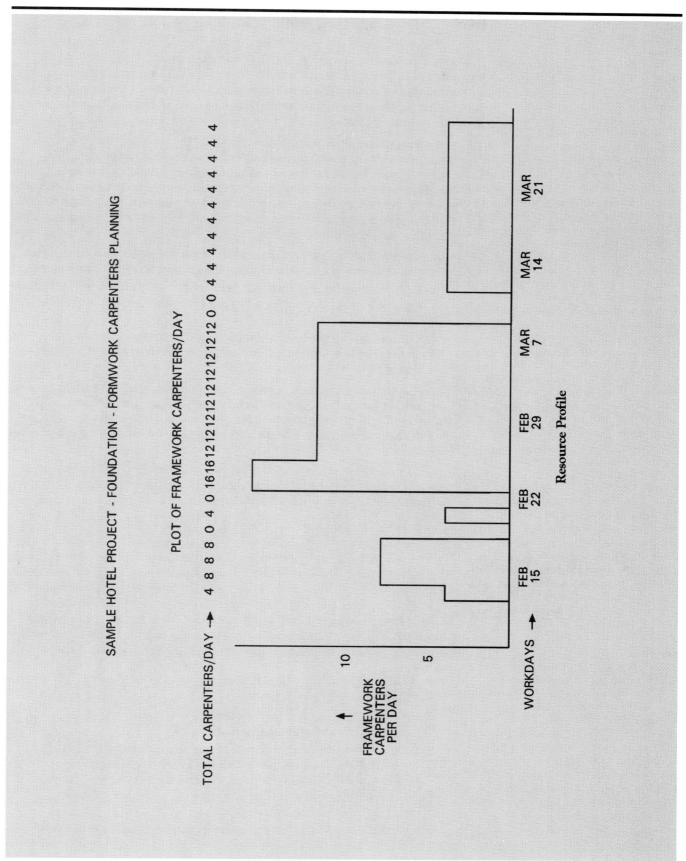

Figure 9.5

The following example shows how schedule adjustments might be made. Figure 9.6 is a bar chart showing the detail of the waffle slab structural work on the sample office building. In this case, it is assumed that the superintendent has broken the work down into three separate placements. Each placement consists of *Forming*, then *Placing*, followed by *Stripping* after an interval of 10 days to allow for curing. It should also be noted that for *Forming* the three segments are sequential, and the crew moves immediately from one segment to the next. It can also be seen that there are gaps in the schedule for *Stripping*.

Comparing the bar chart to the resource profile for this set of activities, Figure 9.7, it can be seen that there is a peak demand for formwork carpenters on three days, beginning on 31 July. Also, the demand falls to zero on 7 August, then carpenters are needed again for 3 days beginning on 12 August, then no demand again until 24 August, at which time they are needed again for 3 days to strip segment 3. It can also be seen that the peak demand periods are caused by noncritical activities, which gives the superintendent more attractive options.

Using the principle that it is better to move noncritical activities than critical ones, the superintendent might consider adjusting the stripping activities as follows:

1. Begin the stripping of segment number 1 on the day after the forming of segment 3 ends. Also, begin the *Stripping* of segment 2 immediately after segment 1.

2. Change the durations for stripping segments 1 and 2 as necessary to take up the time between the end of *Forming* and the beginning of *Stripping* segment 3.

The effect of these changes can be seen in Figure 9.8. Now the superintendent has an even crew size for the forming process, then moves a few carpenters to other work, and keeps an even crew size on for the stripping process. The overall time of erecting the waffle slab has not changed, yet the work flow and crew sizes have been smoothed out considerably.

Also, it should be noted that while it may have been possible to perform this simple resource-leveling task by hand, consider the difficulty in doing it if multiple structures and forming had been involved. Clearly, computerization is a useful tool in these situations.

Practical Aspects of Resource Management

Some people in the construction industry claim that resource management techniques are relatively precise. This may be true on huge projects where the project managers have a large work force that can be moved around. However, on the vast majority of construction projects, precision is extremely difficult to attain. The techniques of resource management are at best an approximation. Nevertheless, it is still a very valuable tool. These techniques can smooth the rough edges and improve the overall project plan. When using resource management, it is helpful to observe the following guidelines.

1. As noted, these techniques offer approximate solutions, so perfection should not even be attempted, much less expected. They are also very much trial and error; be prepared to take several passes at leveling and smoothing out a resource such as *formwork carpenters*.

2. Give priority to the critical and near critical activities, ensuring that they receive enough labor and equipment to stay on schedule. The noncritical activities can be adjusted as necessary, with the activities that have the most float having the greatest flexibility. Be careful, however, not to let the noncritical activities slip by unnoticed.

3. Constant monitoring of labor and equipment use is necessary to ensure

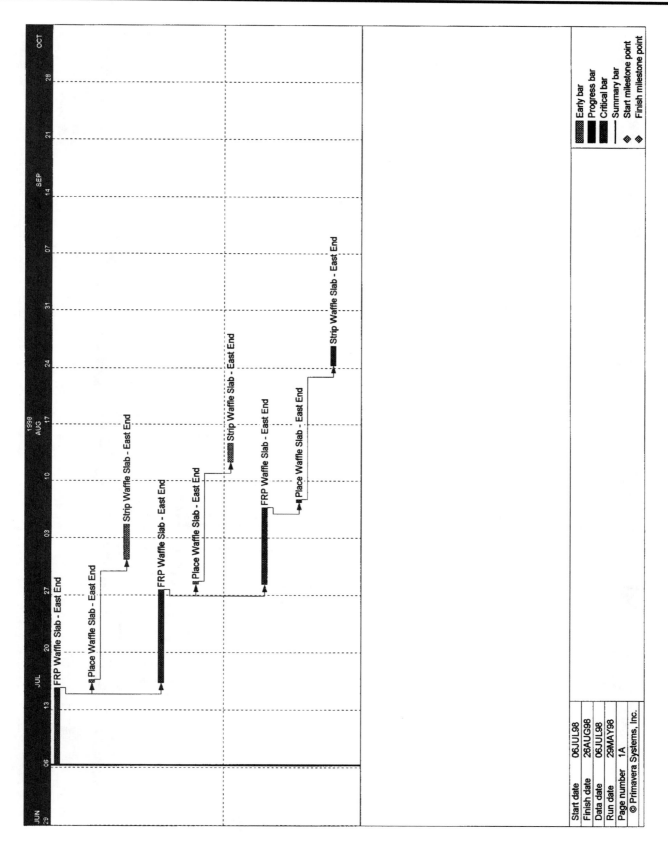

Figure 9.6

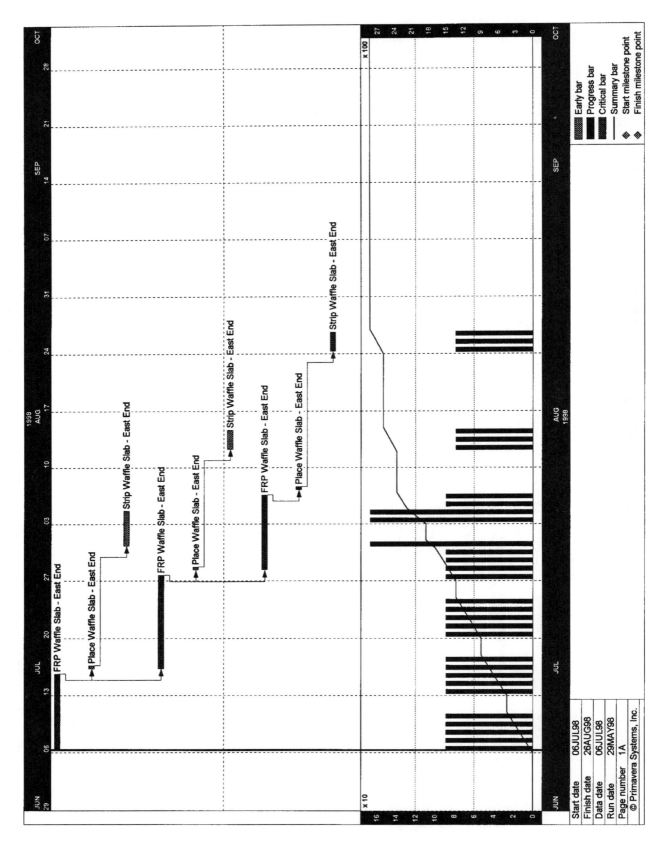

Figure 9.7

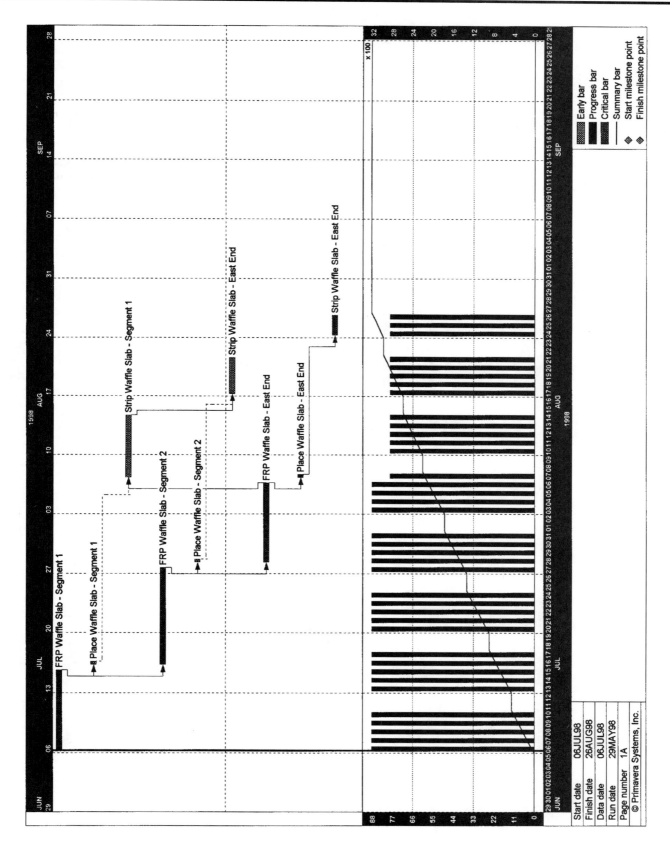

Figure 9.8

153

compliance with the plan, or to notice if the plan is not working. Toward this end, be prepared to revise and re-plan frequently and whenever necessary.

4. It is probably not realistic to look ahead more than a few weeks at a time in an attempt to work things out in detail. The advantage of revising along the way is that it is possible to apply what is learned in the early stages of a job to the later stages.

5. Computers are great for plotting the data, but are terrible for making decisions. Some computer programs have leveling algorithms which can calculate the most efficient redistribution of labor or other resources. As a practical matter, these programs work only on the largest of jobs. These leveling programs are also extremely complex. Thus, one can use them in good faith without completely understanding what they are calculating.

6. The best use of computers is plotting resource profiles. The project manager can take the computer print-out sheet, mark it up with ideas for change, input the changes back into the computer, and find out the result. The computer allows this "what-if" game, where a number of options can be tried out very easily, leading to a better overall solution by the project manager.

Summary

In this last chapter, we looked at the task of planning and monitoring the use of resources, as opposed to controlling time alone. One key point covered was the idea that resource planning need not be complex or difficult, as is sometimes believed. Even the simplest job can sometimes benefit from monitoring key resources, especially with the ease with which modern software products can be used. The reader is encouraged to experiment with these techniques on a small scale and "work up" to larger and more comprehensive problems.

10

Management of Submittal Data and Procurement

Management of Submittal Data and Procurement

The emphasis so far has been on planning and scheduling the physical building tasks necessary to complete a project. The construction process involves more, however, than the actual placement of concrete, steel, and other materials. The technical complexity of many of today's construction projects requires the purchase of materials meeting rigorous specifications, often from remote vendors. Contractors must frequently go through a long review and approval process for these materials, submitting technical data to the owner and/or architect/engineer for determination of a product's suitability for the project. Only after this review and approval can the actual purchase and installation take place.

An entire set of administrative procedures has grown up around this purchasing requirement, which is typically called *submittal data/shop drawing and procurement*.

Submittal data and procurement are proving to be major problems for many contractors. It is an unavoidable process, but one that is often a significant cause of delay in the overall building process. This chapter provides guidelines for the project manager who is interested in setting up a simple, yet effective system. Using these prescribed methods, submittal data and procurements may be tracked and reported accurately. With access to reliable data, potential problems can be recognized and addressed early, thereby minimizing delays.

The Source of the Problem

Clearly, construction work cannot be performed unless the necessary materials are delivered to the job site on time. For readily available materials, this is usually not much of a problem. In the case of more unusual materials, however, and most equipment, the review, approval, and procurement process may create the need for a long lead time. Why are so many delays caused by procurement problems? The reasons are many and varied; some of the most prominent are listed below.

First, the procurement process is inherently cumbersome and involves a considerable amount of detailed record keeping and paperwork. Consequently, there is ample opportunity for error and oversight.

Second, most construction professionals are oriented not to the administration of paperwork, but rather to physical action. Many of their careers have been built around the management of actual construction tasks, not "office work." It is only natural for such individuals to concentrate on the problems in the field, paying less attention to off-site planning.

Third, most of the tasks necessary for good procurement management take place off the site. As a result, the project management team may tend to take an "out of sight, out of mind" attitude. Unless a distinct effort is made to do the necessary administrative tasks, the progress of the procurement process is not visible and is therefore ignored.

Fourth, many parts of the process are controlled by others who may not share the project manager's sense of time, schedule, and priorities. For example, the architect/engineer is not contractually obligated to the contractor in any way. He is acting as the agent of the owner, and as such has a limited legal obligation to act expeditiously in carrying out the review tasks required of him. The subcontractors, while legally obligated to the contractor, often do not have the same priorities as the general contractor, and may have equally pressing obligations to other projects. The subcontracting firms may be manned by personnel even less office-oriented than the general contractor, further compounding the "out of sight, out of mind" point of view. Finally, suppliers of materials and equipment have their own schedules for production—schedules that may have only the remotest connection with the general contractor's project. Their production schedules are typically determined by the order in which the materials required for their products are purchased, leaving the contractor with little, if any, control over the fabrication schedule which affects his specific project.

Procurement is an essential process. It has the potential for causing significant delays, yet the project manager has only limited control over many parts of the process. It is therefore critical that the project manager pay extra attention and take every action to overcome the problems, thereby ensuring a smooth, steady flow of materials to the job.

Basic Procurement Procedures

The basic procurement procedures are typically specified by the architect/engineer and detailed in the project specifications. These procedures typically resemble those outlined schematically in Figure 10.1.

Generally, the project manager begins by issuing a purchase order or subcontract to the appropriate supplier or subcontractor. The supplier or subcontractor then prepares what is known as *submittal data*, which is transmitted to the contractor at the job site. This submittal data can take many forms. One common type of submittal is shop drawings, engineered drawings that further amplify the working drawings for the project. Also, suppliers typically provide *catalog cuts*, which are simply pages from their catalogs that provide technical information.

Certificates of compliance or inspection reports may also be required. In any case, the exact requirements should be stated in the project specifications. After a general review by the project manager or other member of the project team, the requirements are transmitted to the owner and architect/engineer for review and approval. Once approved, the submittal documents are transmitted back down the chain to the appropriate parties, who then carry out the tasks of fabrication and delivery. Only after all this has taken place can the material be installed on the project.

Key Elements in Successful Procurement

Procurement is a straightforward process in most cases. If the quantities of data transmitted are small, there should be few, if any, problems in carrying the procurement out effectively. However, the amount of data on a typical job is usually very large. To manage procurement activities effectively, the project manager must keep certain key principles in mind, and adapt the process to the specific job at hand.

First, it is vital to identify not only the firm (subcontractor or supplier) used at each stage of construction, but also a personal contact at each firm. For example, the architect and/or engineer's offices generally assign project captains to monitor the designer's reviews. Each subcontractor assigns a project manager; each supplier assigns a salesperson. The project manager (or whoever he assigns to the task of tracking submittal data) should establish a personal working relationship with these representatives and maintain regular contact with them, keeping them informed of concerns and problems at the job site. This contact will in many cases be daily.

Second, a good tracking system must be maintained. The purpose of this system is to provide the project manager with a record of each piece of submittal data—including where it is at any time in the process. In this way, the project manager can follow up on those items that are not progressing through the process quickly enough, and take action to ensure timely delivery of material to the job. This system also allows the project manager to find out which parties are consistently holding up the process. In the event of a claim for extension of time or other compensation, the project manager can use the tracking records to make a case concerning others causing delays to the job.

Third, communication and follow-up are crucial. For example, it does no good for the project manager to know that the architect is holding up several key shop drawings if no one calls the architect's project captain to promote action on the reviews. Submittal data/procurement probably involves more parties than any other aspect of the overall construction process, and communication problems always increase as the number of communicants grows. In addition to personal contacts with the various parties, it is also an excellent idea to include detailed reviews of submittal data status in the weekly or monthly job schedule meetings. At these meetings, responsibility can be assigned to project team members for tracking down delayed submittals and deliveries (as identified in the meetings).

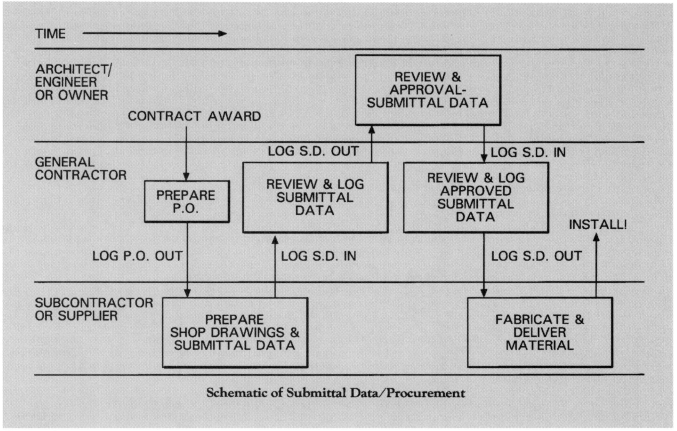

Schematic of Submittal Data/Procurement

Figure 10.1

Record Keeping and Tracking

The first task in the management of the procurement process is setting up an efficient record keeping system. A good system can be maintained easily by the project team members and provides data about the mass of submittals to be developed and submitted during the course of construction. Setting up and maintaining this system is basically a three step procedure:

1. Making a list of the items that require submittal data;
2. Keeping records of their progress in a log;
3. Coordinating the submittal data processing with the construction schedule.

Making a List of Submittal Items

The first and probably the most difficult task is determining all of the documents that must be submitted to the owner and architect for approval prior to purchasing the material. Unfortunately, this list will probably be voluminous on all but the smallest jobs. It takes some time to put such a list together; the day after the contract award is not too soon to begin. The starting point for this task is the *project specifications*. If the architect and engineers have done their job properly, each required submittal will be listed in the beginning of each specification section or sub-section. Ideally, the specifications should list exactly what documentation is required. If this is not the case, some judgment based on experience is required of the person developing the actual list. Ideally, development of this list is best assigned to one person in order to prevent gaps. However, on some jobs, preparing a list of submittals may be too large a task for one person to finish in a reasonable period of time.

Once a comprehensive list of submittal items is drawn up, it must be determined exactly who is responsible for the preparation of each item. Most of the submittal items come to the general contractor from subcontractors. If the subcontractor has an organized and professional management system, the general contractor can probably expect submittal items to be delivered on time. If they are not on time, there is a need for follow-up. The person writing the submittal list must be aware of which subcontractor has the contract for the various elements of each section. For example, while Division 15 includes both plumbing and HVAC systems, these two elements are typically performed by separate contractors.

Once the list is developed by the general contractor, the various sub-lists should be transmitted to the persons responsible for submitting the data. It is a good idea to present these lists to each subcontractor in an initial meeting. At this time, the subcontractor may be asked for commitments on submittal times and delivery. Based on this information, the project manager can get a better feel for whether or not any of the subcontractor's material deliveries can be expected to cause delay problems. The contractor should also make clear to all subcontractors and suppliers the *procedures* for submitting data. (For example, should the material be sent to the home office or to the job site?)

Finally, it is impossible to be too thorough in drawing up a list of submittal data items. Nothing is more frustrating to a project manager than to have a job going along smoothly only to discover that everything must come to a halt because a key piece of equipment has not arrived.

Keeping a Log of Submittal Data Approvals

Once the list of items has been developed and all parties are aware of their responsibilities for submittal and procurement, the submittal items begin to come to the job site for review. The project manager must ensure that detailed and thorough records are kept of the progress of items up and down the chain (See Figure 10.1). The easiest and best method involves maintaining a log similar to that shown in Figure 10.2. This example is not the only acceptable format; other possibilities for workable log formats are shown in Figures 10.3 through 10.5.

The procedure for record keeping is quite straightforward: each time a document passes through the project manager's office, it is logged in the appropriate column. As shown in Figures 10.1 and 10.2, the log is simply a recording of actions taken by the project team members on the job. For example, when the documents reach the job office, the package or submittal number is assigned and the receipt date is logged under *Preparation and Receipt*. When the documents are sent to and then returned by the architect and/or owner, these dates are logged under *Review/Approval*, and so on.

The problems with record keeping arise primarily because the volume of documents becomes so great on many jobs. In such cases, hard and fast rules should be pre-established regarding the *processing* of documents. It is important, for example, to establish the maximum amount of time that the documents are permitted to stay in the contractor's offices being reviewed. This time limit varies from contractor to contractor, but should be consistent within the company to ensure that the contractor is not the cause of any delays. Equally important is the establishment of procedures for *transmitting* documents. The project manager should ensure that documents are not allowed to accumulate for several days after approval; there should be a requirement that all processed documents be sent out no later than the following day. Whatever the specific rules, they should ensure *regular, daily* handling of all submittal data.

Coordinating Submittals with the Construction Schedule

One of the keys to effective project management is knowing that *the procurement process should serve the construction schedule, not the other way around.* If work on the job site is to proceed efficiently and smoothly, then the material must reach the craftsmen before it is to be installed. Otherwise, the work sequence is interrupted and must be altered to accommodate disjointed delivery schedules. This situation cannot help but have an adverse effect on overall project time and profit.

To ensure timely delivery of materials, the project manager needs a way to determine from the construction schedule the latest acceptable delivery dates. He must then take all possible action to ensure delivery by that date. The best way to accomplish this goal is to treat the submittal data and procurement tasks as *activities*, just like the construction activities. Figure 10.6 shows that it is possible to convert the sequence of *prepare purchase order, prepare submittal data, review and approve submittal data*, etc.—as shown on the log—to a sequence of critical path activities which are (like construction activities) dependent on one another. The submittal and procurement *activities* can then be assigned scheduled durations in the same way, and the entire string of events which make up the procurement process can be tied to the appropriate construction activity.

For example, the activities necessary to purchase hollow metal door frames are shown in Figure 10.7. The times for these activities are based on various factors, as follows. *Prepare purchase order* is an activity within the control of the project manager and can therefore be assigned a time according to job procedures. Other activity times can be determined by talking to the parties responsible for them: the architect may say that *review and approval* will take four weeks; the subcontractor may require four weeks to *prepare shop drawings*, and 17 weeks to *fabricate and deliver* the hollow metal frames. For each time period indicated by each party, the project manager should add extra time to account for turnaround at the job site. In the case of hollow metal door frames, the adjusted times for each activity are as follows.

Prepare purchase order	5 days
Prepare shop drawings	22 days
Review and approve shop drawings	22 days
Fabricate and deliver door frames	85 days
Total time for submittal data, review, fabrications, & delivery	134 days

Figure 10.8 is a planning schedule showing the first activity that requires hollow metal door frames, Activity 50020, "Erect HM frames/Studs—main Lvl." The date provided for the early start of this activity is July 28, 1998. This date occurs 127 working days from

Shop Drawing/Submittal Control Log

Spec. Section	Description	P.O. or Sub-contractor		Preparation for Submission		A/E Review & Approval		Fabricate & Deliver			Comments
		No.	Date Sent	Received From Sub.		Date to A/E	Date From A/E	Transmit to Sub.	Deliver to Site	Install	
				SCH ACT SCH ACT SCH ACT SCH ACT							

Figure 10.2

Subcontractors Shop Drawings/Materials Data

Greene & Associates, Inc.

100 Smith Lane
Kingston, MA 02364
Tel: 555-1212

Project _____
Our Job No. _____

Contractor _____
Trade _____

Material/Equipment Item	Contract Award Date	Shop Drawing Submittal			Review			Fabricate & Deliver		
		Est. Weeks	Est. Date	Actual	Return Date	Status		Est. Weeks	Est. Date	Actual

Figure 10.3

Subcontractors Shop Drawings / Material Control

Greene and Associates
Construction Management Consultants

100 Smith Lane
Kingston, MA 02364
Telephone: 555-1212

Sheet ___ of ___
Date ___

Project ___
Our Job No. ___

Contractor ___
Trade ___

Spec. Sect.	Item	Contract And Date	Shop Drawing Submittals			Arch. Review/Approval			Fabrication & Delivery			Work Item Tie-In Point
			Sched. Submit Date	Crit. Submit Date	Actual Submit Date	Sched. Appr. Date	Crit. Appr. Date	Actual Appr. Date	Sched. Del. Date	Crit. Del. Date	Actual Del. Date	

Figure 10.4

the beginning of the job, which means that, given the times provided to the project manager for the submittal and procurement tasks for hollow metal doors, the first doors will reach the site approximately nine days after the early start of the first activity for which they are needed.

Clearly, the project manager must take action to speed up some part of the submittal data/procurement process if he wishes to meet the early start schedule. There are several options at this point. One is to simply allow the installation to start a little later since it has over 100 days of float. If, however, there is no float, the situation is quite different. In this case, the project manager might have to make the architect aware of the need for a particularly quick review in this one case. Or, he could contact the supplier of

Greene & Associates
Construction Management Consultants

Shop Drawing Checklist
Date: _____

Project: _____
Project No.: _____

Specification Section	Submittal Item	Submitted to Architect?			Approved?			Returned to Subcontractor		
		Yes	No	Date	Yes	No	Date	Yes	No	Date

Figure 10.5

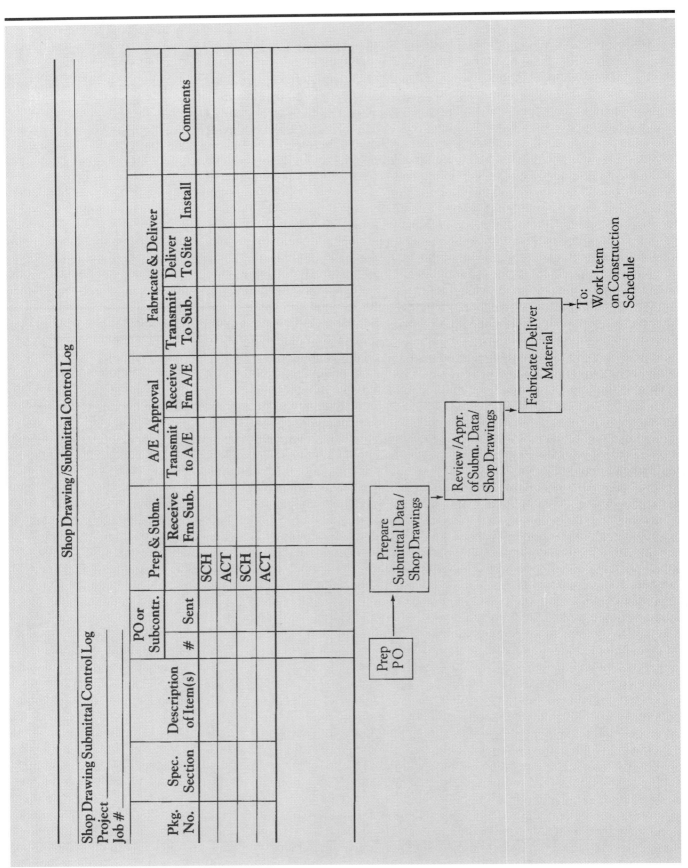

Figure 10.6

Project Planner

Activity ID	Orig. Dur.	Rem. Dur.	Pct.	Code	Activity Description	Early Start	Early Finish	Late Start	Late Finish	Total Float
1010	5	5	0	OFFC	Prepare Purch. Order — HM Door Frames	1FEB98	5FEB98	5OCT98	11OCT98	177
1020	22	22	0	OFFC	Prep. Subm. Data — HM Door Frames	8FEB98	8MAR98	12OCT98	10NOV98	177
1030	22	22	0	OFFC	Rvw. & Appr. Subm. Data — HM Door Frames	9MAR98	7APR98	11NOV98	12DEC98	177
1040	85	85	0	OFFC	Fab. & Del. — HM Door Frames	8APR98	4AUG98	13DEC98	10APR99	177

Figure 10.7

Project Planner

Activity ID	Orig. Dur.	Rem. Dur.	Pct.	Code	Activity Description	Early Start	Early Finish	Late Start	Late Finish	Total Float
50010	10	10	0	HVAC	Rough-in HVAC-Main Lvl	14JUL98	27JUL98	23DEC98	5JAN99	116
50020	10	10	0		Erect HM Frmes/Studs—Main Lvl	28JUL98	10AUG98	6JAN99	19JAN99	116
50040	10	10	0		Rough Plumbing—Main Lvl	11AUG98	24AUG98	20JAN99	2FEB99	116
50030	8	8	0	ELEC	Rough in Elec—Main Lvl	11AUG98	22AUG98	24JAN99	2FEB99	118
50050	6	6	0		Rough In Spnklr Piping, Main Lvl	11AUG98	18AUG98	26JAN99	2FEB99	120
50060	10	10	0		Hang & Tape GWB—Main Lvl	25AUG98	7SEP98	3FEB99	16FEB99	116

Figure 10.8

hollow metal doors, and ask that special attention be given to the doors to be installed in the shear walls on the second floor. In any case, scheduling and then enforcing the time limits on submittal data tasks is just as necessary to the timely completion of the job as is the monitoring of construction activities. The key is maintaining a good tracking system.

Scheduling the Procurement Activities

Scheduling procurement activities is relatively easy from an administrative standpoint. The basic sequence of events is typically standard for a given project, and a project manager can set up a chain of activities for each procurement item, as shown in Figure 10.9. These chains of activities can then be connected to the construction logic diagram, using the hexagonal symbol to show the connection. The forward pass, backward pass, and float calculations work in exactly the same manner as before, and a schedule of start and finish times for procurement activities can be generated just as they are for construction.

The project manager must then decide whether or not the procurement should be connected to the construction activity as part of the overall schedule, and calculated at the same time. Based on the principle that the procurement schedule should not drive the construction schedule, the answer is that they should *not* be connected, nor calculated concurrently. In the case of hollow metal door frames, the early start of activity 50020 could be delayed a week to August 5, 1998. In this specific case, such an adjustment should not be a problem, since there is so much float available on the activity. The project manager might never realize that the procurement is determining the start of the erection of the hollow metal door frames. This lack of awareness is not ideal from a project management control standpoint. In a large project schedule where many procurement chains are connected to the construction schedule, it can become very difficult to determine where the procurement is affecting the overall

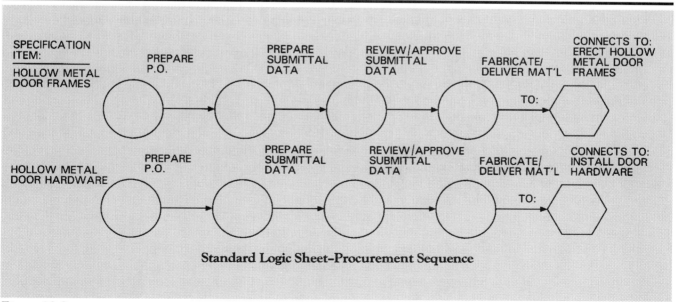

Standard Logic Sheet–Procurement Sequence

Figure 10.9

project. Practically speaking, it is probably better to maintain a separate CPM schedule for the procurement activities, then transfer the dates to the procurement log and compare them by hand to the affected activities on the construction schedule. In this way, the project manager can be sure that the integrity of the construction sequence he has set up is maintained.

Reporting

Once the tracking procedures are underway and operating normally, the project manager must use the information developed to see that the submittals and purchases are carried out. The first step is to determine where the hold-ups exist in the process. The data must be viewed from two perspectives.

First, which pieces of submittal data are not meeting the scheduled dates? This determination should be done no less than weekly. It requires a detailed examination of the control log, and flagging of those submittals which have not met their dates. The list of flagged items should be broken down by the party responsible, i.e., subcontractors, architect, owner, etc. Separate lists should be made for each responsible party, showing how many submittals are in their hands, and the status of each submittal relative to the scheduled date. These lists can then be used in weekly job review meetings or in one-on-one sessions to review status and devise solutions for problem areas.

Developing status lists for submittal data can be done manually, by simply going through each log one at a time and picking out the behind-schedule submittals. This task is much easier if there is a separate log maintained for each subcontractor and supplier. The submittal control log can be kept on an ordinary microcomputer spreadsheet program, which will make the analysis somewhat less tedious. If a spreadsheet program is used, it is a good idea to keep a hand log as well, for back-up purposes.

Follow-up on the Information

Finally, follow-up is essential to the successful management of submittal data and procurement. The daily pressures of a construction project are such that it is very easy to fall into a pattern of performing the update and review on only an occasional basis. Unfortunately, this is an almost certain path to disaster. The procurement process requires regular, consistent, thorough record keeping and follow-up if the materials are to arrive on time, and if the process is to support the construction effort and not vice versa. In the case of our hollow metal door frames, 17 weeks is a long time for a purchase order to be out. This situation needs follow-up at no less than monthly, and probably two-week intervals. With this kind of regular monitoring, the manufacturer of the hollow metal door frames cannot let the fabrication schedule slip without the project manager knowing about it.

Summary

Finally, we discussed in this last chapter the task of tracking procurement and submittal data. As the reader has seen, this process is always necessary, but hopefully the principles and techniques presented will reduce the task from being onerous and cumbersome to one which is merely tedious.

Appendix

DIV.	DESCRIPTION	MATERIAL	LABOR	EQUIPMENT	SUBCONTRACT	TOTAL

CONDENSED ESTIMATE SUMMARY

PROJECT Office Building
LOCATION
ARCHITECT
PRICES BY:

TOTAL AREA / VOLUME
COST PER S.F. / C.F.
EXTENSIONS BY:

SHEET NO.
ESTIMATE NO:
DATE:
NO. OF STORIES
CHECKED BY:

DIV.	DESCRIPTION	MATERIAL	LABOR	EQUIPMENT	SUBCONTRACT	TOTAL
1	General Requirements	$112,377	$101,872	$0	$0	$214,249
2	Site Work	$206,849	$41,319	$40,812	$33,415	$322,395
3	Concrete	$264,758	$201,353	$7,163	$0	$473,274
4	Masonry	$50,353	$0	$0	$0	$50,353
5	Metals	$0	$0	$0	$521,797	$521,797
6	Wood & Plastics	$5,232	$2,509	$0	$0	$7,740
7	Thermal & Moisture Protection	$8,051	$6,973	$0	$103,240	$118,264
8	Doors & Windows	$24,681	$4,492	$0	$15,835	$45,007
9	Finishes	$109,217	$76,214	$0	$254,539	$439,970
10	Specialties	$12,939	$2,092	$0	$0	$15,031
11	Equipment	$0	$0	$0	$0	$0
12	Furnishings	$0	$0	$0	$0	$0
13	Special Construction	$0	$0	$0	$0	$0
14	Conveying Systems	$0	$0	$0	$128,647	$128,647
15	Mechanical	$0	$0	$0	$1,529,994	$1,529,994
16	Electrical	$251,984	$146,988	$0	$0	$398,972
	Subtotals	$934,065	$481,939	$47,974	$2,587,467	$4,051,445
	Sales Tax 6%	$56,044				$56,044
	Overhead & Profit 10/45.9/10/10%	$93,407	$238,560	$4,797	$258,747	$595,510
	Subtotal	$1,083,516	$720,498	$52,772	$2,846,213	$4,702,999
	Bond ($12 /M)					$56,436
	Contingency 2%					$94,060
	Adjustments					$4,853,495
	TOTAL BID					$4,853,000

Figure A.1

COST ANALYSIS

PROJECT: Office Building
LOCATION:
TAKE OFF BY:

CLASSIFICATION: Division 2
ARCHITECT:
QUANTITIES BY:
PRICES BY:
EXTENSIONS BY:

SHEET NO. 1 of 4
ESTIMATE NO:
DATE: 1/93
CHECKED BY:

DESCRIPTION	SOURCE	QUANT	UNIT	MATERIAL COST	MATERIAL TOTAL	LABOR COST	LABOR TOTAL	EQUIPMENT COST	EQUIPMENT TOTAL	SUBCONTRACT COST	SUBCONTRACT TOTAL	TOTAL COST	TOTAL
Sitework - Div. 2													
Site Clearing													
Med. Trees - Cut	021 104 0200	0.46	Acre			1525	702	1650	759.00				1461
Grub & Remove Stumps	021 104 0250	0.46	Acre			570.00	262	1575	724.50				987
Light Clearing	021 108 0300	2.6	Acre			193.00	502	415.00	1079.00				1581
Earthwork													
Bulk Excavation	022 238 1300	5430	C.Y.			0.29	1575	0.81	4398				5973
Load Trucks (Loose)	022 238 1550	3212	C.Y.			0.47	1510	0.49	1574				3084
Haul (Loose)	022 266 0400	3212	C.Y.			1.02	3276	2.54	8158				11435
Compact Fill	022 222 0300	2860	C.Y.			0.23	658	0.42	1201				1859
Excess Excavation @ Foundation	022 242 5220	272	C.Y.			0.38	103	1.40	381				484
Backfill & Compact @ Foundation	022 204 1300	302	C.Y.			0.25	76	0.69	208				284
	0600	302				2.75	831	1.12	338				1169
Backfill & Compact @ Elev. Pit	022 204 0010	30	C.Y.			11.80	354	1.12	354				354
	0600	30				2.75	83	1.12	34				116
Footing Excavation, Spread	022 254 0060	305	C.Y.			1.93	589	1.44	439				1028
	2400	305				0.58	177	0.43	132				308
Footing Excavation, Continuous	022 254 0060	85	C.Y.			1.93	164	1.44	122				286
Backfill @ Footings Incl. Spread Excess	022 204 1900	390	C.Y.			0.34	133	0.92	359				491
Subtotals							$10,992		$19,908				$30,899

Figure A.2a

173

COST ANALYSIS

| PROJECT: | Office Building | | | | | | | |
| LOCATION: | | | | | | | | |

		SHEET NO.	2 of 4
CLASSIFICATION:	Division 2	ESTIMATE NO:	
ARCHITECT:		DATE: 1/93	

TAKE OFF BY: QUANTITIES BY: PRICES BY: CHECKED BY: EXTENSIONS BY:

SOURCE		DESCRIPTION	QUANT	UNIT	MATERIAL		LABOR		EQUIPMENT		SUBCONTRACT		TOTAL	
					COST	TOTAL	COST	TOTAL	COST	TOTAL	COST	TOTAL	COST	TOTAL
		Division 2: (Cont'd)												
		Earthwork (Cont'd)												
		Utility Excavation,												
022	254 0300	24" Drain Excavation	230	C.Y.			2.08	478	3.13	720				1198
022	204 0600	Backfill & Compact	287	C.Y.			2.75	789	1.12	321				1111
022	258 2600	Gas, Water, Sewer	240	L.F.			0.32	77	0.32	77				154
022	258 3200	Compaction	240	L.F.			0.16	38	0.16	38				77
022	262 1300	Sub Drain Gravel	46	C.Y.	8.65	398	4.78	220	0.67	31				649
022	262 0600	Floor Slab Gravel, 6" Compacte	19000	S.F.	0.17	3230	0.12	2280	0.02	380				5890
022	274 0400	Mobilization, Dozer, Loader	4	Ea.			49.50	198	256.00	1024				1222
		Backhoe, Compactor												
		Site Drainage & Utilities												
027	152 1120	Catch Basin & Grate	3	Ea.	410.00	1230	246.00	738	67.50	203				2171
	2100		3	Ea.	188.00	564	69.50	209	27.50	83				855
026	852 0650	Gas Service 3"	80	L.F.	6.95	556	3.71	297	0.19	15				868
026	686 1430	Water Service 6"	80	L.F.	9.95	796	6.30	504	1.24	99				1399
151	960 2300	Gate Valve 6"	1	Ea.	670.00	670	236.00	236						906
027	168 2040	Sewer, 6" PVC	80	L.F.	3.96	317	1.61	129						446
027	106 2020	Foundation Drain	620	L.F.	1.50	930	0.67	415						1345
027	162 2040	Drain Pipe 24" Concrete	310	L.F.	18.50	5735	10.55	3271	2.14	663				9669
		Subtotals				$14,426		$9,879		$3,654				$27,959

Figure A.2b

COST ANALYSIS

PROJECT: Office Building
LOCATION:
TAKE OFF BY:

CLASSIFICATION: Division 2
ARCHITECT:
QUANTITIES BY: PRICES BY:

ESTIMATE NO:
DATE: 1/93
CHECKED BY:

EXTENSIONS BY:

DESCRIPTION	SOURCE		QUANT	UNIT	MATERIAL		LABOR		EQUIPMENT		SUBCONTRACT		TOTAL	
					COST	TOTAL	COST	TOTAL	COST	TOTAL	COST	TOTAL	COST	TOTAL
Division 2: (Cont'd)														
Roads & Walks														
Base Course 9"	022	308 0200	8530	S.Y.	11.55	98522	0.47	4009	0.97	8274				110805
Paving – Bituminous														
Binder	025	104 0160	8530	S.Y.	3.89	33182	0.41	3497	0.35	2986				39665
Wearing	025	104 0460	8530	S.Y.	4.61	39323	0.45	3839	0.40	3412				46574
Concrete Curb														
Precast Straight	025	254 0550	2050	L.F.	6.25	12813	1.80	3690	0.89	1825				18327
Precast Radius	025	254 0600	240	L.F.	7.75	1860	3.87	929	1.92	461				3250
Line Painting														
Stalls	025	804 0800	203	Stall	1.80	365	2.30	467	1.14	231				1064
Arrows	025	804 0620	150	S.F.	0.45	68	0.44	66	0.22	33				167
Precast Bumpers	028	408 1000	203	Ea.	21.50	4365	7.00	1421						5786
Concrere Sidewalks	025	128 0310	1625	S.F.	0.96	1560	0.97	1576						3136
Concrete Steps	028	416 0500	95	L.F.	3.86	367	10.05	955	0.30	29				1350
from (033-130-6850)														
Lawns & Plantings														
Landscaping	TELEPHONE QUOTE													
Sprinkler			15700	S.F.							0.56	8792		8792
Lawn, Top Soil, Fert., Seed			15.71	MSF							570.00	8952		8952
Trees (60) & Shrubs (200),												15671		15671
including planting														
Subtotals						$192,423		$20,449		$17,250		$33,415		$263,537

Figure A.2c

COST ANALYSIS

PROJECT:	Office Building	CLASSIFICATION:	Division 2		SHEET NO.	4 of 4
LOCATION:		ARCHITECT:			ESTIMATE NO:	
TAKE OFF BY:		QUANTITIES BY:		PRICES BY:	DATE: 1/93	
					CHECKED BY:	

DESCRIPTION	SOURCE	QUANT	UNIT	MATERIAL		LABOR		EQUIPMENT		SUBCONTRACT		TOTAL	
				COST	TOTAL	COST	TOTAL	COST	TOTAL	COST	TOTAL	COST	TOTAL
Division 2: (Cont'd)													
Sheet 1 Subtotals							10992		19908				30899
Sheet 2 Subtotals					14426		9879		3654				27959
Sheet 3 Subtotals					192423		20449		17250		33415		263537
Division 2 Totals					$206,849		$41,319		$40,812		$33,415		$322,395

Figure A.2d

COST ANALYSIS

PROJECT: Office Building
LOCATION:
TAKE OFF BY:
CLASSIFICATION: Division 3
ARCHITECT:
QUANTITIES BY:
PRICES BY:
EXTENSIONS BY:

SHEET NO. 1 of 5
ESTIMATE NO:
DATE: 1/93
CHECKED BY:

DESCRIPTION	SOURCE		QUANT	UNIT	MATERIAL		LABOR		EQUIPMENT		SUBCONTRACT		TOTAL
					COST	TOTAL	COST	TOTAL	COST	TOTAL	COST	TOTAL	TOTAL
Division 3: Concrete													
Formwork													
Spread Footings	031	158 5150	2008	SFCA	0.55	1104	1.93	3875	0.00	0			4980
Dowel Supports	031	158 6100	28	Ea.	13.50	378	40.00	1120	0.00	0			1498
		6150	28	Ea.	22.00	616	47.00	1316	0.00	0			1932
Continuous Footings	031	158 0150	2205	SFCA	0.78	1720	1.65	3638	0.00	0			5358
Dowel Supports	031	158 0500	1031	L.F.	0.64	660	1.60	1650	0.00	0			2309
Keyway (excl. stairs & core)	031	158 1500	791	L.F.	0.21	166	0.40	316					483
Walls:													
Pit (10")	031	182 2000	336	SFCA	1.87	628	3.35	1126	0.00	0			1754
Ramp & Stoops (8")	031	182 2000	1528	SFCA	1.87	2857	3.35	5119	0.00	0			7976
Perimeter (12' x 10')	031	182 2550	9926	SFCA	0.67	6650	3.14	31168	0.00	0			37818
Deduct Openings													
Garage													
Above Grade													
Box Openings	031	182 0150	466	L.F.	1.85	862	4.15	1934	0.00	0			2796
Columns - 28" diam, 9 @ 9', 1 @ 12'	031	142 1850	93	L.F.	12.35	1149	6.40	595	0.00	0			1744
Pilasters	031	182 8600	793	SFCA	2.19	1737	4.59	3640	0.00	0			5377
Subtotals						$18,528		$55,497		$0			$74,024

Figure A.3a

177

COST ANALYSIS

PROJECT: Office Building	CLASSIFICATION: Division 3
LOCATION:	ARCHITECT:
SHEET NO. 2 of 5	ESTIMATE NO:
	DATE: 1/93

TAKE OFF BY: QUANTITIES BY: PRICES BY: CHECKED BY: EXTENSIONS BY:

DESCRIPTION	SOURCE	QUANT	UNIT	MATERIAL COST	MATERIAL TOTAL	LABOR COST	LABOR TOTAL	EQUIPMENT COST	EQUIPMENT TOTAL	SUBCONTRACT COST	SUBCONTRACT TOTAL	TOTAL COST	TOTAL
Division 3: (Cont'd)													
Formwork (Cont'd)													
Chamfer 3/4"	031 112 2200	288	L.F.	0.40	115	0.40	115						230
4" Slab Edge Form @ Pit & Openings	031 170 3000	65	L.F.	0.43	28	1.33	86	0.00	0				114
Waffel Slab (1st Floor)	031 150 4500	18220	S.F.	4.27	77799	3.06	55753	0.00	0				133553
Deduct, Stairs Shaft													
Opening Edge Forms	031 150 5000	273	SFCA	3.08	841	6.50	1775	0.00	0				2615
Perimeter Edge Forms	031 150 7100	600	SFCA	0.43	258	2.29	1374	0.00	0				1632
Perimeter Work Deck	031 150 8000	200	L.F.	9.15	1830	8.90	1780	0.00	0				3610
Bulkhead Forms	031 150 6000	5000	L.F.	1.65	8250	2.48	12400	0.00	0				20650
Reinforcing Steel													
Footings	032 107 0500	5.75	T	520.00	2990	450.00	2588						5578
Walls	032 107 0700	9.49	T	520.00	4935	315.00	2989						7924
Columns	032 107 0250	9.43	T	525.00	4951	410.00	3866						8817
Waffle Slab	032 107 0400	23.59	T	575.00	13564	325.00	7667						21231
Subtotals					$115,561		$90,393		$0				$205,954

Figure A.3b

COST ANALYSIS

SHEET NO. 3 of 5

PROJECT:	Office Building	CLASSIFICATION:	Division 3	ESTIMATE NO:	
LOCATION:		ARCHITECT:		DATE:	1/93
TAKE OFF BY:		QUANTITIES BY:	PRICES BY:	CHECKED BY:	
				EXTENSIONS BY:	

DESCRIPTION	SOURCE	QUANT	UNIT	MATERIAL COST	MATERIAL TOTAL	LABOR COST	LABOR TOTAL	EQUIPMENT COST	EQUIPMENT TOTAL	SUBCONTRACT COST	SUBCONTRACT TOTAL	TOTAL COST	TOTAL TOTAL
Division 3: (Cont'd)													
Reinforcing Steel													
WWF: 6 x 6 10/10													
Elevated Slabs		37800											
Garage Slab		18900											
Penthouse Floor		2100											
Deduct-Stair		-1200											
Elevator		-360											
		57240	SF										
Total WWF	032 207 100	572.4	CSF	8.35	4780	12.45	7126						11906
Cast in Place Concrete													
Spread Footings													
Concrete - Incl. 5% waste	033 126 0150	180	CY	48.00	8640								8640
Placing	033 172 2600	180	CY			8.55	1539	0.59	106				1645
Continuous Footings													
Concrete - Incl. 5% waste	033 126 0150	52	CY	57.50	2990								2990
Placing	033 172 1900	52	CY			8.70	452	0.54	28				480
Walls													
Concrete - Incl. 5% waste	033 126 0300	233	CY	60.50	14097								14097
Placing	033 172 5100	233	CY			13.00	3029	6.45	1503				4532
Finishing	033 458 0010	6000	SF	0.02	120	0.38	2280						2400
Columns													
Concrete - Incl. 5% waste	033 126 0300	18	CY	60.50	1089								1089
Placing	033 172 1000	18	CY			10.20	184	5.05	91				275
Finishing	033 458 0010	730	SF	0.02	15	0.38	277						292
Subtotals					$31,730		$14,888		$1,728				$48,345

Figure A.3c

COST ANALYSIS

PROJECT: Office Building	
LOCATION:	
TAKE OFF BY:	
CLASSIFICATION: Division 3	
ARCHITECT:	
QUANTITIES BY:	
PRICES BY:	
EXTENSIONS BY:	
SHEET NO. 4 of 5	
ESTIMATE NO:	
DATE: 1/93	
CHECKED BY:	

DESCRIPTION	SOURCE	QUANT	UNIT	MATERIAL COST	MATERIAL TOTAL	LABOR COST	LABOR TOTAL	EQUIPMENT COST	EQUIPMENT TOTAL	SUBCONTRACT COST	SUBCONTRACT TOTAL	TOTAL COST	TOTAL TOTAL
Division 3: (Cont'd)													
Cast in Place Concrete													
Pilasters													
Concrete - Incl. 5% waste	033 126 0300	20	CY	50.50	1010								1010
Placing	033 172 4950	20	CY			14.30	286	7.05	141				427
Finishing	033 458 0010	793	SF	0.02	16	0.38	301						317
Slab on Grade													
Concrete - Incl. 5% waste	033 126 0150	348	CY	57.50	20010								20010
Placing	033 172 4600	348	CY			6.35	2210	0.45	157				2366
Finishing	033 454 0150	18210	SF			0.30	5463	0.00	0				5463
Pit Slab													
Concrete - Incl. 5% waste	033 126 0150	3	CY	57.50	173								173
Placing	033 172 4600	3	CY			6.35	19	0.45	1				20
Finishing	033 454 0150	80	SF			0.30	24	0.00	0				24
Waffle Slab													
Concrete - Incl. 5% waste	033 126 0300	555	CY	60.50	33578								33578
	033 126 1000	555	CY	6.05	3358								3358
Placing	033 172 1400	555	CY			10.20	5661	5.05	2803				8464
Finishing	033 454 0150	18900	SF			0.30	5670	0.00	0				5670
5 1/2" Elevated Slab													
4" Lt.Wt. Concrete - Incl. 5%	033 126 0300	462	CY	60.50	27951								27951
	033 126 1010	462	CY	15.13	6988								6988
Placing	033 172 1400	462	CY			10.20	4712	5.05	2333				7046
Finishing	033 454 0150	37800	SF			0.30	11340	0.00	0				11340
													0
Curing - 3 floors	033 134 0300	567	CSF	2.53	1435	3.48	1973						3408
Subtotals					$94,517		$37,660		$5,435				$137,611

Figure A.3d

180

COST ANALYSIS

SHEET NO.   5 of 5

PROJECT: Office Building CLASSIFICATION: Division 3
LOCATION: ARCHITECT:
TAKE OFF BY:
QUANTITIES BY: PRICES BY: EXTENSIONS BY:

ESTIMATE NO:
DATE: 1/93
CHECKED BY:

DESCRIPTION	SOURCE			QUANT	UNIT	MATERIAL		LABOR		EQUIPMENT		SUBCONTRACT		TOTAL	
						COST	TOTAL	COST	TOTAL	COST	TOTAL	COST	TOTAL	COST	TOTAL
Division 3: (Cont'd)															
Cast in Place Concrere (Cont'd)															
Stair Treads & Landings	033	184	1750	1436	SF	3.08	4423	2.03	2915						7338
Subtotal							$4,423		$2,915						$7,338
Sheet 1 subtotals							18528		55497		0				74024
Sheet 2 subtotals							115561		90393		0				205954
Sheet 3 subtotals							31730		14888		1728				48345
Sheet 4 subtotals							94517		37660		5435				137611
Sheet 5 subtotals							4423		2915						7338
Division 3 Total							$264,758		$201,353		$7,163				$487,950

Figure A.3e

COST ANALYSIS

PROJECT: Office Building   CLASSIFICATION: Division 4   SHEET NO. 1 of 1
LOCATION: ARCHITECT: ESTIMATE NO:
TAKE OFF BY: QUANTITIES BY: PRICES BY: EXTENSIONS BY: DATE: 1/93   CHECKED BY:

DESCRIPTION	SOURCE	QUANT	UNIT	MATERIAL COST	MATERIAL TOTAL	LABOR COST	LABOR TOTAL	EQUIPMENT COST	EQUIPMENT TOTAL	SUBCONTRACT COST	SUBCONTRACT TOTAL	TOTAL COST	TOTAL TOTAL
Division 4: Masonry													
Regular Block 8" x 16" x 8"	R042-200	11189	Ea.	0.99	11077								11077
Split Face Block 8" x 16" x 6"	042 220 6150	2420	Ea.	2.24	5421								5421
Mortar	041 024 2100	804	CF	3.70	2975								2975
Reinforcing	041 512 0010	6	MLF	270.00	1620								1620
Labor: Masons		80	MD	216.40	17312								17312
Helpers - Reg		40	MD	167.60	6704								6704
OT		20	Hr.	40.58	812								812
Equip: Mixer	016 406 1900	20	Day	66.50	1330								1330
Scaffolding (24 Sections)	R015-100	1	Mo.	208.15	208								208
Crane	016 460 2500	4	Hr.	73.75	295								295
Forklift	016 420 2040	10	Day	210.00	2100								2100
Masonry Saw	016 420 6000	10	Day	50.00	500								500
Division 4 Total					$50,353								$50,353

Figure A.4

COST ANALYSIS

PROJECT: Office Building CLASSIFICATION: Division 5 SHEET NO. 1 of 3

LOCATION: ARCHITECT: ESTIMATE NO:

DATE: 1/93

TAKE OFF BY: QUANTITIES BY: PRICES BY: EXTENSIONS BY: CHECKED BY:

DESCRIPTION	SOURCE	QUANT	UNIT	MATERIAL COST	MATERIAL TOTAL	LABOR COST	LABOR TOTAL	EQUIPMENT COST	EQUIPMENT TOTAL	SUBCONTRACT COST	SUBCONTRACT TOTAL	TOTAL COST	TOTAL TOTAL
Division 5: Metals													
Structural Steel													
Columns		53,885	lbs.										
2nd & 3rd Fl. beams		190,554											
Roof		60,631											
Penthouse		8,440											
		313,510	lbs.										
10 % connections		31351											
		344,861	lbs.										
Base PL		5,275											
		350,136	lbs.										
Total	051 255 0800	175	T							1875	328125		328125
High strength Bolts 20/Ton (77)	051 255 5200	3500	Ea.							6.15	21525		21525
Anchor Bolts (Mat. Only)	031 110 0500	112	Ea.							9.50	1064		1064
Subtotals					$0.00						$350,714		$350,714

Figure A.5a

COST ANALYSIS

PROJECT:	Office Building	CLASSIFICATION:	Division 5	SHEET NO.	2 of 3
LOCATION:		ARCHITECT:		ESTIMATE NO:	
TAKE OFF BY:				DATE:	1/93

EXTENSIONS BY: QUANTITIES BY: PRICES BY: CHECKED BY:

DESCRIPTION	SOURCE			QUANT	UNIT	MATERIAL COST	MATERIAL TOTAL	LABOR COST	LABOR TOTAL	EQUIPMENT COST	EQUIPMENT TOTAL	SUBCONTRACT COST	SUBCONTRACT TOTAL	TOTAL COST	TOTAL TOTAL
Division 5: (Cont'd)															
Metal Joists & Decks															
Joists	051	255	0800	36110	lbs.										
Bridging				3379											
				39489	lbs.										
Total	051	255	0800	19.75	T							1830	36143		36143
Bottom chord extensions	052	110	1650	32	Ea.							10.07	322		322
Composite Deck- 3" 22 ga.	053	104	5200	40570	SF							1.38	55987		55987
Roof- 1 1/2" 22 ga.	053	104	2400	18900	SF							1.05	19845		19845
Edge form	053	104	7100	2160	LF							3.94	8510		8510
Shear studs, 3/4" x 4 3/16"	050	560	0300	3172	Ea.							1.94	6154		6154
Subtotals													$126,960		$126,960

Figure A.5b

COST ANALYSIS

SHEET NO. 3 of 3

PROJECT: Office Building
LOCATION:
TAKE OFF BY:

CLASSIFICATION:
ARCHITECT:
QUANTITIES BY:

Division 5

ESTIMATE NO:
DATE: 1/93
CHECKED BY:

PRICES BY:
EXTENSIONS BY:

DESCRIPTION	SOURCE			QUANT	UNIT	MATERIAL		LABOR		EQUIPMENT		SUBCONTRACT		TOTAL	
						COST	TOTAL	COST	TOTAL	COST	TOTAL	COST	TOTAL	COST	TOTAL
Division 5: (Cont'd)															
Miscellaneous Metals															
Stairs 3' - 6" w/ rails	055	104	0200	188	R							128.13	24088		24088
Landings 10' - 8" x 4'	055	104	1500	320	SF							49.19	15741		15741
Exterior Alum. Rails	055	203	0010	150	LF							23.45	3518		3518
Lintels (Matl. only)	051	232	2100	34	Ea.							22.82	776		776
Subtotal													44123		44123
Sheet 1 subtotal													350714		350714
Sheet 2 subtotal													126960		126960
Sheet 3 subtotal													44123		44123
Division 5 Total													$521,797		$521,797

Figure A.5c

COST ANALYSIS

PROJECT:	Office Building		SHEET NO.	1 of 1
LOCATION:		CLASSIFICATION: Division 6	ESTIMATE NO:	
		ARCHITECT:	DATE:	1/93
TAKE OFF BY:	QUANTITIES BY:	PRICES BY:	CHECKED BY:	
			EXTENSIONS BY:	

DESCRIPTION	SOURCE			QUANT	UNIT	MATERIAL COST	MATERIAL TOTAL	LABOR COST	LABOR TOTAL	EQUIPMENT COST	EQUIPMENT TOTAL	SUBCONTRACT COST	SUBCONTRACT TOTAL	TOTAL COST	TOTAL TOTAL
Division 6: Wood & Plastics															
Rough Carpentry															
Blocking	061	102	2740	0.1	MBF	575.00	58	1500	150						208
Fire Treatment	063	102	0400	0.1	MBF	266.00	27								27
Finish Carpentry															
Paneling @ Elevator Lobby	062	504	2600	1800	SF	1.91	3438	1.06	1908						5346
Vanities	064	140	8150	6	Ea.	177.00	1062	37.00	222						1284
Arch. Woodwork															
Vanity Top, with backsplash	062	408	1000	24	LF	26.00	624	7.05	169						793
Cutouts	062	408	1900	9	Ea.	2.63	24	6.60	59						83
Division 6 Totals							$5,232		$2,509						$7,740

Figure A.6

COST ANALYSIS

PROJECT:	Office Building	CLASSIFICATION: Division 7			SHEET NO. 1 of 2
LOCATION:		ARCHITECT:			ESTIMATE NO:
TAKE OFF BY:		QUANTITIES BY:	PRICES BY:	EXTENSIONS BY:	DATE: 1/93
					CHECKED BY:

DESCRIPTION	SOURCE	QUANT	UNIT	MATERIAL COST	MATERIAL TOTAL	LABOR COST	LABOR TOTAL	EQUIPMENT COST	EQUIPMENT TOTAL	SUBCONTRACT COST	SUBCONTRACT TOTAL	TOTAL COST	TOTAL TOTAL
Division 7: Moisture & Thermal Protection													
Waterproofing													
Asphalt Coating	071 602 0600	3000	SF	0.15	450	0.38	1140						1590
Protective Board 1/4"	071 602 4000	3000	SF	0.35	1050	0.38	1140						2190
Vapor Barrier - 6 mil poly	071 922 0900	208	Sq.	2.90	603	5.70	1186						1789
Insulation													
3 1/2" Fiberglass Ext.	072 118 0420	17600	SF	0.26	4576	0.13	2288						6864
3 1/2" Fiberglass Int.	072 118 0820	7620	SF	0.18	1372	0.16	1219						2591
Roof Deck (Incl. Penthouse) 2 5/8" Urethane/Fiberglass	072 203 1300	18900	SF	SUBCONTRACT	SUBCONTRACT	SUBCONTRACT	SUBCONTRACT	SUBCONTRA		1.68	31752		31752
Roofing													
4 - ply Built-up	075 102 0500	189	Sq.							182.00	34398		34398
4 x 4 cant	075 103 0010	800	LF							1.88	1504		1504
Subtotals					$8,051		$6,973				$67,654		$82,678

Figure A.7a

COST ANALYSIS

PROJECT: Office Building
LOCATION:
TAKE OFF BY:
CLASSIFICATION: Division 7
ARCHITECT:
QUANTITIES BY:
PRICES BY:
EXTENSIONS BY:
SHEET NO. 2 of 2
ESTIMATE NO:
DATE: 1/93
CHECKED BY:

DESCRIPTION	SOURCE			QUANT	UNIT	MATERIAL		LABOR		EQUIPMENT		SUBCONTRACT		TOTAL	
						COST	TOTAL	COST	TOTAL	COST	TOTAL	COST	TOTAL	COST	TOTAL
Division 7: (Cont'd)															
Sheet Metal															
Gravel Stop	077	105	0350	800	LF	SUBCONTRACT		SUBCONTRACT		SUBCONTRA		7.60	6080		6080
Alum. Flashing	076	204	0100	200	SF							3.66	732		732
Accessories															
Smoke Hatches (Stairs)	077	206	1200	3	Ea.							1300	3900		3900
Smoke Vent (Elevator)	077	208	0200	1	Ea.							1150	1150		1150
Subtotals													$11,862		$11,862
Sheet 1 Subtotals							$8,051		$6,973				$67,654		$82,678
Sheet 2 subtotals													$11,862		$11,862
Division 7 Totals							$8,051		$6,973				$103,240		$118,264

Figure A.7b

COST ANALYSIS

PROJECT: Office Building   CLASSIFICATION: Division 8

LOCATION: ARCHITECT:

TAKE OFF BY: QUANTITIES BY: PRICES BY: EXTENSIONS BY:

SHEET NO.   1 of 3

ESTIMATE NO:

DATE: 1/93

CHECKED BY:

DESCRIPTION	SOURCE			QUANT	UNIT	MATERIAL		LABOR		EQUIPMENT		SUBCONTRACT		TOTAL	
						COST	TOTAL	COST	TOTAL	COST	TOTAL	COST	TOTAL	COST	TOTAL
Division 8: Doors, Windows & Glass															
H.M.															
Frames 16 ga. 3' x 7'															
8"	081	118	4400	2	Ea.	91.00	182	28.00	56						238
8" "B"	081	118	6200	10		104.00	1040	28.00	280						1320
4 3/4" "B"	081	118	5400	21		90.00	1890	28.00	588						2478
6' x 7'															
8"	081	118	6240	1		122.00	122	35.50	36						158
Metal Doors 18 ga.															
3' x 7'	081	103	1160	2		191.00	382	25.00	50						432
3' x 7' "B"	081	110	0180	12		216.00	2592	26.50	318						2910
10" x 10" lites	081	110	0240	12		56.50	678								678
Wood Doors – Flush Oak															
3' x 7' "B" 1 1/2 hr.	082	070	0890	9		195.00	1755	35.50	320						2075
3' x 7' "B" 1 hr.	082	070	0190	12		185.00	2220	35.50	426						2646
Hardware															
Locksets	087	120	1400	8	Ea.	147.00	1176	21.00	168						1344
Panic Hardware	087	127	0020	17	Ea.	360.00	6120	42.50	723						6843
Closers	087	206	2400	35	Ea.	125.00	4375	35.50	1243						5618
Subtotals							$22,532		$4,206						$26,738

Figure A.8a

COST ANALYSIS

SHEET NO. 2 of 3

PROJECT:	Office Building	CLASSIFICATION: Division 8	ESTIMATE NO:
LOCATION:		ARCHITECT:	DATE: 1/93
TAKE OFF BY:	QUANTITIES BY:	PRICES BY:	CHECKED BY:

DESCRIPTION	SOURCE			QUANT	UNIT	MATERIAL COST	MATERIAL TOTAL	LABOR COST	LABOR TOTAL	EQUIPMENT COST	EQUIPMENT TOTAL	SUBCONTRACT COST	SUBCONTRACT TOTAL	TOTAL COST	TOTAL TOTAL
Division 8: (Cont'd)															
Hardware (Cont'd)															
Push / Pull	087	129	0100	9	Ea.	4.58	41	17.65	159						200
Kickplates	087	118	0010	9	Ea.	15.45	139	14.10	127						266
Hinges	087	116	1400	52.5	Ea.	37.50	1969								1969
Special Doors															
Roll Up Grills	083	402	0010	200	SF							24.50	4900		4900
Motorized	083	402	1100	2	Ea.							1800	3600		3600
Entrances and Storefronts															
Front Entrances (2)	084	105	1000	240	SF							16.65	3996		3996
Black (36% Mat.)	084	105	1600	240	SF							4.05	972		972
Basement Entrance	084	105	1000	54	SF							16.65	899		899
Black (36% Mat.)	084	105	1600	54	SF							4.05	219		219
Glazing															
Bathroom Mirrors	088	144	0200	135	SF							9.25	1249		1249
3 - 3' x 8'															
3 - 3' x 7'															
Subtotals							$2,149		$286				$15,835		$18,269

Figure A.8b

COST ANALYSIS

PROJECT:	Office Building	CLASSIFICATION:	Division 8				SHEET NO.	3 of 3
LOCATION:		ARCHITECT:					ESTIMATE NO:	
TAKE OFF BY:		PRICES BY:		EXTENSIONS BY:			DATE: 1/93	
	QUANTITIES BY:						CHECKED BY:	

DESCRIPTION	SOURCE			QUANT	UNIT	MATERIAL COST	MATERIAL TOTAL	LABOR COST	LABOR TOTAL	EQUIPMENT COST	EQUIPMENT TOTAL	SUBCONTRACT COST	SUBCONTRACT TOTAL	TOTAL COST	TOTAL TOTAL
Division 8: (Cont'd)															
Window/Curtain Wall	Telephone Quote														
	089	206	0050	25060	SF							38.00	952280		952280
Sheet 1 subtotals							$22,532		$4,206						$26,738
Sheet 2 subtotals							$2,149		$286				$15,835		$18,269
Sheet 3 subtotals															
Division 8 Totals							$24,681		$4,492				$15,835		$45,007

Figure A.8c

COST ANALYSIS

PROJECT: Office Building CLASSIFICATION: Division 9
LOCATION: ARCHITECT:
TAKE OFF BY: QUANTITIES BY: PRICES BY:
ESTIMATE NO:
DATE: 1/93
CHECKED BY:
EXTENSIONS BY:

DESCRIPTION	SOURCE			QUANT	UNIT	MATERIAL		LABOR		EQUIPMENT		SUBCONTRACT		TOTAL	
						COST	TOTAL	COST	TOTAL	COST	TOTAL	COST	TOTAL	COST	TOTAL
Division 9: Finishes															
Framing: Metal Studs															
6" - 25 ga.	092	612	2500	300	SF	0.33	99	0.52	156						255
3 5/8" - 25 ga.	092	612	2300	13664	SF	0.24	3279	0.49	6695						9975
1 5/8" - 25 ga.	092	612	2000	7344	SF	0.19	1395	0.47	3452						4847
Accessories															
7/8" Furring	092	804	0900	31.5	CLF	17.50	551	81.50	2567						3119
J - Bead	092	804	1120	34.1	CLF	17.35	592	71.50	2438						3030
Corner Bead	092	804	0300	58.4	CLF	9.65	564	53.00	3095						3659
Drywall															
5/8" F.R. @ Columns	092	608	4050	5640	SF	0.60	3384	1.41	7952						11336
5/8" F.R. @ Core	092	608	2150	7720	SF	0.30	2316	0.44	3397						5713
5/8" Standard	092	608	2050	16008	SF	0.29	4642	0.44	7044						11686
Shaftwall: @ Elevator	092	624	0300	2040	SF	1.13	2305	2.35	4794						7099
Subtotals							$19,128		$41,590						$60,718

Figure A.9a

COST ANALYSIS

PROJECT: Office Building	CLASSIFICATION: Division 9		SHEET NO. 2 of 4	
LOCATION:	ARCHITECT:		ESTIMATE NO:	
TAKE OFF BY:	QUANTITIES BY:	PRICES BY:	EXTENSIONS BY:	DATE: 1/93
				CHECKED BY:

DESCRIPTION	SOURCE			QUANT	UNIT	MATERIAL		LABOR		EQUIPMENT		SUBCONTRACT		TOTAL	
						COST	TOTAL	COST	TOTAL	COST	TOTAL	COST	TOTAL	COST	TOTAL
Division 9: (Cont'd)															
Fireproofing: @ Beams	072	554	0400	40500	SF							1.17	47385		
Total Fireproofing													47385		
Ceramic Tile:															
Walls	093	102	5400	1584	SF							5.15	8158		
Bull Nose	093	102	2500	396	LF							7.45	2950		
Cove Base	093	102	0700	396	LF							7.35	2911		
Floors	093	102	3300	960	SF							7.20	6912		
Total Ceramic Tile													20930		
Acoustical Ceilings:															
Grid	091	304	0050	56700	SF	0.30	17010	0.26	14742						
Tile	095	104	3740	53735	SF	1.36	73080	0.37	19882						
Total Ceiling							90090		34624						

Figure A.9b

COST ANALYSIS

PROJECT: Office Building CLASSIFICATION: Division 9
LOCATION: ARCHITECT:
TAKE OFF BY:
QUANTITIES BY: PRICES BY: EXTENSIONS BY:

SHEET NO. 3 of 4
ESTIMATE NO:
DATE: 1/93
CHECKED BY:

DESCRIPTION	SOURCE			QUANT	UNIT	MATERIAL		LABOR		EQUIPMENT		SUBCONTRACT		TOTAL	
						COST	TOTAL	COST	TOTAL	COST	TOTAL	COST	TOTAL	COST	TOTAL
Division 9: (Cont'd)															
Flooring:															
Carpet	096	852	3200	5850	SY							25.98	151983		
Cove Base	096	601	1150	2530	LF							1.52	3846		
Parquet @ lobby & elevators	095	604	6500	1800	SY							7.30	13140		
Total Flooring													168969		
Painting:															
Walls (Drywall)	099	224	0840	27784	SF							0.45	12503		
Wood Doors	099	216	1800	21	Ea.							36.50	767		
Metal Doors (Primed)	099	216	1000	14	Ea.							31.50	441		
Block Walls	099	224	2880	9846	SF							0.36	3545		
Total Painting													17255		

Figure A.9c

COST ANALYSIS

PROJECT: Office Building
LOCATION:
TAKE OFF BY:
CLASSIFICATION: Division 9
ARCHITECT:
QUANTITIES BY:
PRICES BY:
EXTENSIONS BY:

SHEET NO. 4 of 4
ESTIMATE NO:
DATE: 1/93
CHECKED BY:

DESCRIPTION	SOURCE	QUANT	UNIT	MATERIAL COST	MATERIAL TOTAL	LABOR COST	LABOR TOTAL	EQUIPMENT COST	EQUIPMENT TOTAL	SUBCONTRACT COST	SUBCONTRACT TOTAL	TOTAL COST	TOTAL
Division 9: (Cont'd)													
Drywall & Framing	Sheet 1				$19,128		$41,590						$60,718
Fireproofing	Sheet 2										$47,385		$47,385
Ceramic Tile	Sheet 2										$20,930		$20,930
Acoustical Ceiling	Sheet 2				$90,090		$34,624						$124,714
Flooring	Sheet 3										$168,969		$168,969
Painting	Sheet 3										$17,255		$17,255
Division 9 Totals					$109,217		$76,214				$254,539		$439,970

COST ANALYSIS

		SHEET NO. 1 of 1
PROJECT: Office Building	CLASSIFICATION: Division 10	ESTIMATE NO:
LOCATION:	ARCHITECT:	DATE: 1/93
TAKE OFF BY:	QUANTITIES BY:	PRICES BY: EXTENSIONS BY: CHECKED BY:

DESCRIPTION	SOURCE			QUANT	UNIT	MATERIAL COST	MATERIAL TOTAL	LABOR COST	LABOR TOTAL	EQUIPMENT COST	EQUIPMENT TOTAL	SUBCONTRACT COST	SUBCONTRACT TOTAL	TOTAL COST	TOTAL TOTAL
Division 10: Specialties															
Bathroom Accessories:															
Towel / Waste	108	204	0610	9	Ea.	274.00	2466	21.00	189						2655
Grab Bar	108	204	1100	6	Ea.	44.50	267	10.60	64						331
Napkin Dispenser	108	204	4200	6	Ea.	360.00	2160	14.10	85						2245
Mirrors (Handicapped)	108	204	3000	3	Ea.	63.00	189	10.60	32						221
Soap Dispenser	108	204	4600	15	Ea.	38.50	578	10.60	159						737
S. S. Shelves	108	204	5700	6	Ea.	60.50	363	13.25	80						443
T. P. Holder	108	204	6100	18	Ea.	9.60	173	7.05	127						300
Ash Trays	108	204	7800	12	Ea.	69.00	828	11.75	141						969
Toilet Partitions:															
Floor Mounted, Headrail	101	602	2500	15	Ea.	360.00	5400	70.50	1058						6458
Urinal Screens	101	602	4700	3	Ea.	172.00	516	53.00	159						675
Division 10 Totals							$12,939		$2,092						$15,031

Figure A.10

COST ANALYSIS

| PROJECT: | Office Building | | CLASSIFICATION: | Division 14 | | | | | SHEET NO. | 1 of 1 |

LOCATION: ESTIMATE NO:

ARCHITECT: DATE: 1/93

TAKE OFF BY: QUANTITIES BY: PRICES BY: EXTENSIONS BY: CHECKED BY:

DESCRIPTION	SOURCE	QUANT	UNIT	MATERIAL		LABOR		EQUIPMENT		SUBCONTRACT		TOTAL	
				COST	TOTAL	COST	TOTAL	COST	TOTAL	COST	TOTAL	COST	TOTAL
Division 14: Conveying Systems													
Pass. Hydraulic - Base	36500												
2500 lbs. capacity	1300												
Travel 37'	12025												
Stops (plus 2)	6700												
Speed - 100 fpm													
S. S. Doors	805												
Carpet	320												
P. L. Walls													
S. S. Entrance - Doors	805												
- Frame	805												
Each Elevator	#####	2	Ea.								118520		118520
Automatic Controls		1	Ea.							3475	3475		3475
Fire Service		1	Ea.										
Hall Lanterns		8	Ea.							425.00	3400		3400
Position Indicators		4	Ea.							315.00	1260		1260
Maintenance		1	Ea.							1992	1992		1992
Division 14 Total											$128,647		$128,647

Figure A.11

COST ANALYSIS

PROJECT:	Office Building
LOCATION:	
TAKE OFF BY:	
CLASSIFICATION:	Division 15
ARCHITECT:	
QUANTITIES BY:	
PRICES BY:	
EXTENSIONS BY:	
SHEET NO.	1 of 5
ESTIMATE NO:	
DATE:	1/93
CHECKED BY:	

DESCRIPTION	SOURCE	QUANT	UNIT	MATERIAL COST	MATERIAL TOTAL	LABOR COST	LABOR TOTAL	EQUIPMENT COST	EQUIPMENT TOTAL	SUBCONTRACT COST	SUBCONTRACT TOTAL	TOTAL COST	TOTAL TOTAL
HVAC Sheet Metal Duct Work													
Supply Duct 3" Floor (Insul)		6800	lb.										
Supply Duct (Not insulated)		14000	lb.										
Return Duct (Not insulated)		4800	lb.										
Toilet Exhaust Duct Work		325	lb.										
Total Duct Work	157 250 0580	25925	lb.	0.40	10370	2.40	62220						72590
9" x 9" Supply Diffusers	157 450 2020	3	Ea.	67.50	203	17.45	52						255
15" x 15" Supply Diffusers	157 450 2060	132	Ea.	92.00	12144	22.00	2904						15048
24" x 24" Framed Eggcrate	157 460 4040	19	Ea.	80.00	1520	15.25	290						1810
Splitter Damper, 1 Foot Rod	157 480 7000	12	Ea.	14.30	172	10.15	122						293
6" Flexible Toilet Exhaust Duct	157 250 1560	200	LF	1.02	204	1.57	314						518
4" Flexible Toilet Exhaust Duct	157 250 1520	90	LF	0.78	70	1.22	110						180
8" x 6" Exhaust Register	157 470 5040	3	Ea.	17.60	53	10.15	30						83
8" x 4" Exhaust Register	157 470 5020	1	Ea.	17.60	18	9.40	9						27
Roof Exhaust Fan 4600 CFM	157 290 7240	1	Ea.	1225	1225	141.00	141						1366
24" Double Wall Galv. Chimney	155 680 0340	12	LF	143.00	1716	21.50	258						1974
24" Roof Flashing Collar	155 680 1170	1	Ea.	240.00	240	57.00	57						297
24" Double Wall Tee	155 680 1330	1	Ea.	705.00	705	57.00	57						762
24" Tee Cap	155 680 1590	1	Ea.	46.50	47	32.50	33						79
24" Rain Cap & Screen	155 680 1880	1	Ea.	660.00	660	34.00	34						694
Subtotals					$29,345		$66,631						$95,976

Figure A.12a

COST ANALYSIS

PROJECT: Office Building
LOCATION:
TAKE OFF BY:

CLASSIFICATION: Division 15
ARCHITECT:
QUANTITIES BY:
PRICES BY:

SHEET NO. 2 of 5
ESTIMATE NO:
DATE: 1/93
CHECKED BY:
EXTENSIONS BY:

DESCRIPTION	SOURCE		QUANT	UNIT	MATERIAL COST	MATERIAL TOTAL	LABOR COST	LABOR TOTAL	EQUIPMENT COST	EQUIPMENT TOTAL	SUBCONTRACT COST	SUBCONTRACT TOTAL	TOTAL COST	TOTAL TOTAL
Division 15: (Cont'd)														
Air - Conditioning														
Chiller, 175 Tons	157	190 1600	1	Ea.	83000	83000	16200	16200						99200
30 Ton Fan Coil Unit	157	150 0260	6	Ea.	6225	37350	1200	7200						44550
175 Ton Tower	157	240 1900	175	Ton	83.50	14613	5.65	989						15601
6" Thermometer 30° - 40° F	157	420 4500	4	Ea.	24.00	96	7.95	32						128
3 1/2" Dial Pressure Gague	157	420 2300	6	Ea.	13.50	81	7.95	48						129
7 1/2 HP Condenser Water Pum	152	410 4420	1	Ea.	1850	1850	285.00	285						2135
5 HP Chill Water Pump	152	410 4410	2	Ea.	1900	3800	285.00	570						4370
4" Steel Pipe, Bevel End	151	701 2110	180	LF	8.45	1521	12.30	2214	1.31	236				3971
2" Steel Pipe, Thread & Coupled	151	701 0610	340	LF	4.12	1401	7.10	2414						3815
4" Weld Tee	151	720 3440	15	Ea.	33.50	503	152.00	2280	16.15	242				3025
4" Weld Elbow	151	720 3130	20	Ea.	16.95	339	91.00	1820	9.70	194				2353
4" Weld Neck Dlange	151	720 6500	14	Ea.	25.50	357	45.50	637	4.35	61				1055
4" Sets, Nuts, Bolts & Gaskets	151	720 0670	30	Ea.	9.80	294	31.50	945						1239
2" Cast Iron Tee	151	716 0580	12	Ea.	9.55	115	41.50	498						613
2" Cast Iron Elbow	151	716 0140	24	Ea.	6.80	163	25.50	612						775
4" OS & Y Gate Valve 1B	151	960 3680	8	Ea.	222.00	1776	152.00	1216						2992
4" Wafer, Check Valve	151	960 6670	3	Ea.	198.00	594	91.00	273						867
2" Bronze Gate Valve	151	955 3480	6	Ea.	65.50	393	23.00	138						531
4" Balancing Valve, Flanged	151	990 7030	3	Ea.	355.00	1065	152.00	456						1521
2" Stop and Balance Valve	151	990 1080	6	Ea.	128.00	768	31.50	189						957
4" Flanged Y Strainer	156	612 1060	3	Ea.	191.00	573	153.00	459						1032
ASME 31 Gal. Expan. Tank	155	671 3020	1	Ea.	1350	1350	57.50	58						1408
Subtotals						$152,001		$39,532		$733				$192,265

Figure A.12b

COST ANALYSIS

PROJECT: Office Building	CLASSIFICATION: Division 15	SHEET NO. 3 of 5	
LOCATION:	ARCHITECT:	ESTIMATE NO:	
TAKE OFF BY:	QUANTITIES BY:	DATE: 1/93	
	PRICES BY:	CHECKED BY:	

EXTENSIONS BY:

DESCRIPTION	SOURCE			QUANT	UNIT	MATERIAL COST	MATERIAL TOTAL	LABOR COST	LABOR TOTAL	EQUIPMENT COST	EQUIPMENT TOTAL	SUBCONTRACT COST	SUBCONTRACT TOTAL	TOTAL COST	TOTAL TOTAL
Division 15: (Cont'd)															
Heating															
3500 MBH, Gas, CI Water Heat	155	115	3400	1	Ea.	17000	17000	3750	3750						20750
Electric Duct Heater	155	408	0160	1	Ea.	1400	1400	43.50	44						1444
79 Gal. ASME Expansion Tank	155	671	3060	1	Ea.	2025	2025	92.00	92						2117
3" Steel Pipe, Bevel End	151	701	2090	120	LF	5.95	714	10.60	1272	1.13	136				2122
1 1/2" Stl Pipe, Thread & Couple	151	701	0600	3200	LF	3.05	9760	5.70	18240						28000
3" Wled Tee	151	720	3430	15	Ea.	23.50	353	114.00	1710	12.10	182				2244
3" Weld Elbow	151	720	3120	12	Ea.	9.90	119	65.00	780	6.95	83				982
3" Weld Neck Flange	151	720	6480	8	Ea.	21.50	172	32.50	260	3.46	28				460
3" Sets, Bolts, Nuts & Gaskets	151	720	0650	16	Ea.	5.40	86	23.00	368						454
1 1/2" cast Iron Tee	151	716	0570	12	Ea.	6.95	83	35.00	420						503
1 1/2" cast Iron Elbow	151	716	0140	24	Ea.	6.80	163	25.50	612						775
3" OS & Y Iron Boot Gate Valve	151	960	3660	4	Ea.	157.00	628	101.00	404						1032
3" Water Check Valve	151	960	6660	2	Ea.	155.00	310	57.00	114						424
1 1/2" Bronze Gate Valve	151	955	3470	6	Ea.	48.00	288	9.45	57						345
3" Balancing Valve, Flanged	151	990	7020	2	Ea.	280.00	560	101.00	202						762
1 1/2" Stop & Balance Valve	151	990	1070	6	Ea.	109.00	654	23.00	138						792
3" Iron Body, Flanged Strainer	156	612	1040	2	Ea.	112.00	224	102.00	204						428
3" Air Control Fitting	156	205	0100	1	Ea.	840.00	840	115.00	115						955
6" Thermometer, 40° to 249° F	157	420	4500	2	Ea.	24.00	48	7.95	16						64
3 1/2" Dial Pressure Gague	157	420	2300	4	Ea.	13.50	54	7.95	32						86
5 HP Hot Water Pump	152	410	4300	2	Ea.	1325	2650	253.00	506						3156
Subtotals							$38,131		$29,335		$428				$67,894

Figure A.12c

COST ANALYSIS

PROJECT: Office Building CLASSIFICATION: Division 15 SHEET NO. 4 of 5

LOCATION: ARCHITECT: ESTIMATE NO:

TAKE OFF BY: QUANTITIES BY: PRICES BY: EXTENSIONS BY: DATE: 1/93

CHECKED BY:

DESCRIPTION	SOURCE	QUANT	UNIT	MATERIAL		LABOR		EQUIPMENT		SUBCONTRACT		TOTAL	
				COST	TOTAL	COST	TOTAL	COST	TOTAL	COST	TOTAL	COST	TOTAL
HVAC: Miscellaneous													
Record Drawings		8	Hr.										
Operating Instructions		8	Hr.										
Maintenance Manuals		4	Hr.										
Cleaning Systems		16	Hr.										
	Total	36	Hr.	####		988						988	
Subcontracts													
Insulation										22424		22424	
Balancing										9113		9113	
Controls										43550		43550	
Crane									1530			1530	
Subtotals					0		$988		$1,530		$75,087		$77,605

COST ANALYSIS

PROJECT: Office Building	CLASSIFICATION: Division 15
LOCATION:	ARCHITECT:
TAKE OFF BY:	QUANTITIES BY:
	PRICES BY:

SHEET NO. 5 of 5
ESTIMATE NO:
DATE: 1/93
CHECKED BY:
EXTENSIONS BY:

DESCRIPTION	SOURCE	QUANT	UNIT	MATERIAL COST	MATERIAL TOTAL	LABOR COST	LABOR TOTAL	EQUIPMENT COST	EQUIPMENT TOTAL	SUBCONTRACT COST	SUBCONTRACT TOTAL	TOTAL COST	TOTAL
Division 15: (Cont'd)													
HVAC: Summary													
Ductwork	Sheet 1				$29,345		$66,631		$0		$0		$95,976
													$0
Air Conditioning	Sheet 2				$152,001		$39,532		$733		$0		$192,265
													$0
Heating	Sheet 3				$38,131		$29,335		$428		$0		$67,894
													$0
Miscellaneous	Sheet 4				$0		$988		$0		$0		$988
													$0
Subcontracts	Sheet 4				$0		$0		$1,530		$75,087		$76,617
Material Subtotal					$219,477								
Sales Tax				6%	$13,169								
Bare Cost Totals					$232,646		$136,486		$2,691		$75,087		$446,910
Overhead & Profit				10%	$23,265	46.1%	$13,649	10%	$269	10%	$7,509		$44,691
Totals					$255,910		$150,134		$2,960		$82,596		$491,601
Total Bid													$491,601

Figure A.12e

COST ANALYSIS

PROJECT:	Office Building	CLASSIFICATION:	Division 15		SHEET NO.	1 of 1
LOCATION:		ARCHITECT:			ESTIMATE NO:	
TAKE OFF BY:		QUANTITIES BY:	PRICES BY:		DATE: 1/93	
					CHECKED BY:	

DESCRIPTION	SOURCE		QUANT	UNIT	MATERIAL		LABOR		EQUIPMENT		SUBCONTRACT		TOTAL	
					COST	TOTAL	COST	TOTAL	COST	TOTAL	COST	TOTAL	COST	TOTAL
						EXTENSIONS BY:								
Division 15: Mechanical														
	SUBCONTRACTOR QUOTATIONS													
Plumbing:														
Base Price											144539			144539
Pipe Insulation (HW only)											4336			4336
											0			0
Total Plumbing											148875			148875
											0			0
Fire Protection:											0			0
Standpipes											42589			42589
Sprinklers											68766			68766
											0			0
Total Fire Protection											111355			111355
											0			0
HVAC:											0			0
Base Price											419211			419211
Insulation											24666			24666
Balancing											10024			10024
Controls											47905			47905
Crane											2960			2960
											0			0
Total HVAC											504767			504767
Division 15 Totals					0		0		0		$1,529,994			$1,529,994

Figure A.13

COST ANALYSIS

PROJECT: Office Building
LOCATION:
TAKE OFF BY:
QUANTITIES BY:

CLASSIFICATION: Division 16
ARCHITECT:
PRICES BY:

SHEET NO. 1 of 2
ESTIMATE NO:
DATE: 1/93
CHECKED BY:
EXTENSIONS BY:

DESCRIPTION	SOURCE			QUANT	UNIT	MATERIAL		LABOR		EQUIPMENT		SUBCONTRACT		TOTAL	
						COST	TOTAL	COST	TOTAL	COST	TOTAL	COST	TOTAL	COST	TOTAL
Division 16: Electrical															
Lighting															
Fixtures:															
Type															
A 2'x4' w/4L	166	130	0600	725	Ea.	56.00	40600	52.50	38063						78663
B 1'x4' w/2L	166	130	0200	28	Ea.	46.00	1288	43.00	1204						2492
C 6"x4' w/1L	166	130	2020	29	Ea.	59.00	1711	31.00	899						2610
D 6"x8' w/1L	166	130	2600	53	Ea.	39.00	2067	36.50	1935						4002
E 6"x4' mirror light	166	130	6900	9	Ea.	80.00	720	31.00	279						999
G 4' surface mount	166	130	2200	27	Ea.	26.00	702	29.00	783						1485
H 150 W HPS wall pk	166	115	1170	2	Ea.	230.00	460	61.50	123						583
K 70 W HPS wall pk	166	115	1160	3	Ea.	195.00	585	61.50	185						770
L Exit, single face	166	110	0080	23	Ea.	35.00	805	31.00	713						1518
M Remote head	166	110	0780	4	Ea.	19.00	76	9.20	37						113
N Emergence battery unit	166	110	0500	13	Ea.	215.00	2795	61.50	800						3595
															0
															0
															0
Raceways:															
1/2" EMT	160	205	5000	9080	LF	0.40	3632	1.45	13166						16798
Set screw conn.	160	205	6500	1052	Ea.	0.52	547	2.05	2157						2704
Com. pr. conn.	160	205	8800	104	Ea.	1.55	161	2.55	265						426
															0
Greenfield	160	270	0050	4430	LF	0.23	1019	1.23	5449						6468
Connectors	160	270	0420	1482	Ea.	0.95	1408	2.46	3646						5054
															0
															0
															0
															0
															0
															0
															0
Subtotals							$58,576		$69,701		$0		$0		$128,277

Figure A.14a

COST ANALYSIS

SHEET NO.　2 of 2

PROJECT:	Office Building	CLASSIFICATION:	Division 16		ESTIMATE NO:
LOCATION:		ARCHITECT:			DATE:　1/93
TAKE OFF BY:	QUANTITIES BY:	PRICES BY:	EXTENSIONS BY:		CHECKED BY:

DESCRIPTION	SOURCE	QUANT	UNIT	MATERIAL		LABOR		EQUIPMENT		SUBCONTRACT		TOTAL	
				COST	TOTAL	COST	TOTAL	COST	TOTAL	COST	TOTAL	COST	TOTAL
Division 16: (Cont'd)													
Lighting: (Cont'd)													
Conductors:													
THHN copper # 12	161 165 1200	405	CLF	7.40	2997	22.50	9113						12110
													0
Boxes & Devices:													0
Box - 4" octagon	162 110 0020	394	Ea.	1.44	567	12.30	4846						5414
4" Blank cover	162 110 0250	394	Ea.	0.68	268	3.84	1513						1781
Box - 4" square	162 110 0150	23	Ea.	1.90	44	12.30	283						327
Plaster rings	162 110 0300	23	Ea.	1.14	26	3.84	88						115
Switch box	162 110 0650	20	Ea.	2.11	42	9.10	182						224
S. P. switch 20A	162 320 0500	20	Ea.	6.60	132	9.10	182						314
Switch plate	162 320 2600	20	Ea.	1.70	34	3.08	62						96
Subtotals					$4,110		$16,268		$0		$0		$20,379
Sheet 1 subtotals					$58,576		$69,701		$0		$0		$128,277
Sheet 2 subtotals					$4,110		$16,268		$0		$0		$20,379
Total Lighting					$62,686		$85,970		$0		$0		$148,656

Figure A.14b

COST ANALYSIS

PROJECT:	Office Building		SHEET NO.	1 of 1
LOCATION:		CLASSIFICATION: Division 16		
TAKE OFF BY:		ARCHITECT:	ESTIMATE NO:	
	QUANTITIES BY:		DATE: 1/93	
		PRICES BY:	CHECKED BY:	

						MATERIAL		LABOR		EQUIPMENT		SUBCONTRACT		TOTAL	
DESCRIPTION	SOURCE	QUANT	UNIT	COST	TOTAL		COST	TOTAL		COST	TOTAL		COST	TOTAL		COST	TOTAL
Division 16: Electrical															
Lighting					$62,686			$85,970							$148,656
															$0
Service & Distribution					$72,320			$21,932							$94,252
															$0
Branch Circuits					$77,793			$23,050							$100,843
Incl. under carpet system															$0
															$0
Motors					$18,493			$3,730							$22,223
															$0
Fire Alarm					$20,692			$12,306							$32,998
Division 16 Total					$251,984			$146,988			$0			$0			$398,972

Figure A.15

QUANTITY SHEET

PROJECT: Office Building   Division 3   SHEET NO. 1 of 1
LOCATION: ARCHITECT: ESTIMATE NO:
TAKE OFF BY: EXTENSIONS BY: DATE:
                                             CHECKED BY:

DESCRIPTION	NO.	DIM	DIM	DIM	Forms	UNIT	Volume	UNIT	Reinf.	UNIT	Finish	UNIT
Spread Footings	6	11.5'	11.5'	2'	552	SFCA	1587	CF				
	4	9.5'	9.5'	2'	304		722					
	18	8'	8'	2'	1152		2304					
					2008	SFCA	4613	CF				
Dowel Supports	28 Ea.						171	CY	8892	Lbs.		
									4.45	T		
Continuous Footings												
Perimeter	(	600'	2'	1'	1200	SFCA	1200	CF				
Deduct Spr. Footings		8'	2'	1'	-288		-288	)				
Ramp		166'	1.5'	0.67'	498		166					
Stoop		25'	1.5'	0.67'	75		25					
Stairs	2	40'	1.5'	0.67'	240		81					
Core		160'	1.5'	0.67'	480		161					
					2205	SFCA	1345	CF				
Dowel Supports		1031	LF				50	CY	2600	Lbs.		
Keyway		791	LF						1.30	T		
Deduct Stairs / Core												
Walls - Perimeter		600'	1'	10'	12000	SFCA	4020	CF			6000	SF
Pit		42	0.83'	4'	336		140					
Ramp & Stoop		191'	1'	~4'	1528		512					
Deduct - Doors	(	10'	1'	10'	-400		-134	)				
Openings	(	31'	1'	~4.5'	-1674		-561	)				
					11790	SFCA	3977	CF				
Box Openings		466	LF				148	CY	18988	Lbs.		
									9.49	T		
Columns 28" diam.	9	30" diam.	9'		81	LF	398	CF			636	
	1	30" diam.	12'		12		59				94	
					93	LF	457	CF			730	SF
							17	CY	8908	Lbs.		
									4.45	T		
Pilasters 3 Sides	14	2'	1.67'	9'	673	SFCA	421	CF				
2 Sides	4	1.67'	1.67'	9'	120		100					
					793	SFCA	521	CF	9956	Lbs.	793	SF
							19	CY	4.98	T		
Chamfer	32	9'			288	LF						

Figure A.16

QUANTITY SHEET

PROJECT: Office Building
LOCATION:
TAKE OFF BY:

Division 5
ARCHITECT:
EXTENSIONS BY:

SHEET NO. 1 of 2
ESTIMATE NO:
DATE:
CHECKED BY:

DESCRIPTION	NO.	L	W	Lbs.	UNIT	Lbs.	UNIT	Total Lbs.	UNIT	Acc.	UNIT
Columns											
W8 x 40	18	31.27'				22514	Lbs.				
W8 x 24	18	11.33'				4895					
W8 x 67	4	31.23'				8370					
W8 x 31	4	11.33'				1405					
W12 x 58	6	31.20'				10857					
W8 x 48	6	20.29'				5844		53885	Lbs.		
PL 1 1/2"	18	1.33'	1.33'	61.2		1949	Lbs.				
2"	4	1.75'	1.75'	81.6		1000					
2 3/8"	6	2'	2'	96.9		2326		5275	Lbs.		
3/4" Anchor Bolts		24"								112	Ea.
Beams - 2nd & 3rd Floors											
W14 x 26	4	34'				3536	Lbs.				
	8	35'				7280					
	4	25'				2600					
	1	27'				702					
	1	20'				520					
W14 x 30	8	34'				8160					
	30	35'				31500					
W14 x 34	5	34'				5780					
W12 x 19	5	9'				855					
W21 x 44	4	29'				5104					
W18 x 40	2	30'				2640					
	2	30'				2400					
W24 x 55	10	29'				15950					
	5	30'				8250					
Each Floor						95277	Lbs.				
Both Floors								190554	Lbs.		
3/4" Shear Studs	4	3/16"								2636	Ea.

Figure A.17a

QUANTITY SHEET

PROJECT: Office Building
LOCATION:
TAKE OFF BY:

Division 5
ARCHITECT:
EXTENSIONS BY:

SHEET NO. 2 of 2
ESTIMATE NO:
DATE:
CHECKED BY:

DESCRIPTION	NO.	DIMENSIONS L	DIMENSIONS W	DIMENSIONS Lbs.	UNIT	Lbs.	UNIT	Total Lbs.	UNIT	Acc.	UNIT
Beams - Roof											
W16 x 26	4	34'				3536	Lbs.				
	8	35'				7280					
W21 x 44	7	35'				10780					
W18 x 24	1	26'				1040					
W21 x 49	4	29'				5684					
W21 x 49	2	30'				2940					
W21 x 62	10	29'				17980					
	3	30'				5580					
W27 x 94	2	30'				5640					
W12 x 19	1	9'				171	Lbs.	60631	Lbs.		
3/4" Shear Studs		4 3/16"								536	Ea.
Beams - Penthouse											
W21 x 49	2	30'				2940	Lbs.				
W21 x 62	1	30'				1860	Lbs.				
W16 x 26	4	35'				3640	Lbs.	8440	Lbs.		
Joists - Roof & Penthouse											
2447	30	34'		11.5		11730	Lbs.				
	52	35'		11.5		20930					
	10	30'		11.5		3450	Lbs.	36110	Lbs.		
Bottom Chord Ext.	32									32	Ea.
Bridging	36	88'		0.8		2534	Lbs.				
	24	29'		0.8		557					
	12	30'		0.8		288	Lbs.	3379	Lbs.		
Deck (22 ga.)											
3" - 2nd & 3rd Floor	2	210'	90'		39900 SF						
Incl. Penthouse		70'	30'								
1 1/2" - R & P	2	210'	90'		18900 SF						
		210'	30'								
Edge Form	3	210'	90' + Opening							2160	LF

Figure A.17b

209

QUANTITY SHEET

PROJECT: Office Building
LOCATION:
TAKE OFF BY:

Division 9
ARCHITECT:
EXTENSIONS BY:

ESTIMATE NO:
DATE:
CHECKED BY:

DESCRIPTION	NO.	L	W	H	Studs	UNIT	5/8" Std. Drywall	UNIT	5/8" F.R. Drywall	UNIT	Acc.	UNIT
Partitions - 25 ga.												
Bath Chase 6"	3	10'		10'	300	SF			600	SF		
Interior 3 5/8"												
Lobby	1	86'		10'	860	SF			1720	SF		
Core	3	90'		10'	2700	SF			5400	SF		
Corner Bead	27			10'							270	LF
Furring 16" O.C.	3	140'		10'			4200	SF			3151	LF
Exterior 3 5/8"	3	560'		10'	10104	SF	10104	SF				
Deduct Windows	(	496'		4'-5")								
Corner Bead	6	496'									3408	LF
	96	4.5'										
J - Bead	6	496'									3408	LF
	96	4.5'										
Window Returns	3408'	0.5'			1704	SF	1704	SF				
1 5/8" Studs												
Columns 1 5/8"	3	188'		10'	5640	SF						
Unfinished									5640	SF		
Taped									5640	SF		
Corner Bead	3	72'		10'							2160	LF
Quantity Summary												
Studs: 6"					300	SF						
3 5/8"					13664	SF						
1 5/8"					7344	SF						
Drywall: 5/8" F.R.									13360	SF		
Unfinished: 5/8" F.R.									5640	SF		
5/8" Std.							16008	SF				
Corner Bead											5838	LF
J - Bead											3408	LF
Furring											3151	LF

Figure A.18

PROJECT
OVERHEAD SUMMARY

SHEET NO.

PROJECT: Office Building
LOCATION: ARCHITECT: DATE:
QUANTITIES BY: PRICES BY: EXTENSIONS BY: CHECKED BY:

ESTIMATE NO:

DESCRIPTION	QUANTITY	UNIT	MATERIAL/EQUIP. UNIT	TOTAL	LABOR UNIT	TOTAL	TOTAL COST UNIT	TOTAL
Job Organization: Superintendent	49	WK			1210	59290		59290
Project Manager								
Timekeeper & Material Clerk	40	WK			705	28200		28200
Clerical								
Safety, Watchman & First Aid								
Travel Expense: Superintendent								
Project Manager								
Engineering: Layout	10	DAY			560	5600		5600
Inspection / Quantities								
Drawings								
CPM Schedule								
Testing: Soil								
Materials								
Structural								
Equipment: Cranes								
Concrete Pump, Conveyor, Etc.								
Elevators, Hoists								
Freight & Hauling								
Loading, Unloading, Erecting, Etc.								
Maintenance								
Pumping								
Scaffolding								
Small Power Equipment / Tools	0.5	%						
Field Offices: Job Office Trailer	11	Mo.	215	2365				2365
Architect / Owner's Office								
Temporary Telephones								
Utilities	11	Mo.						
Temporary Toilets								
Storage Areas & Sheds	11	Mo.	70	770				770
Temporary Utilities: Heat								
Light	567	CSF	2.03	1151	4.85	2750		
Power	11	Mo.	101	1111				1111
PAGE TOTALS				$5,397		$95,840		$97,336

Figure A.19a

DESCRIPTION	QUANTITY	UNIT	MATERIAL/EQUIP.		LABOR		TOTAL COST	
			UNIT	TOTAL	UNIT	TOTAL	UNIT	TOTAL
Totals Brought Forward				$5,397		$95,840		$97,336
Winter Protection: Temp. Heat/Protection	567	CSF	5.00	2835	1.50	851		3686
Snow Plowing								
Thawing Materials								
Temporary Roads	750	SY	1.53	752	1.48	751		1503
Signs & Barricades: Site Sign	1	LS	125	125				125
Temporary Fences	1350	LF	1.80	2430	1.95	2633		5063
Temporary Stairs, Ladders & Floors								
Photographs								
Clean Up								
Dumpster	40	WK	575	23000				23000
Final Clean Up	56.7	MSF	3	149	####	1426		1575
Continous - One Laborer	45	WK			8.26	372		372
Punch List	0.2	%		7144				7144
Permits: Building	1	%		47030				47030
Misc.								
Insurance: Builders Risk - Additional Rider	1	LS		23515				23515
Owner's Protective Liability								
Umbrella								
Unemployment Ins. & Social Security								
(SEE ESTIMATE SUMMARY)								
Bonds								
Performance (SEE ESTIMATE SUMMARY)								
Material & Equipment								
Main Office Expense (SEE ESTIMATE SUMMARY)								
Special Items								
Totals:				$112,377		$101,872		$210,348

Figure A.19b

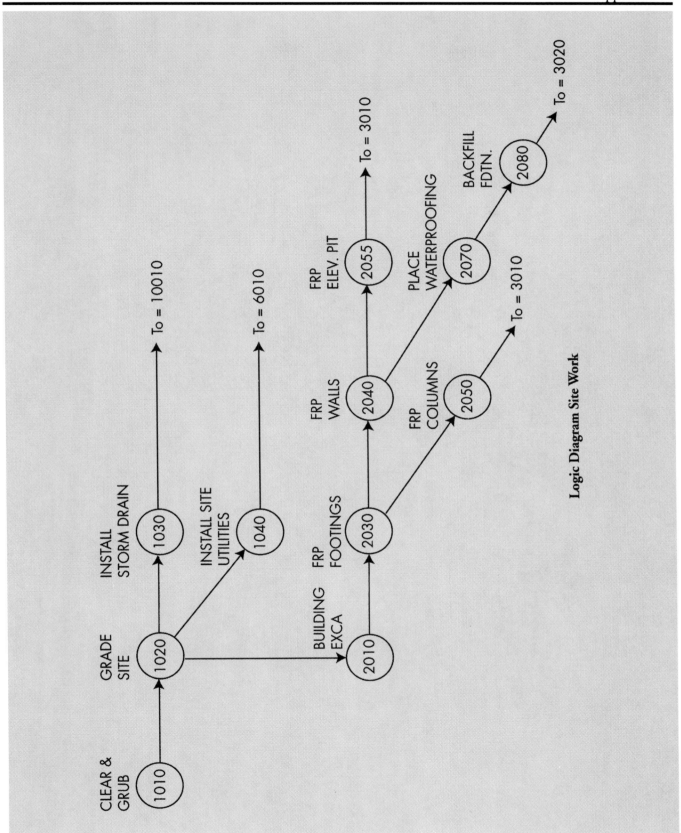

Logic Diagram Site Work

Figure B.1

213

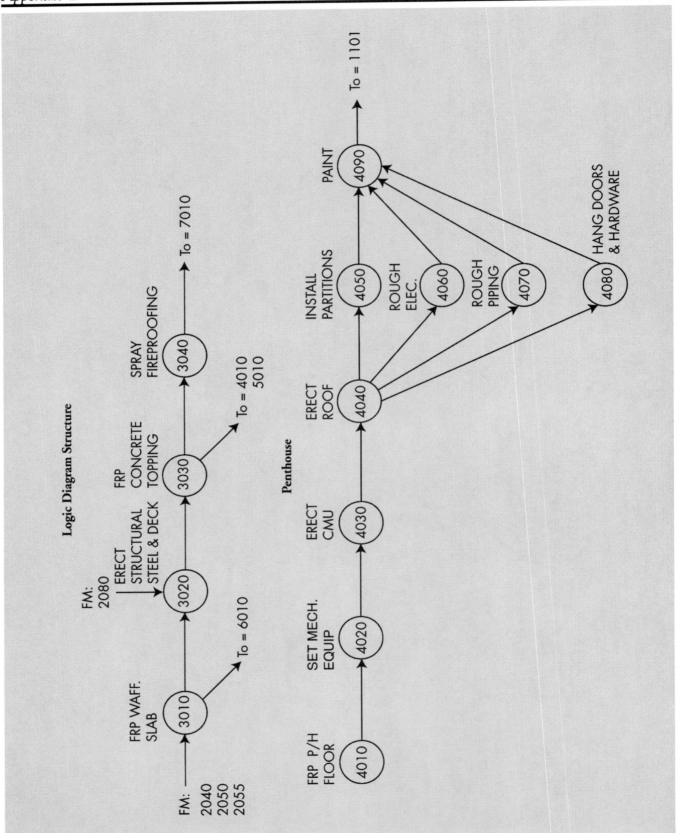

Logic Diagram Structure

Figure B.2

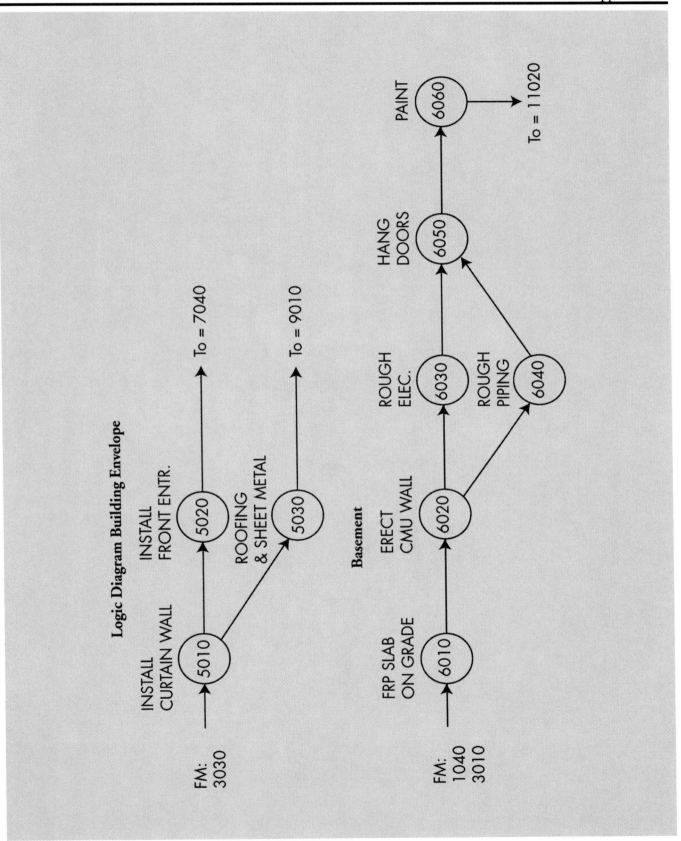

Figure B.3

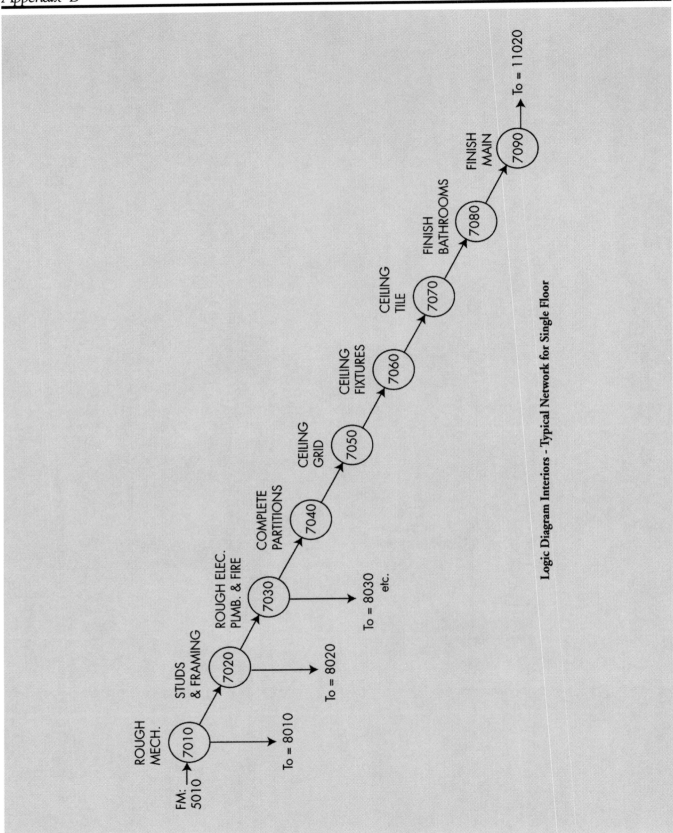

Logic Diagram Interiors - Typical Network for Single Floor

Figure B.4

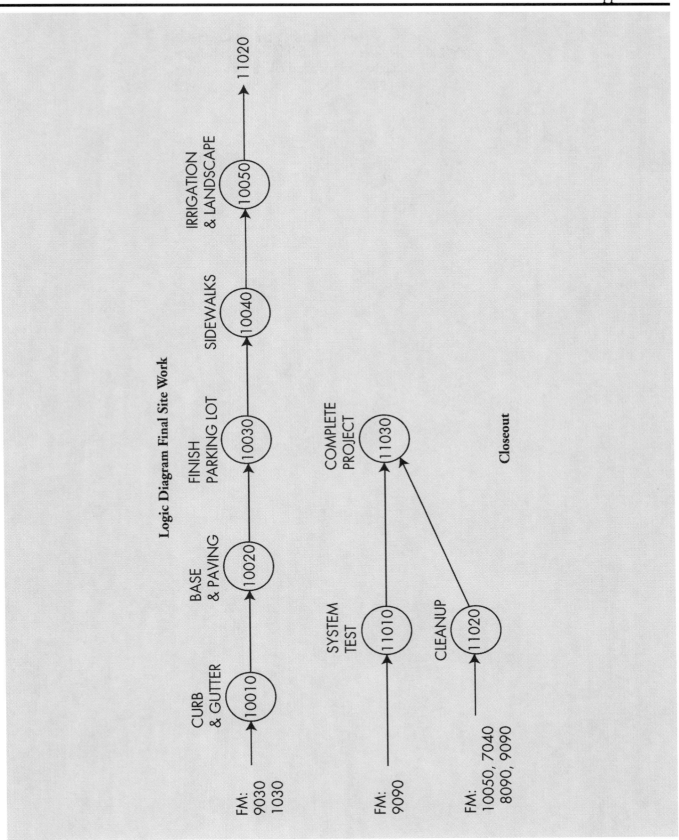

Logic Diagram Final Site Work

Figure B.5

The following planning schedule lists all activities
and predecessors for the R. S. Means Office Building.
This list can be used to trace the logic for the project.

Act ID	Description	Orig Dur	Early Start	Early Finish	Activity ID	Predecessors	
1000	Sitework	17d	05JAN98	27JAN98	1000		
1010	Clear and Grub	3d	05JAN98	07JAN98	1010		
1020	Grade Site	11d	08JAN98	22JAN98	1020	1010	
1030	Install Storm Drain System	7d	19JAN98	27JAN98	1030	1020	
1040	Install Site Utilities	4d	22JAN98	27JAN98	1040	1020	
2000	Foundation	29d	23JAN98	04MAR98	2000		
2010	Building Excavation	2d	23JAN98	26JAN98	2010	1020	
2030	FRP Footings	15d	27JAN98	16FEB98	2030	2010	
2040	FRP Foundation Walls	17d	03FEB98	25FEB98	2040	2030	
2050	FRP Columns	4d	03FEB98	06FEB98	2050	2030	
2055	FRP Elevator Pit	4d	03FEB98	06FEB98	2055	2040	
2070	Place Waterproofing	3d	26FEB98	02MAR98	2070	2040	
2080	Backfill Foundatio	2d	03MAR98	04MAR98	2080	2070	
3000	Structure	58d	26FEB98	18MAY98	3000		
3010	FRP Waffle Slab	24d	26FEB98	31MAR98	3010	2040, 2050, 2055	
3020	Erect Structural Steel and	24d	01APR98	04MAY98	3020	3010	
3030	FRP Concrete Topping	7d	05MAY98	13MAY98	3030	3020	
3040	Spray Fireproofing	14d	29APR98	18MAY98	3040	3030	
4000	Penthouse	40d	14MAY98	10JUL98	4000		
4010	FRP Penthouse Floor	3d	14MAY98	18MAY98	4010	3030	
4020	Set Mechanical Equipment	15d	19MAY98	09JUN98	4020	4010	
4030	Erect CMU Walls -	5d	10JUN98	16JUN98	4030	4020	
4040	Erect Penthouse Roof	3d	17JUN98	19JUN98	4040	4030	
4050	Install Partitions -	5d	22JUN98	26JUN98	4050	4040	
4060	Roughin Electrical -	14d	22JUN98	10JUL98	4060	4040	
4070	Roughin Piping -	4d	22JUN98	25JUN98	4070	4040	
4080	Hang Doors and Hardware	1d	22JUN98	22JUN98	4080	4040	
4090	Paint - Penthouse	2d	29JUN98	30JUN98	4090	4050, 4080	
5000	Building Envelope	41d	14MAY98	13JUL98	5000		
5010	Erect Curtain Wall	30d	14MAY98	25JUN98	5010	3030	
5020	Install Front Entrance	2d	26JUN98	29JUN98	5020	5010	
5030	Roofing and Sheet Metal	15d	22JUN98	13JUL98	5030	4040	
6000	Basement	40d	22APR98	17JUN98	6000		
6010	FRP Slab on Grade	5d	22APR98	28APR98	6010	1040, 3010	
6020	Erect CMU Walls -	5d	29APR98	05MAY98	6020	6010	
6030	Rough Electrical -	25d	06MAY98	10JUN98	6030	6020	
6040	Rough Piping - Basement	17d	06MAY98	29MAY98	6040	6020	
6050	Hang Doors & Hardware -	2d	11JUN98	12JUN98	6050	6030, 6040	
6060	Paint - Basement	3d	15JUN98	17JUN98	6060	6050	
7000	Interiors - 1st floor	10d	05JUN98	09NOV98	7000		
7010	Roughin Mechanical	16d	05JUN98	26JUN98	7010	5010	

Start date	05JAN98	▨ Early bar
Finish date	27JAN99	▬ Progress bar
Data date	05JAN98	▨ Critical bar
Run date	15MAY98	── Summary bar
Page number	1A	◈ Start milestone point
© Primavera Systems, Inc.		◈ Finish milestone point

R. S. Means Office Building

Figure B.6

219

Act ID	Description	Orig Dur	Early Start	Early Finish	Activity ID	Predecessors	
7020	Studs and Framing	5d	29JUN98	06JUL98	7020	7010	
7030	Roughin Elec, Plmbg, Fire	12d	07JUL98	22JUL98	7030	7020	
7040	Complete Partitions	22d	23JUL98	21AUG98	7040	7030	
7050	Ceiling Grid	8d	24AUG98	02SEP98	7050	7040	
7060	Ceiling Fixtures & Registers	14d	03SEP98	23SEP98	7060	7050	
7070	Ceiling Tile	6d	24SEP98	01OCT98	7070	7060	
7080	Finish Bathrooms	15d	02OCT98	22OCT98	7080	7070	
7090	Finish Main Areas	12d	23OCT98	09NOV98	7090	7080	
8000	Interiors - 2nd floor	16d	29JUN98	10DEC98	8000		
8010	Roughin Mechanical	16d	29JUN98	21JUL98	8010	7010	
8020	Studs and Framing	5d	22JUL98	28JUL98	8020	7020, 8010	
8030	Roughin Elec, Plmbg, Fire	12d	29JUL98	13AUG98	8030	7030, 8020	
8040	Complete Partitions	22d	24AUG98	23SEP98	8040	7040, 8030	
8050	Ceiling Grid	8d	24SEP98	05OCT98	8050	8040	
8060	Ceiling Fixtures & Registers	14d	06OCT98	23OCT98	8060	8050	
8070	Ceiling Tile	6d	26OCT98	02NOV98	8070	8060	
8080	Finish Bathrooms	15d	03NOV98	23NOV98	8080	8070	
8090	Finish Main Areas	12d	24NOV98	10DEC98	8090	8080	
9000	Interiors - 3rd floor	22d	22JUL98	13JAN99	9000		
9010	Roughin Mechanical	16d	22JUL98	12AUG98	9010	8010	
9020	Studs and Framing	5d	13AUG98	19AUG98	9020	9010	
9030	Roughin Elec, Plmbg, Fire	12d	20AUG98	04SEP98	9030	9020	
9040	Complete Partitions	22d	24SEP98	23OCT98	9040	8040, 9030	
9050	Ceiling Grid	8d	26OCT98	04NOV98	9050	9040	
9060	Ceiling Fixtures & Registers	14d	05NOV98	24NOV98	9060	9050	
9070	Ceiling Tile	6d	25NOV98	03DEC98	9070	9060	
9080	Finish Bathrooms	15d	04DEC98	24DEC98	9080	9070	
9090	Finish Main Areas	12d	28DEC98	13JAN99	9090	9080	
10000	Final Sitework	23d	08SEP98	08OCT98	10000		
10010	Curb & Gutter	3d	08SEP98	10SEP98	10010	1030, 9030	
10020	Base & Paving	7d	11SEP98	21SEP98	10020	10010	
10030	Finish Parking Lot	4d	22SEP98	25SEP98	10030	10020	
10040	Sidewalks	5d	28SEP98	02OCT98	10040	10030	
10050	Irrigation & Landscape	4d	05OCT98	08OCT98	10050	10040	
11000	Closeout	20d	30DEC98	27JAN99	11000		
11010	Systems Test & Startup	15d	30DEC98	20JAN99	11010	9090	
11020	Cleanup and Punchlist	10d	14JAN99	27JAN99	11020	10050, 7090, 8090,	
11030	Complete Project	0		27JAN99	11030	11010, 11020	

Start date	05JAN98		
Finish date	27JAN99		
Data date	05JAN98		
Run date	15MAY98	**R. S. Means Office Building**	
Page number	2A		
© Primavera Systems, Inc.			

Legend:
- Early bar
- Progress bar
- Critical bar
- Summary bar
- ◈ Start milestone point
- ◈ Finish milestone point

Figure B.7

Notes on Schedule Sequencing

(Suggestions from readers for this appendix would be most welcome. Please contact the author c/o R.S. Means Reference Book Department.)

The following "rules" are included to help the reader visualize some typical sequences of construction. They should be regarded as suggestions, not hard and fast requirements.

Always Schedule the Physical Dependencies First, Then Decide How the Crews will be Sequenced.

Items that rest on top of other things must follow the item below it. For example,

- Column on a footing
- Roofing on top of a roof deck
- Railing attached to a deck
- Roofing which is installed over flashing

Note: Sometimes what rests on top of something else is not readily apparent. For example, electrical conduit embedded in a concrete slab usually goes underneath the reinforcing steel. This is typically not obvious from drawings.

Architectural Work

Sometimes the architectural detail will determine which goes first. For example,

- In commercial work, hollow metal frames must be set before gypsum wall board (GWB) is hung.
- In residential work, prehung frames and doors cannot be set until after GWB is in.
- The difference is in the way the door frames fit with the GWB. The fit shown on the drawing detail will govern.

Items that go inside something must be installed after the enclosing item is built in position.

- Items that go in a wall and depend on the wall for alignment and location—conduit, rough plumbing, cabling, insulation, etc.—can go in only after the studs are up.

  Note: GWB can be hung only after the items inside the wall are installed.

Look at the wall sections for a basic sequence.

Example of a carpentry sequence for residential construction:

- Sill
- Joists
- Subfloor
- Bottom plate, studs, top plate
- Sheathing
- Rafters (or trusses)
- Roof decking

Example of a structural concrete sequence:

- Footings
- Foundation walls
- First floor slab
- Columns to second floor
- Second floor slab

Basic Interior Sequencing

Everything above the ceiling first. Least flexible items go first.

- Ductwork
- Piping (fire protection and any plumbing)
- Electrical conduit
- Flexible wiring (like computer cabling)

Install ceiling grid.

Install everything that rests in the grid:

- Light fixtures
- HVAC registers and grilles
- Sprinkler heads, etc.

Install the ceiling tiles.

Install finishes in the rooms below the ceiling grid, e.g., cabinetry, finish carpentry, carpet, etc.

Some General Rules for Interior Work

Bathrooms:

- Tile goes first, since most things rest on it.
- Cabinets must go in before lavatories, etc.
- Finish plumbing fixtures go in after tile since they rest on the tile.
- Accessories and toilet partitions go in last.

Other interior work ideas:

- Door jambs go in with studs; doors themselves go in later.
- Look at the details to determine order:
    - If item A butts up against item B, then B goes in first, followed by A, e.g., vinyl wall covering must be fitted to cabinetry.
    - It is a good idea to do the finish flooring last to prevent damage by other trades.

Rules About Concurrence

Usually, two activities can go on at the same time if they're not in the same space. For example,

- External siding on a house can be installed while electricians put in panels and wiring inside.
- Landscaping can go on while interior finishes are being done.

Workmen cannot work over others if a hazard is possible. For example,

- Do not install roofing while external siding is being installed. The roofers can drop things which would injure the carpenters below.

Two activities can take place in the same space if they are non-interfering. For example,

- Often mechanical, electrical and plumbing rough-ins can occur on the same floor if the area is large enough so that workmen will not interfere.
- Some activities just can't have other work going on at the same time in the same space, e.g., rough painting using sprayers.

Underground Work

- Generally, bring the site to grade, then put in underground systems (storm drains, water piping, etc.)
- Elevation almost always rules—deepest first.

Mechanical Work

- Install vessel first, then pipe to the vessel. For example, set air handling units, boilers and chillers first, then run the piping lines between them.
- Use same concept with HVAC equipment and ductwork, although the rule is not as hard and fast.
- Ductwork installers like to have a clear floor, i.e., no studs or other building elements in the way.
- Look for pieces of equipment so large that they must be installed first, then have the building built around them and sequence accordingly. For example, mechanical equipment in basements or penthouse structures.

Index

Notes

Notes

Notes

Notes

Notes

Notes

Notes

Notes

Notes